ANTHOLOGY IN LAW AND THE SOCIAL SCIENCES

I0655958

Kenneth K. Mwenda
PhD, LLD, DSc(Econ)

GIFT *Certificate*

TO:

FROM:

DATE:

Would you like to buy a copy of
ANTHOLOGY IN LAW AND THE SOCIAL SCIENCES?

Please visit:
http://www.kennethmwenda.com/books

ANTHOLOGY IN LAW AND THE SOCIAL SCIENCES

VOLUME - 1

Kenneth K. Mwenda
PhD, LLD, DSc(Econ)

www.africa**in**canadapress.com

TORONTO, CANADA – 2016

Anthology in Law and the Social Sciences

Kenneth K. Mwenda

http://www.kennethmwenda.com

PUBLISHED BY:

AFRICA IN CANADA PRESS

18A-100 Westmore Drive, Toronto, ON   M9V 5C3, CANADA
Tel: 1 (416) 644-1106,   Fax: 1 (416) 644-1126
http://www.africaincanadapress.com

AFRICA IN CANADA PRESS is committed to publishing works by authors of African descent in Canada and abroad with excellence.

COVER DESIGN & TYPESETTING BY:

www.diamondbooks.ca

PAPERBACK EDITION -V1 : ISBN: 978-1-988251-10-3 – AFRICA IN CANADA PRESS
PAPERBACK EDITION -V2 : ISBN: 978-1-988251-07-3 – AFRICA IN CANADA PRESS
E-BOOK EDITION   : ISBN: 978-1-988357-03-4   – DIAMOND PUBLISHERS

PRINTED IN CANADA

DEDICATION

In loving memory of my father,
Mr. Joseph T. Mwenda Snr.

Your footprints remain indelible. You taught me to think critically about the virtues of honesty, integrity, love, faith and truth. You inspired in your children the values of continuous learning and erudition. You lived an exemplary life, with the highest standards of integrity and moral character. You will always be my greatest role model. And I know that you are up there teaching angels how to love. We miss you always and forever.

"A wise [man] will hear, and will increase learning; and a man of understanding shall attain unto wise counsels: To understand a proverb, and the interpretation; the words of the wise, and their dark sayings. The fear of the LORD is the beginning of knowledge: but fools despise wisdom and instruction."

Proverbs 1:5-7

ACKNOWLEDGEMENT

To my many students and former students worldwide at the various international universities where I have taught, thank you for being promising leaders for the next generation. That a number of my former law students have gone on to become notable Supreme Court judges, Constitutional Court judges, Court of Appeal judges and High Court judges, including an eminent Chief Justice, while others continue to serve as law professors, diplomats and ambassadors, as well as judicial clerks and prominent Cabinet Ministers, is only the beginning of the story. For, there are also those that have held or continue to hold senior positions at the World Bank, the African Development Bank, the Common Market for Eastern and Southern Africa, and many other international organizations. I am truly humbled and grateful to God, Jehovah, Almighty, for all these blessings.

Special thanks also go out to all friends and colleagues (as well as my family members, including my wife and son) who provided comments on the various sayings, musings and metaphors in this book. Their tireless contributions helped to sharpen my views on a number of issues. My other thanks go out to **Africa in Canada Press** for the timely and efficient publication of the book. **Diamond Books - Canada** is also hereby acknowledged for the excellent typesetting work and the preparation of the cover design.

TABLE OF CONTENTS

THE FOLLOWING CHAPTERS ARE AVAILABLE IN **VOLUME – 2**

- Kenneth K. Mwenda

PART - B

PART - C

PREFACE

While this book does not purport or pretend to have all the answers to the many social challenges that we face in life, it certainly does raise some thought-provoking questions for us to think through. I hasten to add, however, that the book is not a work of fiction. Neither is it about motivation like many motivational books that are on the bookshelves today. Rather, it is an example of public intellectualism in Law and the Social Sciences. The book distills complex ideas that are often confined to the academic world into more easily discernible ideas by everyone, including the laity. Such is a cardinal objective of the book – to provoke some critical thinking across a broad spectrum of society on certain topical themes pertaining to Law and the Social Sciences. With an inter- and multi-disciplinary focus, the book cuts across many contemporary themes in the Law and Social Science discourse.

What started out first as a series of short intellectually stimulating and thought-provoking articles published in a number of media outlets in Zambia and elsewhere culminated into the publication of this anthology: that is, a collection of short articles in the Law and Social Science discourse. Over the years, I have made significant contributions to contemporary debate on various political, economic and social issues. Many individuals that have followed my scholarly and public contributions have encouraged me to bring together into a book a collection of some of my well-received media articles. And so, this is how the idea of this book came about. The writing of the book was a response to the increasing and growing demand from the readership. I have included in this book new and updated material whose 'footage' has not been seen before. It has not been an easy path to tread where you sometimes have to raise certain 'unorthodox' and out-of-the-box questions that many folks would rather ignore or pretend not to have some idea about. But avoiding a problem only provides temporary relief for you to face the same problem again tomorrow. So, to avoid facing the same problem the next day, it is best to confront it – like the taking of a bull by the horns!

In putting this book together, I carefully crafted the aforesaid material along the lines of certain themes examined in a number of my media articles. For example, the chapters on religion and the law follow one another in one section of the book. And while the book presents an eclectic taste of the Law and the

Social Science discourse, such that many a reader might find it hard to put the book down once they start reading, a deliberate effort is made to set the discussion in its proper socio-political and socio-economic contexts. Indeed, law does not exist or operate in a vacuum. It must be situated in its proper socio-political and socio-economic contexts. Thus, the book presents a valuable 'Law in Context' contribution. Much of the analyses are made through the prism of the social sciences.

The paperback edition of the book is arranged in **two (2) volumes** whilst the **electronic edition** is **a single publication** containing both Volumes 1 and 2. For those accessing the book as a paperback, you are encouraged to read both Volumes 1 and 2. For those accessing the electronic edition, you are encouraged to read the whole book. In this book, a number of themes pursued are closely interrelated. They cut across intertwined disciplines. Against this background, it would benefit the reader to get a good grasp of both Volumes 1 and 2 of the paperback edition or the whole of the electronic edition. Elsewhere, I have authored several scholarly books and journal articles that are now widely cited in academia and by major policy institutions as well as by the courts of law. The current book is, therefore, not my maiden effort at writing. The reader is encouraged to consult also, if need be, my many

- Kenneth K. Mwenda

scholarly works that are abundantly available in almost all of the world's leading academic libraries.

In this book, I endeavour to stand back from my notable scholarly work of authoring for an academic and intellectual audience. What I propose to do instead is to seek dialogue with a broader section of society, ranging from the most intellectually sophisticated to the least enlightened person. Very often, as scholars, our ideas tend to be detached from the real world, particularly when we use technical language and jargon or other forms of communication that only our fellow intellectuals can understand or decipher. Take, for example, the case of a PhD economist who is in the habbit of using complex mathematical formula to write or report on contemporary economic issues in the media. How useful is such writing and information to the common man on the ground that has little interest in learning about complex mathematical equations?

A notable role of public intellectualism is to stand back from the intimidating language of a technocrat so as to avoid some kind of tunnel-vision where only you, the author, and your fellow technocrats are the ones who can understand what you are talking about. And this is exactly what this book endeavours to do. People from different walks of life will find the book an easy read, whether they are travelling on a train or they are on a long flight. The book will give them a valuable companion. And even though some of the readers may not be in full agreement with some contentious arguments that the author advances in certain parts of the book, many a readers' thoughts are likely to be provoked to some greater degree. That, really, is what matters most. Indeed, it is that stimulation of debate that lies at the centre of this book.

Closely related to the foregoing, although the debate continues on the meaning of the term 'public intellectual', it is not far from a truism that such an individual cannot be pigeon-holed into a dogmatic or single way of expressing and communicating his or her ideas. A public intellectual often transcends the boundaries of academic pedagogy, while avoiding the chasm that divides scientific inquiry and intellectualism from the typical practitioner role of unscientific advocacy. A public intellectual often remains focused on translating complex theoretical and conceptual ideas into easily discernible scientific and objective analyses that even wananchi (*i.e.* the public citizens) can understand. In doing so, the public intellectual should try to communicate and speak the language of the common man, without stifling debate or intimidating the audience with all manner of intellectual sophistry. To that end, the

- *Kenneth K. Mwenda*

use of metaphors, adages, and illustrations becomes handy in breaking down certain ideas that would ordinarily be seen as too complex for the common man to understand. This book takes such an approach, breaking down complex ideas into easily discernible ideas.

Although some illustrations and examples provided in the book are drawn from specific jurisdictions and localities, a good number of them are of wider application to many other contexts and situations. This is not a book about Africa only or about America and Europe alone. Rather, it is a book about the human condition everywhere in the world. Every single reader will be able to relate to one or more illustrations and arguments contained in the book. For example, while the issue of tribalism is often rife in developing countries, the closely related issue of racism is often rife in the developed Western world. In tackling these issues, the book does so with honesty and critically insightful wit.

As noted above, a good many of chapters in this book have appeared as short articles in the media. However, I have made significant efforts to revise and update these articles, capturing now much of the feedback that has been received from many sections of the readership. The revised articles are set alongside new material that has never been published before. And it is expected that a wide section of society will find the book a valuable read, irrespective of their level of intellectual sophistication or their race, gender, creed or ideological belief.

The analyses, arguments, interpretations and conclusions expressed in this book are entirely those of the author. They do not represent the views of any institution, person or body to which the author is affiliated.

Professor Kenneth K. Mwenda
PhD, LLD, DSc(Econ).

Washington DC, USA.
Tuesday, March 1, 2016

CHAPTER

1

WHAT THEY DO NOT TEACH YOU
IN BUSINESS SCHOOL

In Business School, they teach you many great things about how to manage and run a business. But they do not teach you how to get your dream job, how to grow a professional career, or how to get promoted at work. Neither do they teach you how to survive organizational politics and adverse corporate cultures at work. A spouse, for example, will sometimes not understand why her husband looks very tired and depressed when he gets home from work. She may not realize that it has to do with the politics at the office. Yes, organizational politics can be overwhelmingly de-motivating if not handled properly.

It is such issues that are hardly captured in much of the literature on Organizational Behaviour and Industrial Psychology. One of the reasons for this lacuna is that there are no straight jacket-answers to these issues. At the outset, I must stress that while I do not subscribe to the culture of corporate

- Kenneth K. Mwenda

hustling, as described below, the views set forth hereunder are only meant to help those that subscribe to corporate hustling. And we must be mindful that different contexts require different emphasis. But, then, what is 'corporate hustling'?

In the English vocabulary, the word "hustle" means, *inter alia*, to obtain by aggressive or illicit means, to push or force one's way, to jostle or shove, or to be aggressive, especially in business or other financial dealings. Thus, hustling often entails some degree of dishonesty, including unethical posturing as well as craftiness and shrewdness, just to get your way around. It knows no rules or boundaries, and can sometimes tread on the fringes of illegality and criminality. Let us now take the example of a young female who is a university graduate seeking employment in Zambia.

Armed with her CV, the young lady applies for a job and is called in for interviews only to find that the prospective male employer is asking her for some sexual favours before he can give her the job. Even if she were to comply with his lustful demands, there is no guarantee that he will honour his promise. Also, whether it is through indulging in protected sex or unprotected sex, the notion of "carpet interviews", as it is sometimes called, is just unethical and intolerable in any decent society. But, then, how do young females deal with such social pressures in an economy with a growing population but with very few jobs?

Ace Hood, one of the famous US rappers, in his

official remix of the title song "Hustle Hard", featuring other lead rappers such as Rick Ross and Lil Wayne, shouts out: "But it's the same sh***... Just a different day...I should try to get it... Mama need a house, baby needs some shoe, guess what I'm gonna do? Hustle, hustle, hustle..."! And Beyonce Knowles, Jay-Z's lovely wife, singing her "Diva" song, put it more aptly: "I'm a, I'm a, a diva, hey... Na, na, na... A diva is a female version of a hustler..."! And so it is in the corporate world. While Business Schools will teach you much about what you need to know to execute business deals and to increase profit margins or to win market-shares and make sound investment decisions, the art of navigating the corporate culture terrain is something that most Business Schools do not teach you effectively. Such issues are hard to capture in a formalized learning environment.

From a systemic and holistic perspective, there are mainly four dimensions to any organization, including a church, and these are: (a) business processes; (b) organizational design and information flows; (c) corporate culture; and (d) organizational politics. And many Business Schools are well-equipped to teach you about handling business processes or realigning the organizational design and information flows. But hardly will you find a management guru that has all the answers to organizational politics and corporate culture. That is the most complex area of problem-solving for any organization. Not even the theories of Total Quality Management (TQM), Six Sigma or Business Process-Re-Engineering have all the answers to such issues.

4

And to find the answers, you have to go beyond organizational processes and designs.

As much as I do not subscribe to the idea of corporate hustling, especially because hustling, like patronage and cronyism, is a form of insidious corruption, the corporate world is often full of hustlers and those that thrive on cronyism and patronage. And such individuals end up rising on the corporate ladder, surpassing even the hardworking and honest folks. Some critics may argue that corporate hustling is all about using emotional intelligence in a smart way. But I have difficulties appreciating that line of thought. Emotional intelligence, it must be stressed, is not about corporate hustling, cronyism or patronage. Rather, it is about the ability of an individual to identify, assess and control his or her emotions as well as those of others. Viewed from this angle, emotional intelligence is the innate potential to identify, feel, describe, learn from, use, communicate, recognize, remember, manage, understand and explain emotions. Kendra Cherry, writing Online for *About.comPsychology* (July 22, 2011), observes that John D. Mayer and Peter Salovey, two of the leading researchers on the topic, contend that emotional intelligence is "the ability to monitor one's own and others' feelings and emotions, to discriminate among them and to use this information to guide one's thinking and actions." In a sense, emotional intelligence, unlike corporate hustling, is not about mere chancing of opportunities through, say, craftiness or some dubious form of human behaviour like cronyism or patronage. By

4

contrast, it represents an ability to reason systematically with emotions and to use emotions to enhance thought. And these are qualities that are missing in corporate hustling.

In general, corporate hustling, cronyism and patronage are predicated on a culture of mediocrity. Hustlers are almost always trying to suppress meritocracy. And they often lack the emotional intelligence to figure out how others perceive their behaviour or conduct. The concept of the Johari Window for helping people better understand their relationship with the self and with others is almost always missing in a hustler. Ocassionally, where a hustler is conscious of how he or she is perceived by others, the hustler cares little as long as he or she gets what he or she wants. As Charles Bukowski once observed, "The problem with the world is that the intelligent people are full of doubts, while the stupid ones are full of confidence." Indeed, many a hustler lacks intellectual sophistication. They are usually technically incompetent and professionally unsound, but try to leverage their way up the corporate ladder through what they call "networking". And if it means stepping on the heads of others to get ahead, the hustlers will do just that. They will even talk ill of others, or betray their better qualified and more technically competent colleagues.

And where a hustler manages to get up the corporate ladder, his or her immediate preoccupation is to entrench the *Dunning–Kruger* effect that brings about cognitive bias where he or she does not realize that he or she suffers from illusory superiority of mistakenly rating his or her ability much higher than average. This bias, psychologists tell us, is attributed to a metacognitive inability of the 'unskilled' or 'semi-skilled' manager failing to recognize his or her own mistakes. In such cases, dishonesty in dealings, treacherous acts, jealousies against hardworking colleagues, deceitful conduct and promises, as well as vindictiveness, vendettas and retaliatory measures against subordinates, including cajoleries to win support of other colleagues, will be the hallmarks of the hustler-manager. It does not matter that the hustler has now become a manager. He or she will still feel insecure. And most hustlers have no moral conscience or integrity. They often do not feel an iota of shame or guilt. Hustlers are often driven by their own insecurity. And they tend to be quite envious of those that are technically much better than them, and thus would do anything to bring such gifted people down.

If a new boss joins the institutional unit, the hustlers will be the first to befriend the new boss, faking smiles and giggling much of the time and volunteering themselves for chores or assignments that have not been asked for by the boss. For the hustlers, it is all about wanting to get ahead of others. Such is life. But the Business School curriculum does not teach us about all this hustling, cronyism or patronage in the corporate world. By contrast, the Business School uses euphemism and refers to such machinations as "networking". But, you do not need an Oxford Dictionary to know that, with a few exceptions, much of what most Business Schools are talking about here is basically hustling, cronyism and patronage. Look, if, for example, you know that today is your boss' birthday, according to the culture of hustling, cronyism and patronage, you should be seen to be eager and resourceful enough to surprise your boss with some token of appreciation. And if your boss accidently drops his wallet or car keys while you are standing right next to him, you are expected to quickly and proudly pick up the wallet or the car keys for him! Do not stand by and just watch. Likewise, if you are standing next to your boss and he accidentally steps on your foot, you should be quick to apologize notwithstanding the excruciating pain that you have suffered. And you should wear a smile as you apologize, and as you meekly say: "I am sorry, sir. I placed my foot under your shoe." That way, you will be seen to be a good team-player.

Recently, I visited an African brother who works for a multinational corporation in London. The guy is now a corporate executive. He seems to be doing fine. But when I asked him how he managed, as a black man, to get such a prestigious position in a white-dominated and well-established large multinational company, he looked back at me and smiled intently, asking: "Do you really want to know?" I responded that it would not hurt to know. He smiled again, and then explained in a low voice to prevent people that were nearby from listening into our conversation. "Man, when I first got here, I noticed that this is a muzungus (whiteman's) company. So, immediately, I started strategising on which a** to lick until I get to the top! In such places, you just have to lick a**. And the euphemism in this part of the world is known as 'networking'! Yet, we all know that it is all about 'a** licking'. Indeed, that is the easiest way to get a promotion, my brother. You gotta kiss and lick a**!"

Well, maybe my African brother was right. But, personally, I wouldn't do such a thing. Just as in the case of tribalism or nepotism in some parts of Africa, where some bosses appoint or promote relatives or tribal folks, many individuals that suck up to bosses easily get promoted. By contrast, many decent individuals, with admirable integrity, are ignored or left out. Indeed, it is not always the smartest and hard working people that get promoted. In many corporations, your hard work accounts only for a smaller fraction of the much sought-after promotion. By contrast, what matters most is corporate hustling, cronyism and patronage. As the African brother in London would said, "If you wanna get that promotion, you gotta kiss a**!"

Later, I met a mutual friend of ours, also working for the same multinational company. He, too, was African. He complained bitterly that ever since the other African brother got his promotion as a corporate executive he had stopped mingling and interacting with fellow black folks at work or outside work. The complaining guy went on to say that 'our' new black corporate executive would actually pretend not to have seen other black people whenever he was in the company of white people. I asked him what could have caused such a transformation, and he replied: "My brother, you know our skin...we have a problem! Many of us are not confident of ourselves. There are very few black brothers who will stand up for a fellow black brother in a white-dominated corporate world. Many people of our colour often feel insecure and unsafe to help out fellow black folks. Look, we are not like the whites. They protect their own kind. But for us, if a black brother gets promoted, he will pull away the ladder so that no other black brother can climb up like him. If anything, he will even appoint white people to surround him. That way, he feels that he has now 'arrived'... It's a serious inferiority complex! Such black brothers fear even their own shaddows, constantly thinking about what the whiteman will say or think should they reach out to help or support a fellow black person. But the whites, Asians and Hispanics do it all the time without shame. They actually look out for their own kind. It's just us, the muntus, who are so insecure, whereby we are constantly looking over the shoulder...and even fearing our very own shaddows."

A closely related metaphor can be found in a village setting where a young lad is trying very hard to impress the village elders so that he can be seen to be well-cultivated. As one commentator put it, "It is like muli pa nsaka naba-fyashi nangu ba shikulu elyo umukalamba abifya umwela. We mwaice kwima bwangu bwangu nokuyebelela ati, 'Mukwayi kuti ba njelelako, nine nabifya umwela...' (i.e. when you are with the elders in the village, and then one of them fouls the air, you have to offer yourself up quickly as the one who has fouled the air and seek their forgiveness). That way the elders will trust you with deep secrets of life and how to get around village politics."

Similarly, at the office, when your boss cracks a dry joke, you are expected to laugh the loudest, pretending to appreciate his "great" sense of humour. That is how hustlers operate. But, Business School does not teach you such things. Instead, you are taught business ethics. Please do not get me wrong. I am not saying we do not need business ethics. It is just that much of the real world is not like that. Even a pretty young lady that wants to get married knows full well that she has to hustle to get the right man. And the man, too, knows that for him to get that chic for his bride he has to hustle because we cannot, as humans, eat love. He has to show that he is worth more than just the words 'I love you' *simpliciter*. Some pastors, too, are in the habit of hustling as they milk off some finances from some of the church congregants' tithing. As a fable would show, three pastors met and agreed most sincerely to share amongst themselves each others' problems, and that the sharing would be kept confidentially as a secret. And so, the first pastor openned up: "My problem is money...I do steal even from the church offering. Please pray for me." Then, the second pastor also confessed: "Mine is women...whenever I see any woman my desire will be to go to bed with her. In fact, I have slept with most of the church (female) members." It was now the third pastor's turn to offer his testimony, so to speak. Suddenly, he fell into a fit of uncontrollable tears as he started to sob. It took his friends some effort to calm him down.

When they asked him to continue, the third pastor was still crying though he managed to utter the following confession: "My problem is gossiping, when we leave this place everybody will hear all what the two of you have just told me. Please pray for me!" The two other pastors fainted.

I must confess that I am one person who really loathes gossiping or hustling. It is not about pride or arrogance. It's about being principled. I would rather retain my own sanity and personal integrity. I really cannot see myself stooping so low. Wherever I am, and whatever I do, I believe in meritocracy. But many others out there are willing to bite the bullet and just stoop low if that is what it takes to get up the corporate ladder. And the corporate world is readily willing to reward those who suck up to the bosses more frequently. In many cases, such people do not have to be a genius, but simply hold out as very resourceful to the boss. For example, they will attend almost every funeral of any important person in town even if the deceased hardly knew them. They will still go to the funeral and appear to be one of the chief mourners. For all you know, the powers-that-be might just spot them and mistakenly believe that they, too, are important people. It's called hustling through fraudulent misrepresentation.

For a hustler, even if your finances are low, you are expected to talk and act big. In the culture of hustling, you are expected to act as if everything is under control but only to fall into tears of economic destitution when you are alone at home. A hustler is a fighter. Even when he has no idea of how to smoke a cigar, a hustler will puff away just to keep up appearances while choking on the smoke and holding back tears. Hustlers come in many different shapes and forms. Some are very subtle networkers, with highly polished and finesse maneuvers, while others are plain crude and thuggish. The corporate world loves the former, the finesse ones. And these types of hustlers tend to dress very well and quite expensively, and they often drive the latest cars in town. They also love to acquire and use expensive smart-phones and apps, such as iPaDs and iPhones, exuding an air of sophistry, yet remaining limited in overall intellectual depth. Hustlers are good at picking up spontaneous but uncoordinated anecdotes and conjectures of news from such international sources as CNN, BBC, the Economist and other foreign media so as to appear to be ahead of the game. And they often watch and discuss passionately foreign soccer matches in the English league, ignoring much of what is going on in their own domestic soccer league at home. The bottom-line for many a hustler is that he or she seeks to gain some influence. To do this, hustlers can be quite astute politically, switching hard facts for fiction, cajoleries and half-truths, as expediency permits. And hustlers are willing to go for it, whether by hook or crook. If it means wearing a short skirt that has a high slit exposing parts of the inner light thigh, so as to raise false hopes in the weak heart of a male boss, some female hustlers will go for it. Others may even drop the skirt eventually, if need be. But do not get me wrong. I am not advocating for such vices. All I am saying is that the corporate world is not as decent as it appears out there. People use all sorts of survival tactics which are not taught in Business School. But it is for you to judge whether what you are doing is morally acceptable or not.

As a fable would show, a fine-looking and well-dressed mid-aged man is seen in the company of young cute Zambian lady, Misozi, sipping some expensive wine over dinner at some trendy restaurant. Naïve and unsuspecting, Misozi has just met this sharp-looking guy. He tells Misozi that he is African-American from New York, US, and that he is in Zambia on a business trip. Misozi is flattered. He explains to Misozi that his name is Denzel. Misozi begins to fantasize, and she is imagining US dollars raining all over her. She begins to visualize a wedding in New York. In the meantime, Denzel who watches too many African-American movies has perfected his fake American accent so well that he can even pass for an American until you see his African childhood vaccination mark on the upper arm. Denzel tactfully complains about the hot weather in Africa. And after dinner, the couple retires to Denzel's rented quarters for a night of endless love and passion. But just before dawn, the couple is awoken to a loud knock on the door. It is Denzel's nephew. He has come to collect some money Denzel owes him. And he calls out: "Ba Chiti...!!! Ba Chiti...!!!", to which Denzel responds without much thought, "Aaahh, mwaice naiwe, ni shani kanshi? Ni'ndala..." (*i.e.* Youngman, I am fast asleep. What's the problem?). Shocked by what she hears from the so-called Denzel, Misozi is in tears, as she laments: "But, but..., I thought you said you are Denzel, an American from New York?" Embarrassed, but holding his cool, "Ba Chiti", simply turns to the other side of the bed. He is a hustler and has just beaten her to the game. The young lady is shocked beyond belief.

The corporate world, too, has such hustlers, although they come in much finer shades than Ba Chiti. Name-dropping in conversations, for example, is one of the attributes of the corporate hustler. The corporate hustler pretends to know all the rich and influential people in town, including all the major political players. Now and again, the corporate hustler will throw into a social conversation the name of a major city or country that he or she recently visited, leaving the unsuspecting audience dazzled and perplexed. And the corporate hustler knows which social gatherings to attend and which ones to turn down. On the one hand, if it suits him or her well, he or she will attend a social gathering of snobs, hyping up his or her English accent accordingly. On the other hand, if it suits him or her well, he or she will speak local lingua to the street boys so that they can help him or her replace the flat tire on his or her car.

A hustler has unbelievable antennas for reading the social weather so as to maximize his or her social capital (*i.e.* social capital is about the value of social networks, bonding similar people and bridging between diverse people, with norms of reciprocity (Dekker and Uslaner 2001; Uslaner 2001)). He has no permanent friends and no permanent enemies. Whenever there is a new boss at work, the hustler quickly befriends the new boss, volunteering and offering to do all sorts of chores. A hustler knows his boss' weaknesses and strengths. If the boss is a womanizer, the hustler will run around to organize strategically some females for the boss without making it so obvious. He will also cover up for the boss when others inquire. That's what a hustler does. He ensures that the boss feels safe and well-taken care of. But, if you are a person of principles, morals and virtues, it is hard to compete with such people. You may be alone out there waiting on meritocracy to get you that promotion, but the hustler knows full well how to bend the rules. As noted above, if he has to climb on people's heads to get to the top, the hustler will not hesitate to do so. But do not feel discouraged, my dear reader, with the hustler. You are not alone in trying to do the right thing morally and ethically. Someone Greater is watching up there. Though seemingly hard, it is, however, possible to excel and succeed in life without really hustling. It is just that, quite often, the absence of hustling appears a tougher route for many.

Hustlers, also known as "ba punka" in Bemba, are chancers and opportunists, pretending to know even what they do not know. That is how the capitalist world works. A hustler, knowing that he or she may not be that good as a technocrat, invests heavily in networking and other forms of social capital. A hustler endeavors to ensure that his hustling overshadows the competences of the competent. And if it means criticizing unfairly those that are actually more competent than the hustler or back-stabbing and rumor mongering against such competent people, the hustler will do just that. The idea for him is to eliminate all possible threats. This type of behavior is also found in the world of politics. Some Cabinet Ministers and politicians, it is alleged, often try to outdo each other by feeding wrong and misleading information to the Head of State so that only they can be seen as indispensible and resourceful. Others are even known to be in the habit of "uku-kunkula" (*i.e.* crawling) before the Head of State so as to secure their political fortunes. And only when they are faced with frustration do they jump ship to join the opposition and begin insulting. It is called political hustling.

Not long ago, I was having a drink with a childhood friend of mine in the company of his workmate. I asked my friend about a mutual friend of ours, inquiring how he was doing. My friend smiled and replied: "Oh, he is doing fine now. He is business seems to be running better now." Then, my friend's workmate, gulping down his pint of beer, chipped in: "Pa Zambia, mdala, pa liba ba punka na ba fighter!!! Lelo wa sanga ati na ba sa-pula, but mailo wa sanga ati bale tutuka pa town after uku-kelenka abantu..." (*i.e.* In our beloved Zambia, we have many hustlers, my man. You will find that some of them are broke today, but tomorrow they are back in business after swindling someone somewhere. It goes on like that). I simply smiled and did not say a word. I thought that perhaps the guy was being a bit harsh, referring to other people's entrepreneurial zeal, motivation, passion and ambition as simply hustling.

Anyhow, a hustler is a fighter. A hustler can even

sell sand to the Sahara desert. You can ask him to bring you a live crocodile overnight for a lucrative price, and he will surely find one and deliver it as promised. Nothing is impossible with a hustler. A hustler is a risk-taker, with little to lose but all to gain. And when you have such people in the corporate world, the poor moralist Christian employee finds himself or herself at a loss. The moralist fails to understand how some few people are able to manipulate the system. Sometimes it can be about tribalism, ethnicity or nepotism. At other times, it can be about discrimination, racism or gender bias. Then, there is also cronyism on whether or not you are part of the hustling team. In the corporate world, like in politics, because of cronyism, sometimes you are forced to hustle a bit no matter how well-qualified you are. Ideally, it should not be like that. But experience teaches you that there is very little idealism out there, and that your CV alone is not enough.

For those that subscribe to hustling, if your boss is an elderly Ngoni, try to learn some Ngoni language and, occasionally, if possible, try to greet him in Ngoni, unless he shows that he is not interested in such tribal issues. The biggest mistake you can make is to continue greeting him in Bemba, "Shani tata?", every time you meet him in the corridors at work. Also, as a fundamental rule of corporate hustling, do not try to be smarter than your boss. Even if you are more educated than your boss, he or she is deemed to be "always" right. As a matter of common etiquette, you do not criticize your boss in the presence of others. That would be like trying to commit suicide. As a hustler, always make sure that your boss looks smart and intelligent by quietly arming him or her with the right ideas before any meeting. If your boss is asked what colour is his shirt, and he responds by saying that his shirt is navy blue, when it is clear that the shirt is sky blue, do not laugh. As a hustler, you should simply pretend that everything is fine. And when you are asked what colour is your boss' shirt, you should simply say: "The shirt is navy blue, like the boss said, although from a distance it looks somewhat like sky-blue..." That way, you will not have embarrassed your boss, but you will also have euphemistically qualified your expected conformity. That's what a hustler does.

Likewise, in politics, if, say, the President is from Eastern Province, an astute political hustler knows that he or she should not start pushing behind the President's back the Bantu-Botatwe agenda, or that of other tribes, thinking that the President will not know. He will get to hear about it, and you will be in trouble. It is all about understanding the art of hustling. Like I said earlier, I am not endorsing hustling, but merely aiding those that subscribe to it. Hustling, it must be noted, goes beyond diplomacy. By parity of reasoning, if, say, some hustler is a private business consultant, he or she may want to befriend some of the major donors that provide financial support to most of the major donor-funded projects. By befriending such people the hustler is not committing corruption, although he or she may be deemed to be hustling too much. Also, befriending those in government and political power, as well as some strategic individuals in the opposition, is not corruption, although it can be termed as hustling. The same analogy extends to situations where a hustler embarks on befriending the President's son or the President's brother to appear to be in the right circles and to push for possible business opportunities.

Hustlers know that if they, their spouse or children strike a good friendship with the Chief Executive Officer (CEO) of one of the donor agencies in Zambia or with the said CEO's spouse or children that in itself is not corruption. In the Western world, it is called "networking". In fact, such ties are a great source of social capital for the hustler. To put matters in context, if, say, a house servant's wife strikes a good and respectful friendship with the boss' wife, it would be hard for the boss to get rid of the servant, not so? Likewise, the house servant or security guard who smokes marijuana secretly with the boss is the boss' close confidant. Even if the house servant or security guard is lazy or reports for work late, and the boss' wife is nagging her husband to fire him, the boss will be reluctant to fire the house servant or security guard. As they say in Bemba, "Aba lya imbulu taba lubana..." That, you cannot learn in Business School, but in the real world.

20

CHAPTER

2

TO WEAR OR NOT TO WEAR
SECONDHAND UNDERWEAR

In a book titled, "Salaula: The World of Second Clothing and Zambia," published in 2000 by the University of Chicago Press, Prof. Karen T. Hansen observes that secondhand clothing business is wildly popular in many African economies, to the point of threatening the indigenous textile industry. Hansen advances a view that wearing secondhand clothes is about much more than imitating Western styles, and that it is about taking a garment and altering it to something entirely local, something that adheres to current cultural norms of etiquette. By unraveling how these garments become entangled in the economic, political, and cultural processes of contemporary Zambia, Hansen also raises provocative questions about environmentalism, charity, recycling, and thrift.

In this paper, we stand back from Hansen's thesis to focuss instead on a particular type of secondhand clothing; that is, used underwear! Can it be argued that the selling, buying or wearing of secondhand underwear is about taking a garment and altering it to something entirely local, something that adheres to current cultural norms of etiquette in a particular African country? In many parts of the world, it is not a crime for a man or woman to buy, sell or wear secondhand underwear. In Zambia, however, the Zambia Bureau of Standards has promulgated a quality control standard for textile apparel, namely, the Inspection and Acceptance Criteria for Used Textile Products (ZS 559 :2004). And since the Code of Practice for Inspection and Acceptance Criteria for Used Textiles Products – Salaula (ZS 559) is a 'compulsory' quality control standard issued by the Minister, through a statutory instrument, pursuant to section 7 of Zambia's Standards Act 1994, it has the force of law. Any contravention of this quality control standard will thus attract criminal sanctions. But, had ZS 559 been issued as a 'voluntary' quality control standard by the Zambia Bureau of Standards under section 6 of the Standards Act 1994, it would have lacked the force of law, carrying only the weight of a policy statement.

And so, a recent Zambia Daily Mail article titled, "Ndola second-hand pants dealers defy ban," published on Friday, September 21, 2012, posits that: "MOST traders in Ndola have continued selling second-hand underwear despite the ban on the clothes by the Zambia Bureau of Standards (ZABS), which has raised hygiene concerns. A survey by the *Daily Mail* in Ndola…found most traders at both Ndola town centre and Main Masala market selling the banned merchandise normally. One of the traders at the town centre, Anna Mulenga, said she and her friends have no information regarding the ban on the sale of second-hand underwear. She said no-one has approached them to say they are not allowed to sell second-hand pants. 'No-one has told us anything about that. These pants cost between K1,500 and K2,000,' (*i.e.* between US$1.50 and US$2.50) Ms Mulenga said. She said ZABS should have sensitised traders of second-hand clothes before making a decision to avoid catching them unaware. 'Some of us have well established customers. They (ZABS) will then have to give us time to finish the stocks we are still selling,' Ms Mulenga said. She said she spent a lot of money to purchase a bale of second-hand underwear, and asked ZABS to give her enough time to finish selling the stock she has for her to recover the money spent on buying the clothes."

The said Zambia Daily Mail article continues: "It was also established during the same survey that new underwear was costing between K5,000 and K10,000 while that of high quality was selling at between K15,000 and K20,000. And some people who were found at Main Masala market buying underwear said they prefer second hand pants to new ones because they are durable and affordable. They said ZABS should leave it to the people to choose whether to go for second-hand pants or new ones rather than dictate the kind of underwear people should be putting on... ZABS swung into action and confiscated several bales of second-hand pants following hygiene concerns... Zambia is not the first country to ban the sale of second-hand pants. Countries such as Zimbabwe have done the same because of hygiene concerns. Zimbabwe has also banned the importation of second-hand underwear, describing it as a health hazard."

In Zambia, the Inspection and Acceptance Criteria for Used Textile Products (ZS 559 :2004) criminalises the selling or buying of second-hand underwear. Indeed, it is a criminal offence to sell or buy second-hand underwear. In an article titled, "Exchanging underwear not Zambian," published on October 4, 2012 in the Zambia Daily Mail, that newspaper's reporter, Emelda Mwitwa, observes:

"EFFECTING the ban on the sale of second-hand underwear is timely yet is not going to be an easy battle. The Zambia Bureau of Standards needs to marshal enough resources and manpower to stop the trade across the country. From my own informal survey carried out among friends, respondents seem to be split between proponents and opponents without an apparent majority – both arguing from either the point of economic rationality or morality (public health). If one chooses to argue on the basis of morality, one will outrightly condemn the sale of second-hand underwear or rather exchanging of underwear if I may bluntly put it that way. However, the truth of the matter is that the sale of second-hand clothes, including underwear is big business with a big clientele. Salaula as the business is called, is a blessing in my lower-middle income countries to many families who are financially constrained to shop for brand new clothes in expensive retail outlets."

According to Ms. Mwitwa, "There is no doubt that second-hand wares from the Western world have made life easier for a cross section of the population who are now able to spend more money on food and other basic necessities of life because of the cheaper and durable clothes on the market. Salaula business is also renowned for creating jobs and providing a steady income to thousands of people who otherwise would have been languishing without this imported merchandise. Second-hand goods – underwear, clothes, towels, shoes, bags, socks, bedding are consumed by both the income-poor and the middle class; of course including some of the rich people. These products, especially clothes are renowned for their durability, because most of it comes with designer labels, sold at affordable prices."

Positing further, Ms. Mwitwa laments: "With all due respect to salaula business, I have not been comfortable with the sale of used underwear, which in my view is as good as exchanging undergarments. How else would you call it if someone uses their underwear – it does not matter how short the period – and puts it up for sale in a foreign country. It is simply exchanging underwear, which is a taboo in our culture. Even in the villages where you expect to find the poorest of the poor, we may share other garments, but not underwear. Similarly at funerals, when someone dies – it does not matter how rich or smart they were, their underwear is not just on the list of items to be shared among close relatives. Our tradition without any influence from experts, appreciates the fact that exchanging underwear is unhygienic, but I wonder why second-hand underpants are treated differently. Is it because second-hand clothes are well packaged and supposedly fumigated to make them safe for transference from one person to the other? From what the Zambia Bureau of Standards are telling us, second-hand underwear are not safe with all the fumigation requirements before these products are shipped to developing countries. According to the bureau's public relations officer, Dingase Makumba, the ban on second-hand underwear was necessitated by the bacteria found on these garments. Ms Makumba argued that used underwear contain some level of moisture which create a breeding ground for bacteria such as yeast and molds, responsible for highly infections conditions such as skin irritations and urinary tract infections. She also warned that second-hand underwear usually contain bacteria such as staphylococcus which cause boils."

In general, however, the buying or wearing of secondhand (or used) underwear remains one of the most embarrassing, humiliating and tightly guarded 'secrets' in many parts of the developing world. Hence, in some parts of Zambia, underwear clothing is referred to as 'tu secret'. There is a story of a young migrant man from some rural part of Zambia who had just secured a job in Lusaka. No sooner had he gotten his first pay-check in Lusaka than he sent some money to his uncle and auntie in the village. He included in the parcel some secondhand underwear for his uncle. A week later, the uncle called, complaining that he needed some more clothes: "Ala natu sapula sana... Pano umwene, na kaputula wa tumine ulya mulungu, ni ba auntie bobe eba-fwele lelo. Ine, nshikwete nelyo kamo mukati!" (*i.e.* please us send some more clothes because your auntie and I are now sharing the only underwear you sent us and that we have between us). To put matters in context, how many remember inheriting underwear from an elder sibling when they were young, especially if you were too many of you in the family? Don't feel shy. Such things do happen even in the so-called developed world.

Yet, some psychologists in the Western world would call the seemingly romantic African gesture of a poor man sharing underwear with his wife an ailment of 'transvestism', not realizing that it is economic hardship that sometimes leads people to do such things. In any event, the sharing of underwear, it could be argued, like that of taking baths together, can have a bonding effect between a wife and a husband, not so? Be that as it may, in an article titled, "Transvestism and the nature of cross-dressing", Eddy Elmer (1992) observes that transvestism is medically-defined as a psychosexual mental illness, 'the essential feature [of which] is recurrent and persistent cross-dressing by a heterosexual male that during at least the initial phase...is for the purpose of sexual excitement...'. But in situations such as the example of the Zambian uncle noted above it is evident that that is not a case of 'transvestism', but rather economic hardship.

- *Kenneth K. Mwenda*

In an article dated January 9, 2012, and titled, "Zimbabwe outlaws sale of used knickers," a British newspaper, the *Guardian*, reported that the Finance Minister of the Republic of Zimbabwe, Mr. Tendai Biti, successfully pushed for the introduction of a law to ban the sale and use of secondhand underwear in Zimbabwe after discovering that poverty had driven people to buy secondhand underwear at flea markets. According the British newspaper, Mr. Biti was shocked to discover that many Zimbabweans bought used underwear from flea markets or stalls. Quoting Mr. Biti, the British newspaper reported further: "…'I am told we are now even importing women's underwear in this country… How does that happen? If you are a husband and you see your wife buying underwear from the flea market, you would have failed… If I was your in-law, I would take my daughter and urge you to first put your house in order if you still want her back.'…"

At about the same time, a Zimbabwean newspaper, *NewsDay*, commended the Minister's legislative intervention, arguing that, "One of the best laws that our country has put in place in recent years is the total ban on the importation of secondhand underwear. Wearing used underwear is most dehumanising and no government worth its salt should allow its citizens to be abused to this extent. It is a fact that our flea markets receive bales of clothing, some of which is exclusively used underwear, some of which is soiled. What nation have we become that knowingly subjects its people to humiliation and disease? It is inconceivable for a country to open its borders for the importation of used underwear – to allow our women to wear undergarments that other women in other countries have used and discarded."

According to the the British Guardian newspaper, under the recently enacted Zimbabwean law, the Zimbabwe Revenue Authority will charge 40% duty and 15% VAT on all underwear imports and apply a US$3 levy on every kilogram of underwear entering the country. But, we contend, the Zimbabwean people should not feel embarrassed or ashamed over such matters. By contrast, they should be comforted to know that it's not only in Zimbabwe that secondhand underwear have been sold and worn. Even in many poorer parts of Europe, Latin America and Asia, people still buy secondhand underwear. And Zimbabwe is not the first African country to enforce legislation to outlaw the sale of used underwear. Ghana is said to have officially banned the practice in 1994 but started enforcing the law in 2011 following concerns about a health hazard. Rwanda, too, it has been reported, banned the sale of secondhand underwear with effect from December 31, 2011.

In an article dated August 28, 2007, and titled, "'Undignified' underwear the only choice for Kenya's poor", *M&C*, an internet-based publication, observes that: "Used clothes markets like the one at Adam's Arcade in western Nairobi are where most Kenyans come to fill their wardrobe. Beyond the most recent styles, which are shipped to the East African country from trend-setting fashionistas in Europe and North America, *bras and underwear – often used ones –* are sold as well, offering poor Kenyans an alternative to buying them in shops and supermarkets at prices they simply can't afford."

According to *M&C*, the sale of used underwear and bras is banned in Kenya. And the Kenyan Government contends that such clothing is unhygienic and harmful to its wearers. However, the Kenyan Government has not been very successful in weeding out the sale of such used garments, and this type of clothing continues to find its way to second-hand markets. As M&C notes, without an alternative to the cheap pieces, Kenyan vendors will continue to sell used underwear anyway, and people will continue to buy.

The issue of selling, buying or wearing secondhand underwear has become a hot topic. In Ghana, for example, *GhanatoGhana.com,* an internet-based publication, through an article dated April 12, 2012 and titled, "Ghanaians told to avoid second-hand underwear," notes that: "The Ministry of Trade and Industry in collaboration with the Ghana Standard Authority (GSA)...organized a day's forum to educate the general public on the need to refrain from patronizing used-underwear. The event was part of a campaign against the importation and sale of secondhand underwear... addressing participants at the Takoradi Market Circle, Mr Kofi Nagetey, the Deputy Executive Director of GSA, said secondhand underwear contained pores, germs and bacteria from the fluid of the previous user and has the potential of being transmitted to the next user."

In Zambia, some customary practices and superstitious views have often dictated that used and worn out underwear clothing of adults should never be inherited or bequeathed. Neither should such clothing be discarded carelessly, say, in a publicly accessible bin. Rather, the used and worn-out underwear of adults are discarded through a secret and solemn ritual of burning the said clothing into ashes and then throwing away the ashes. The fear here is that if people with bad and ill-motives get hold of the discarded underwear, they can bewitch its previous user or owner. It is said that in the case of, say, a female victim she may end up being barren. And in the case of a male victim, he may end up being impotent or with erectile dysfunction. So, a lot of people guard their underwear jealously, even when such garments are worn out. Some people will not even place on the line to dry their washed underwear. They would rather spread such washed garments on the metal springs of their bed, right beneath the mattress.

Now that Zambia has criminalised the selling or buying of secondhand underwear, what moral and ethical choices remain for those in the habbit of selling, buying or wearing such garments? And do we even have laws in Zambia to deal with 'transvestism', for example? Whereas some fashion-conscious African sisters with limited financial means would rather buy a pair of secondhand

'Victoria Secret' at the flea market than get a locally manufactured 'gwende' underwear, it is also feared that some of these secondhand underwear garments are clothes left behind by some deceased persons in the Western world. Like the case of some threads of the so-called 'human hair', commonly used for platting hair, and which some people suspect could be coming from, among other sources, human corpses in places like Asia, so it is with some secondhand underwear. What to do now? Here is a good opportunity for our local entrepreneurs to design and manufacture high quality underwear garments at affordable prices. The local 'gwende' underwear, many ladies argue, has often proved to be a disappointment, lacking in both quality and romanticism.

CHAPTER

3

LEGALIZING MARIJUANA:
TO SMOKE OR NOT TO SMOKE?

In a *Huffington Post* article titled, "Marijuana legalization: More 100 College Professors Express Support for Colorado's Legal Plot Measure," published Online on August 28, 2012, Matt Ferner reports that: "The more than 100 professors represent many different fields of study from law, health, economics and criminal justice from various universities around the nation including some professors from CSU as well as former colleagues of President Obama's during his time as a professor at University of Chicago Law School."

Fermer continues, as he cites a professorial source: "...'The time has come to take a more rational approach to marijuana policy,' Thomas Ginsburg, University of Chicago Law School professor, said in a statement. 'By criminalizing marijuana, we are wasting scarce law enforcement resources, foregoing needed revenue, and channeling people toward the far more dangerous drug that kills tens of thousands each year – alcohol.'..."

Many a reader might be wondering the purpose of this article or what exactly I am trying to get at. Well, I am trying to argue that as long as society allows or approves the abuse of more harmful drugs such as alcohol and tobacco, which are often consumed on a more regular basis and in large amounts, then we might as well permit adults the free choice to smoke some weed (known also as 'marijuana', 'joint', 'ganja', 'ulu-bangula', 'ibange', 'icamba', 'ili-bishi', 'ci-blow', 'matokwani', 'dobo', etc). Otherwise, let us ban alcohol and tobacco as well. Now, don't get me wrong. I ain't crazy. I am just being real. You just have to dig up statistics to see how many lives are lost from the abuse of alcohol, tobacco and some medical drugs such as painkillers, and then compare those statistics with reliable data on lives that are lost from the abuse of marijuana.

In many countries, Zambia included, the growing and use of marijuana, other than for medicinal purposes as prescribed by the law, is prohibited. But, can Rastafarians in Zambia, for example, bring a court action before the High Court, arguing that the law that prohibits the cultivation, smoking, selling or buying of weed is unconstitutional because it contravenes the petitioners' constitutionally guaranteed freedoms of conscience and expression, especially if the said petitioners can show that the use of marijuana remains a central part of their Rastafarian religion? In an article titled, "DEC's reaction to the debate on legalising cannabis," published in the *Zambia Daily Mail* on October 5,

2012, Zambia's Drug Enforcement Commission, through its Public Relations Officer, Samuel Silomba, reacts forcefully and spiritedly:

"THE Drug Enforcement Commission wishes to respond to the article that appeared in the *Zambia Daily Mail* newspaper on 3rd September 2012 entitled: 'Legalising marijuana; to smoke or not to smoke?' written by Professor Kenneth Mwenda, and to the letter written by Robert Sharpe addressed to the Editor of the same newspaper on 6th September 2012 on the subject of marijuana. It was sad to note that, to a large extent, Professor Mwenda's article was skewed towards inciting Rastafarians to push for the legalisation of cultivation, sale and use of cannabis in Zambia. For instance, the author questioned why Rastafarians in Zambia cannot bring a court order before the High Court against the law that prohibits the cultivation, smoking, selling or buying of cannabis. Although the law on narcotic drugs and psychotropic substances permits the cultivation and use of cannabis for the purposes of medicine and research, it is important to appreciate that cultivation, possession and trafficking in cannabis are criminal offences in Zambia."

Silomba continues: "The control and regulation of the use of dangerous drugs, including cannabis, in Zambia, is traced to the year 1923 when the colonial government enacted what was called 'Opium and habit Forming Drugs Regulation Proclamation No. 10 of 1923'. After independence, Zambia revisited the colonial drug laws and enacted the 'Dangerous

Drugs Act No. 42 of 1967' which prescribed administrative and regulatory provisions in the area of drug use and drug handling. It further created restrictions, prohibitions and specific penalties for possession of drugs without a licence or authorisation." According to Silomba, "In 1989, the Zambian government enacted a piece of legislation called 'Dangerous Drugs (Forfeiture of Property) Act No.7 of 1989, which led to the creation of the Drug Enforcement Commission through Statutory Instrument No. 87 of 1989. In 1993, in consultation with international and regional organisations, Zambia enacted the Narcotic Drugs and Psychotropic Substances Act No. 37 of 1993 (Now Cap 96 of the Laws of Zambia under volume 7). Cap 96 of the Laws of Zambia domesticated the United Nations (UN) Convention on the control and prohibition of cannabis. The UN single convention on Narcotic Drugs of 1961, Article 28 (control of cannabis) forbids member states from cultivating cannabis plants for industrial or horticultural purposes. Hence, legalising the cultivation of cannabis in Zambia would imply the undoing of the International Treaties to which Zambia is a signatory."

That said, many jurisdictions are beginning to re-think the rationale for criminalising the use, selling or buying of marijuana. Some arguments in favour of legalising marijuana include the views that: (i) marijuana is a recognized treatment for several medical disorders; (ii) although the use, selling or buying of marijuana is currently illegal and unregulated, despite marijuana still being peddled out there, the legalisation of marijuana would make the drug regulated; (iii) the legalisation of marijuana would reduce illegal importation of marijuana and other drugs; (iv) the legalisation of marijuana as a cash crop would create jobs in the agriculture and trading sectors and thus boost the economy; (v) the selling, buying or smoking of marijuana for recreational purposes can be subjected to taxation, and thus earn the Government revenue; (vi) marijuana is not as harmful as alcohol, cigarettes or hard drugs; and (vii) the use of marijuana does not necessarily lead to the use of hard drugs.

By contrast, those that are against the legalisation of marijuana often contend that: (i) marijuana is a mind-altering drug that affects the way an individual thinks; (ii) marijuana can also be very expensive to the users; (iii) chemicals in marijuana are inhaled into the lungs and placed in the bloodstream that pumps throughout the heart, brain, muscles and other organs and body parts, and that these chemicals can damage the brain while making the smoker feel temporarily happy; (iii) marijuana can harm the effective and efficient functioning of the brain by attaching to cannabinoid receptors, and that marijuana also increases a person's heart rate by 20 to 50 beats per minute; and (iv) marijuana is a highly addictive drug which causes loss of coordination, memory, judgment and perception. So what to do now? To legalise or not to legalise? Or, to smoke or not to smoke?

It is important to distinguish soft drugs such as marijuana from such hard drugs as cocaine and mandrax. It is not disputable that the use of hard drugs can have some debilitating and severely harmful effects on the human body, and that the use or selling of such drugs must be criminalised. By contrast, how worse off is the smoking of marijuana, compared, say, to heavy drinking of fortified and spirited alcohol like whiskey? Although I am not a physician, I have checked with my physician sources for a medically enlightened view. It would appear that the constant or regular abuse of alcohol and/or cigarettes can be more harmful than the occasional smoking of weed. Yet, society appears alright with people drinking such affluent but harmful drinks as spirits.

Now, you might be wondering and thinking: "Maybe this guy also smokes. Why is he so concerned about legalising marijuana?" But to settle your doubts, let me put it clearly. I do not smoke, not even tobacco. With that disclaimer, please allow me to push my argument a little farther. In many parts of the world, there is often a great stigma associated with smoking marijuana. So, even where a Head of State is alleged to have smoked marijuana as a student at university, he will deny and claim instead that he only attempted to smoke but did not 'inhale' the fumes or smoke. Yet, if we were to subject all Heads of State in the world to strict medical exams, including such tests as lie-detectors, with a view of disqualifying from holding office those who have continued to smoke marijuana as well as those who have at some point smoked, we would probably have few Heads of State retaining their majestic offices. Likewise, if we were to extend the same logic to opposition parties, many would have few leaders standing.

Peter Tosh sang about the need to legalise marijuana, contending that even some medical doctors, lawyers, judges and politicians smoke the weed. But his cry fell on deaf ears. Let us, however, be honest and ask ourselves as well as the person seated right next to us: "Have I, or have you, ever smoked marijuana?" Think again. And if you were to ask your boss this same question, you would see how uncomfortable he or she might become. Instead of answering your question, he or she is likely to rebutt inquisitively, fearing that you may have heard something from the grapevine: "Why are you asking?" Just there and then, you should know the answer.

Young people, be warned: do not ask your parents if they have ever smoked marijuana. It is considered rude and disrespectful in our culture to ask elders such questions. Try instead to ask the priest or pastor at Church because these are considered to be the custodians of moral and ethical values in society, especially for a Christian nation such as Zambia. If either of them blushes, and then responds with the question: "Why are you asking?", it is up to you to infer how a reasonable priest or pastor could have answered, especially if he has never smoked before. But, many people live in a world of pretence and denial.

The truth of the matter is that a good number of people, including some priests, pastors, husbands, bosses, aunties, uncles, grandfathers, bishops, wives, sibblings, neighbours, in-laws, divas, and so forth, have all smoked marijuana before. Some of these people hold very senior government jobs. Others are even Chief Executive Officers of major corporations. And there is also a faction that includes renowned soccer players, boxers and sportsmen, as well as engineers, accountants and so forth. The common thread among them all is that the majority cannot come out of the closet for fear of being stigmatised by society. So, the smoking of marijuana remains a hidden secret by the indulging party, even where a culpable house servant, for example, suddenly becomes too energetic and begins to clear an unbelievably heavy workload within a short period of time, or where a culpable dependant suddenly begins to consume insurmountable amounts of nshima at the dinner table or where he habitually breaks into prolonged and inexplicable laughter. So, it is not only the youths or the blue collar workers who are in the habbit of smoking marijuana. Even some educated and seemingly sophisticated socialites are into this habbit. A friend of mine in the US once told me of a story of how some sophistry-inclined young guys and ladies would apply cocaine to their genitals before indulging in illicit sex so as to experience the most powerful and intense orgasm of their lifetime. I could not believe my ears. People do crazy stuff in the name of 'human rights'. So, should Zambia consider legalising marijuana? Or, should marijuana remain as a prohibited drug while we turn a blind eye to the rampant abuse of alcohol and cigarettes?

An anonymous commentator from Zambia observes that: "…marijuana is not an addictive drug; that is the reason why most people have managed to move on when they so decided. Apparently, alcohol is 'physically addictive' while marijuana and soft drinks are 'psychologically addictive' or habitual, and do not engender any reinforcement or withdrawal symptoms. Another dimension is that…the manufacture and sale of alcohol was prohibited in the USA until the 1933 with the passage of the Twenty-first Amendment to the United States Constitution. Other countries have also had their periods of prohibition. Alcohol's acceptability over marijuana is largely due to political correctness and stigmatisation issues, rather than grounded in objective medical assessment… The creative genius of Bob Marley has largely been credited to his use of marijuana."

But, Reuters, in a recent Online article titled, "Marijuana smoking tied to testicular cancer: study", dated September 11, 2012, observes that: "Young men who had smoked marijuana recreationally were twice as likely to be diagnosed with testicular cancer than men who have never used marijuana, according to a U.S. study." Reuters continues that: "Researchers whose findings appeared in the journal, *Cancer*, said the link appeared to be specific to a type of tumor known as nonseminoma."

So, what to do now? To smoke or not to smoke? Shouldn't the abuse of alcohol and tobacco be prohibited as well? Within a month after this article was published in the *Zambia Daily Mail*, the Drug

Enforcement Commission of Zambia (DEC) issued another rebuttal through a press statement. Citing DEC in a media article titled, "Marijuana smoke: DEC calls Professor Bluff," published on October 4, 2012, *Zambia Daily Mail*'s Caroline Kalombe reports:

"THE Drug Enforcement Commission (DEC) has maintained that marijuana is an illegal substance that shall continue to attract punishment by law in Zambia. The DEC was responding to an opinion authored by US-based Zambian Professor Kenneth Mwenda who wants to see the drug legalised... DEC public relations officer Samuel Silomba told the *Zambia Daily Mail* in a statement that there is no credible research both locally and abroad that supports Prof. Mwenda's desire to have the drug legalised. 'Current research does not support the idea that marijuana is harmless,' Mr Silomba said, adding that many studies indicate that marijuana usage leads to 'crime, violence, drug dependence and the use of other drugs.' Prof. Kenneth Mwenda's article was published as an opinion under the title: 'Legalising marijuana: to smoke or not to smoke?' Mr Silomba said research shows that cultivation of cannabis poses a threat to food security, as most peasant farmers were replacing cultivation of crops such as rice, yam, maize and cassava with cannabis. He said cannabis abuse adversely affects productivity and development in African communities and poses a direct threat to the health of users."

But in the said rebuttal, DEC did not make a good

case to challenge the legal argument I have advanced on the constitutionality of banning marijuana. And the making of a legal argument need not be construed necessarily as an incitement! The courts of law are there to help us understand issues where there is an unsettled argument or querry. That is really the issue, as opposed to the rather emotive rebuttal from DEC against the legalization of weed. Indeed, we need good legal arguments, as well as empirical public health data on what has caused more health-related costs between weed, on the one hand, and alcohol-tobacco, on the other.

Quoting DEC's Public Relations Officer, Mr. Silomba, Zambia Daily Mail's Caroline Kalombe notes further that: "…'Professor Mwenda under-stated the negative effects of cannabis use, by dwelling more on the perceived benefits of the drug,' he said. Mr Silomba said legalising marijuana will not only increase the number of addicts but will also lead to government redirecting money meant for development projects to the treatment and reintegration of addicts. He said the economic argument for legalising cannabis cultivation has been considered as unethical and uneconomic. 'The economic argument is based on poor fiscal logic as any reduction in the cost of drug control will be offset by much higher expenditure on public health,' Mr Silomba said."

But then, to what extent, for example, has the abuse of marijuana in Zambia caused more heath-related costs on the Government than, say, the treatment of aliments relating to alcohol and tobacco abuse? Besides, what could be attributed to less productivity of some Zambian workers today, the abuse of alcohol or the abuse of marijuana? These are critical issues that DEC should have given some thought to. Indeed, as Zambia's *Post* newspaper observes in its editorial of October 4, 2012, titled "Limiting Alcohol Availability":

"...Alcohol is not an ordinary commodity. It is a powerful toxin with undeniable physical, mental and social consequences for drinkers and those around them. Levels of alcohol consumption and related harms are a function of both the demand for the product and its supply or availability, and there is a clear need to intervene in these in order to achieve the balance between the costs and the apparent benefit of alcohol supply and consumption... The restrictions on the sale and supply of alcohol need to be further tightened and strictly enforced. We think that alcohol should be further restricted to prevent some of its negative consequences. Alcohol causes many unnecessary deaths that could be prevented somehow. Alcohol is involved in most of the violent crimes that occur in our country. It is also well-established that alcohol will impair brain development in those under 25. It is addictive, it damages unborn babies, it causes much hardship. How could we as a society watch such a thing and try to do nothing about it? ...Things are out of control in Zambia over the abuse of alcohol."

However, citing DEC's response to this author's article on the issue of marijuana, *Zambia Daily*

Mail's Caroline Kalombe points out further that: "He added that cannabis is the 'gateway to abuse of hard drugs such as cocaine and heroin which can lead to severe health problems.' Mr Silomba expressed sadness that Prof. Mwenda is 'inciting Rastafarians and young people to push for the legalisation of cultivation, sale and use of marijuana.' In the article, Prof. Mwenda argues that as long as society allows or approves the abuse of more harmful drugs such as alcohol and tobacco, which are often consumed on a more regular basis and in large amounts, then the authorities might as well permit adults the free choice to smoke marijuana. 'Otherwise, let us ban alcohol and tobacco as well,' he argues. He says Rastafarians in Zambia, for example, should bring action before the High Court, arguing that the law that prohibits the cultivation, smoking, selling or buying cannabis is unconstitutional because it contravenes the petitioners' constitutionally guaranteed freedoms of conscience and expression, especially if the petitioners can show that the use of marijuana remains a central part of their Rastafarian religion."

- Kenneth K. Mwenda

CHAPTER

4

ALCOHOL AND CIGARETTES:
TO BAN OR NOT TO BAN?

In the early 2000s, I travelled to Libya at the invitation of the Libyan Government. During my stay there, I was priviledged to have a couple of one-on-one meetings with the then Libyan President, the late Col. Muammar Ghaddafi. I was intrigued and humbled by his kind and patient demeanour, as I presented my technical paper before him.

I was approached and invited directly by the Libyan authorities after they had read some of my research work on stock markets in Africa. In Libya, they looked after me very well, especially that I was designated officially as a Guest of the Head of State. It was at a time when the African Union was being born. I was provided with a presidential jet to fly from Tripoli to Sirte where the African Heads of State were meeting.

On my way back from Sirte to Tripoli, I met a number of African Heads of State at the airport.

They had travelled to Libya to attend the inception ceremony of the African Union. Among them was Zambia's first Republican President, Dr. Kenneth Kaunda. Upon noticing Dr. Kaunda, I managed to maneuver my way by asking one of the Libyan security personnel to let Dr. Kaunda know that there was a Zambian nearby who wanted to say hello to a fellow Zambian. The Libyan security officer hesitated a bit, and asked me if I actually knew Dr. Kaunda – to which I simply smiled confidently before pulling a fast one. "Who do you think are my friends?" I asked the Libyan security officer (smile).

Before he could even answer, I continued: "I came here to Libya at the invitation of Brother Leader (*i.e.* Col Ghaddafi) himself." Indeed, that was true. So, the security officer panicked. He then hurried over to Dr. Kaunda to let him know that his 'Zambian friend' wanted to say hello (smile). I was thus ushered through on to the red carpet by security, as they escorted me to where Dr. Kaunda sat. Of course, it was a pleasant meeting. I must admit, however, that I'd made it up that Dr. Kaunda was a close friend (smile). But it worked, and I had a good and cordial chat with Dr. Kaunda before we both boarded the same jet from Sirte to Tripoli. He took a seat in the First Class, while I took a seat in the Business Class. Now, you may be wondering how this Libyan story comes in.

Throughout my stay in Libya, I had no access alcohol. I mean, I am not an alcoholic. But I do enjoy a good drink occasionally. Alcohol was, however, not allowed, although I was made to understand that some foreign diplomats could consume alcohol within the confines of their diplomatic premises only. To fast-forward, however, on Thursday, October 4, 2012, Zambia's Post newspaper carried an excellent editorial, outlining the negative effects of alcohol abuse. And I fully concur with and commend the Post on the said editorial which highlighted also recent regulatory measures in Zambia to lessen alcohol abuse.

Sadly, I am at pains to understand why the Drug Enforcement Commission (DEC) in Zambia hardly says much about possible ways to prevent alcohol and tobacco abuse (as opposed to dealing mainly with the treatment of alcohol abusers), but seems to take a harder stance against proscribed drugs. Perhaps it is because alcohol and cigarettes for adults are not prohibited by law. But, shouldn't we all be concerned with the effects of alcohol as much as we appear concerned with the effects of, say, marijuana or hard drugs? Even if alcohol and tobacco are not proscribed by law, DEC's sustained public awareness campaigns can influence not only behavioral change but also public policy.

However, in an article published in the Zambia Daily Mail on Friday, October 5, 2012, DEC, through its Public Relations Officer, led an onslaught of an insightful article that I had written in the Zambia Daily Mail a few weeks ago, regarding whether or not Zambia should consider legalising marijuana. There was a deliberate effort in the DEC rebuttal to avoid talking about alcohol and tobacco, but to focuss exclusively on the negative effects of marijuana. Look, the medical arguments presented by DEC on the harmful effects of marijuana are not contestable. Rather, the argument is on the deliberate and misleading omission by DEC on the harmful effects of alcohol, which is often consumed in larger amounts and more regularly than the occasional smoking of marijuana by many who smoke. Let us take a more reasoned look on the effects of alcohol abuse.

In the US, for example, the Centers for Disease Control and Prevention (CDC) point out on their 'Alcohol and Public Health' website (accessed on October 5, 2012) that: "There are approximately 80,000 deaths attributable to excessive alcohol use each year in the United States. This makes excessive alcohol use the 3rd leading lifestyle-related cause of death for the nation. Excessive alcohol use is responsible for 2.3 million years of potential life lost (YPLL) annually, or an average of about 30 years of potential life lost for each death. In 2006, there were more than 1.2 million emergency room visits and 2.7 million physician office visits due to excessive drinking. The economic costs of excessive alcohol consumption in 2006 were estimated at \$223.5 billion."

CDC adds further that, over time, excessive alcohol use can lead to the development of chronic diseases, neurological impairments and social problems. These include but are not limited to: (a) neurological problems, including dementia, stroke and neuropathy; (b) cardiovascular problems, including myocardial infarction, cardiomyopathy, atrial fibrillation and hypertension, (c) psychiatric problems, including depression, anxiety, and suicide, (d) social problems, including unemployment, lost productivity, and family problems; and, (e) cancer of the mouth, throat, esophagus, liver, colon, and breast. In general, as CDC observes, the risk of cancer increases with increasing amounts of alcohol.

Other illnesses associated with excessive alcohol use relate to liver diseases, including: (f) alcoholic hepatitis; (g) cirrhosis, which is among the 15 leading causes of all deaths in the United States; (h) among persons with Hepatitis C virus, worsening of liver function and interference with medications used to treat this condition; and (i) other gastrointestinal problems, including pancreatitis and gastritis. What to do now? Can we say ifya ku America fya ku America, and that things are different in Zambia?

Why is it then that our Zambian laws tend to prohibit the production and selling of Zambian traditional liquors such as Kachasu and Utujili-jili, while turning a blind eye to equally strong western-inspired liquors such as spirits? If we can ban Utujili-jili, we might as well ban other liquors. Is it because these other drinks are taken mainly by the urban socialites and the affluent? Indeed, section 6A of Zambia's Traditional Beer Act 1930 (as amended through 1994) provides that: "It shall be unlawful for any person to prepare, use, possess, dispense, sell or expose for sale, the intoxicating liquor, by whatever name called, which is obtained through a process of distillation and is commonly known as kachipembe, kachasu, kapuli or lutuku."

Understand this: even with cigarettes, it took a long time before the wealthy manufacturing companies that make cigarettes could be forced to start including warning messages on cigarette packets that tobacco is a health hazard. Indeed, the power of these multinational corporations cannot be underestimated. By contrast, the poor Kachasu brewer has no such power, and his drink can thus be banned easily. The authorities can just say: "Kachasu is brewed under unhygienic conditions!"

Also, our own socialization often makes us behave or think differently towards the kind of drinks that westerners themselves deem acceptable and alright. In short, we do not have our own indigenous standards over what is acceptable liquor and what is not. But most alcohol, in all honesty, has serious health hazards, especially when it is taken regularly. Now, one could argue that the marijuana has a higher level of toxin concentration than, say, tobacco. But, the latter can also have debilitating effects when taken too often over a long period of time. Besides, many people that smoke cigarettes do so more regularly than many smokers of marijuana.

Finally, to argue that since Zambia is a State Party to a treaty that proscribes marijuana, and that it cannot therefore consider legalising marijuana, is an argument that is not free from illogical difficulties. Such a submission is somewhat disingenuous, and it shows a lack understanding of how international law works. For example, under the Vienna Convention of the Law of Treaties 1969, a State Party to a treaty need not necessarily abrogate or contravene treaty obligations, but it can instead provide notification to other State Parties of its intention to terminate or withdrawal from the treaty. And after withdrawing from the treaty, Zambia can grow marijuana, as a cash crop, for export (*e.g.* as medicinal marijuana). Consider, for example, how western countries manufacture and sell military weapons recklessly to warring factions in Africa! Do they even care?

CHAPTER

CONTEXTUALISING POVERTY
OF THE MIND

Human mortality has no permanent state of existence, yet some people carry on with their lives as if they will live forever. Many years ago, I attended mass at a local Catholic Church in Lusaka, Zambia, and the presiding priest posited as follows: "Many people are obsessed with accumulating money and material things. They never cease to amaze us. If you ask them, 'What next after all this?', they will tell you that they need to make more money or to acquire many more other things. OK, let us assume that they make all that money, or that they acquire all those other things, then what? Will that make them happy? Or, will they continue with their greed to keep adding more and more to what they already have? When does it ever get enough?"

One anonymous commentator observes: "You see, in Zambia, it's what you have, or what people think you have, that will draw them to you. The situation is worse with us women,...we get ourselves into a lot of debt, just to impress. If your friend changes their car, you follow suit and change yours too. It even gets to a point where people borrow for superficial things like hair and makeup. All in the name of keeping up appearances. You even end up putting your children in expensive private schools because all faith is lost in the public school system. It is very difficult to stay afloat in these times, but thankfully, there are those of us who can see through the maze."

The said commentator continues: "Guys also pretend to have what they do not have in order to feel more macho so that they can woo a girl, I don't blame them though, coz who would sit down to listen to a guy who says, he has 'nothing', but love for you? Will I eat love? LOL…" Indeed, we are living in trying times. We begin to see that things are falling apart when what we used to call "servants' quarters" (*i.e.* a small residential quarter reserved for either the houseservant or the maid, standing adjacent to the boss' house) now assumes the new name of "cottage" as these housing quarters enter Zambia's rental market. One need not be surprised to find that the highly publicized "cottages" in Zambia's capital city, Lusaka, are simply the servants' quarters of the olden days. These quarters are now well accepted forms of accommodation for many young and single educated working class individuals, especially when other people are busy acquiring plots and building houses on what used to be called back then as "side-walks" or "pavements". In Zambia, like many other developing countries, residential areas today, unlike in the past, hardly have any side-walks or pavements on which to walk a dog or take a stroll. In fact, dogs now hardly go for walks with their owners! Rather, folks are busy building residential homes and offices even on public land which once hosted parks for social relaxation! Most likely, our public libraries too will soon be turned into building plots by the eagerly excited land-grabbers!!! In many parts of the developing world, the children of today no longer know what a park looks like or should look like. Yet, we have more pubs coming up every other day in countries such as Zambia. Things are culturally falling apart right before our own eyes!

As one respondent notes: "Prof., this trend is very common especially in Lusaka. Apparently the so-called cottages are expensive...going as high as K1,500,000 per month. People go to such lengths just to avoid living in compounds (i.e. high density and poorer parts of the city). Everyone finds pleasure and satisfaction in saying that they live in Woodlands, Kabulonga etc, and not to mention places like Mtendere, Matero, Chaisa. Ala ni pa ZED."

The cottage formula, though innovative, appears to be a deliberate misrepresentation of facts by many landlords so as to woo tenants. You know how it is when people have to embellish facts in all manner of euphemism so as to make things appear cool. In the USA, for example, some folks that have been to prison or done some jail time often say "...they went to school..."; meaning that they were in jail. And their baby-mama would rather say: "My man was incarcerated for an altercation..." instead of just saying, "My man was arrested and jailed for getting into a fight with someone." People use certain euphemism to make things sound lighter or cool.

In Zambia, those cottages, or rather the concerned premises or parcels of land should simply be referred to as 'renovated servants quarters' or 'refurbished servants quarters.' That is, indeed, what they are, unless we are saying the premises' name changes depending on the social standing of the person occupying them. What is even more worrying in many parts of the developing world today, especially in the relatively affluent neighbourhooods, is that many people have to barricade themselves every night behind a heavy brick wall fence with high voltage electrical lines installed on top of the 'prison-like' wall fence! Indeed, that is the now widely accepted form of home security. Imagine if a fire were to break out and people needed to be evacuated urgently, how can they be evacuated with all those wall-fences surrounding them, in addition to the reinforced metal grill doors in their homes as well as the heavy metal burglar-prevention bars outside their home-windows? It just defeats the beauty of the house when people have to add all sorts of Christmas tree security decorations to their house. But many take pride in having such security gadgets as a sign of affluence.

A colleague of mine, whose name is withheld and protected, shared with me this interesting life-drama in Zambia: "I am reminded of a story that my boss told me about his former workmate. The man had studied so much and was away from Zambia for about 8 years. When he returned from abroad armed with is PhD, he landed himself a big job at one of the government ministries, complete with all the trappings and a driver. The funniest thing was that, whenever his father went to visit him, he would instruct his driver to interpret for him what the old man was saying. He claimed that he had forgotten his Nsenga-mother tongue, and that he therefore needed an interpreter to communicate with his own father!" As noted above, we are living in very strange times.

Similarly, a local chap in Lusaka called "Schooner" is in the habbit of walking around town with a hefty-looking wallet tightly fitted in the rear pocket of his pants, pretending to have a lot of money. The pocket would bulge as if he is carrying a grenade. Unknown to the unsuspecting crowd, Schooner, nicknamed after the famous disco shoe of the late 1970s and early 1980s, likes to load his wallet with worthless newspaper cuttings so as to make it appear as though it is loaded with cash. And when he pitches up at a pub, he carries on with his usual walk of airs and confidence. His style is to buy a round of beers for everyone at the main table as soon as he steps into the club. Once he has done that, Schooner then sits back to enjoy the next 'free' rounds bought by others. He knows full well that many will only remember that he bought a round when he arrived, and that that might make them forget about his turn to buy any subsequent round. And as soon as Schooner notices that his turn to buy the next round might be nearing, he conveniently excuses himself to go to the toilet. Schooner has mastered this art so well, and only returns from the toilet when someone else has bought the next round of beers. For Schooner, it is all about keeping up appearances. Don't we all know of folks like Schooner?

Back in the days, Schooner had a different strategy. He would pretend to have forgotten his wallet at home whenever he went out to a nightclub in the company of his friends. He would then ask one of his friends to loan him some money to be repaid the next day. His famous line was: "Mdala, how's about a K50 grand, I will square you up tomorrow. I forgot my wallet..." But, you would be lucky if you ever saw Schooner the next day!

This is a guy who, while wearing small-size schooner shoes borrowed from a friend (and those small shoes would obviously hurt, but that did not stop him from having a good time), would explain London to women even though he had never been to London himself. He would simply study the map of London as well as the map of the London underground train stations, and then package his words nicely for the women as if he has been there. And while his friends were busy studying in school, Schooner would skip classes, preferring to watch American movies and to rehearse an American accent. Schooner had also mastered the names of famous places and cities in the UK and the US. On certain weekends, Schooner would tell his friends, especially the ladies that he was off to the UK or the States. He would then lock himself indoors at home, telling all his family members not to tell anyone asking after him that he was around. Come Monday, Schooner would resurface from his hideout, pretending to have just arrived from London. Indeed, Schooner has evolved over the years, starting with the old times when he used to drink the opaque local beer known as 'chibuku' to the current times when he claims to be an all 'whiskey' man who likes his whiskey on the rocks.

As one correspondent observes: "Pa zedee, you have lads and lasses aba cikwela (*i.e.* hustlers)! Now it's about political and economic cikwela. These fellas know each and every Minister who comes into power, it does not matter which political party the Minister represents, be it UNIP, MMD, PF they have to chase the powers that be! When it comes to rich families, these fellas know the apamwambas to an extent of claiming 'we are family friends!' The lasses are well known for claiming to be very good buddies of children of heads of state or ministers. First, it was President Kaunda's children that they claimed to know, then President Chiluba's children, followed by President Rupiah Banda's children and now President Michael Sata's children…(smile)!"

And closely related to that, another correspondent observes: "Yes, as a matter of fact, I know a lot of Schooners…, one took my two friends for lunch and told them to order whatever they wanted. When it was time to pay, he got a 'very important call' and left in a hurry, leaving them with a bill for three plates." As someone noted in response to my recent article in the *Zambia Daily Mail* on the emergence of a culture of consumption and accumulation, "You should see how many people are deep in debt because of this same culture of consumption and accumulation. As for the church, just check out some bumper stickers on some cars: 'It's a sin to be poor. 2012 the year of reaping etc'. My question is: 'Where have we gotten this culture from, especially when it comes to the church?'...".

I once met an interesting guy at Arcades Shopping Mall in Lusaka through a mutual friend. We met in the parking lot as I was alighting from a taxi. My friend was trying to introduce us, but the other guy carried on with some self-assumed airs of importance. I am not sure that he knew or realised who I was. By contrast, I never made any assumptions about him, and was ready to get introduced. But, the chap started pacing around while playing with his car keys in the hands. In his mind, there was no point in talking to someone who had just come out of an old-looking and 'finished' taxi. So, he moved closer to this very nice car parked near where we were standing and continued to pace around the car, kicking into its tires as if to check whether the tires needed some more air. The guy was trying to tell me that that is his car. But, what amazed me most was that he was trying to play such childish prank with someone he hardly even knew. Indeed, before you pull such stunts, it is always best to find out first who the other person is. When my friend later told him who exactly I was that is when the guy sobbered down and froze in his pants. What a life! It does not have to come to this.

CHAPTER

6

PLIGHT OF AN INSECURE BLACK MAN IN A RACIALLY DIVIDED WORLD

We live in a racially divided world, although sometimes the social class stratifications in society, based on different people's income and wealth, tend to mask these divisions. But the divisions are there. How, then, does the insecure black man and/or black woman respond to the issue of race? The topic of race, like that of tribalism and other ethnic prejudices, is a very sensitive one. But, then, we cannot shy away from reality, even though we are mindful not to push stereotypes. No doubt, to every general rule there is an exception. And we must keep that in mind. Appreciating exceptions here can help us to avoid making unfounded generalisations as well as to avoid overreacting to arguments. For example, the use of the word 'negro' is generally frowned upon in many parts of the world as a derogatory and offensive term. However, in this paper, wherever the word is used, we do not intend or mean to advance any racial slurs. That is far from it. Rather, the term is used only as a direct quote from or reference to current literature on race relations. Besides, this author is also a black man.

Johnny K, an African man married to a white lady, loves to walk their family dog every evening. The couple lives in an affluent white neighbourhood. And they prefer not to have any children. They only have a dog. To impress his white wife and her white relatives and friends, Johnny K wants to behave as though he is some kind of different black brother from the other blacks. Johnny K pretends that he does not speak any African language. Indeed, Johnny K feels that he is now a 'civilised' and 'enlightened' black man who is fortunate enough to have a white lady on his dark-skinned African hairy arm. Yet, Johnny K comes from a very humble and poor background. He grew up in an impoverished neighbourhood. But, Johnny K is now trying to hide that economically deprived background.

Johnny K's friends are mainly from the white community. And he is very proud of that 'achievement'. It might actually be his greatest achievement thus far. With the influx of all these so-called foreign investors in Africa, folks like Johnny K are now commonplace. Indeed, such chaps are ubiquitously found everywhere, constantly falling all over their knees in the rush to befriend these so-called white and Chinese foreign investors. Even in workplaces, there are many Johnny Ks who will not even greet a fellow black person when they are in the company of white people. They want to behave whiter than white, but their skin is just too dark to whiten up!

Someone recently told me of a funny story of how some educated black people try so hard to befriend white people in some workplaces in the hope that that will influence their career progression. He added: "Especially in these multinational corporations...you will even find some married black women showing their teeth aimlessly and exposing their upper legs all in the hope of winning favours from their white male bosses! Such people hardly spend time with fellow black people, pretending to be busy until they meet the next white person in the corridor. I really don't understand what is wrong with some of our black brothers and sisters! And when they get that promotion that they have been craving for – that is, after all the sucking up to the white folks – they think that they have now arrived. They will do everything to keep their fellow blacks on the lower echelons of the ladder. And I mean just that. Look, I once attended a job interview. There were four white guys, one white lady, and a black man. Yet, it was the black man that asked me the stupidest of all questions, hoping to make things for me difficult. For the white woman, I could understand where she was coming from in terms of her aggression and unfriendliness, as she may have preferred a white male to get the job. It is not unusual for them."

So, the argument that we have now moved past the era of racial discrimination, and that a number of international treaties against racial discrimination have now been signed and ratified by various States, is a superficial grasp of race relations. We have not moved past anything, but have only taken a turn into a parallel highway. In the US, for example, the demise of the heightened epoch of the civil rights movement did not signal an end to racism. Neither has racism come to an end in many parts of Europe, Latin America, the Caribbean Islands, South Asia, East Asia and Africa. By contrast, much of what we are now seeing relates to subtle, but more acute forms of racial discrimination. Examples of such prejudices include institutional racism in some workplaces as well as limited job and educational opportunities for those that belong to certain racial groupings.

Someone once remarked: "Why is it that while many Asian people like to give each other jobs, including looking out for their own, we, Africans, don't? What is it that we fear? Look, it is not only the Asians. Even the whites do the same; they also like to look out for their own in the name of 'networking'. Hispanics too are like that. They look out for their own. Yet, we, Africans, don't. Sometimes, we even discriminate amongst ourselves based on things like tribe as well as such other peculiar grounds as whether someone speaks French or English, as if the white English and French people care much about which nigger speaks French or English! You would be lucky to find a courageous African who can stand up for a fellow African in the midst of white people or Asian people. In fact, he or she may be the main adversary or obstacle, as he or she tries to destroy you in order to appease the whites. We are often very quick at back-stabbing each other, hating on each other and even selling out. Why?"

In his 1952 book, "Black Skin White Masks", Frantz Fanon, a black man born in the French colony and island of Martinique, and a medical doctor by profession with a specialisation in psychiatry, articulated a race theory about the impact of inferiority complex of subjugated peoples, in particular black people, and the alienation of some of them from their kind. Fanon posited that such inferiority complex often resulted in a number of these subjugated people wishing and hoping to be identified with the whites or to imitate the European way of life. In his thesis, Fanon drew on examples relating to the black man and his eagerness to learn very quickly, almost to a state of ultimate perfection, the white man's language as well as the white man's accent and pronunciations. Fanon also laments the inferiority complex exhibited by some women of colour who are so eager to marry themselves off to white men. He laments further a similar inferiority complex of some black men who are so eager to marry a white woman, believing themselves to have now attained a higher level of sophistication. In his book, Fanon explores the psycho-affective condition of the person of colour in the midst of a dominating white culture and ideology. He examines additionally the so-called 'dependency complex of colonised' people before shifting to look at what he calls 'the fact of blackness' and the discourse relating to 'the negro and psychopathology' as well as to the 'negro and recognition'.

Closely related to Fanon's work, Malcom X posited that: "There was two kind of slaves. There was the house negro and the field negro." According to Malcom X, "The house negro, they lived in the house, with master. They dressed pretty good. They ate good, cause they ate his food, what he left. They lived in the attic or the basement, but still they lived near their master, and they loved their master, more than their master loved himself. They would give their life to save their masters house quicker than their master would. The house negro, if the master said 'we got a good house here' the house negro say 'yeah, we got a good house here'. Whenever the master would said 'we', he'd say 'we'. That's how you can tell a house negro. If the master's house caught on fire, the house negro would fight harder to put the blaze out than the master would. If the master got sick, the house negro would say 'What's the matter, boss, we sick?'..."

Although Malcom X and Frantz Fanon wrote their works many years ago, their words still ring true today. As Malcom X noted: "...we still got some house niggers runnin' around here. This modern house negro loves his master. He wants to live near him. He'll pay three times as much as the house is worth just to live near his master, and then brag about, 'I'm the only negro out here. I'm the only one on my job. I'm the only one in this school.' 'You're nothing but a house negro. And if someone come to you right now and say 'Let's separate', you say the same thing that the house negro said on the plantation. 'What you mean separate?... Where you gonna get a better job than you get here? I mean, this is what you say!.."

Insightfully, Malcom X concludes: "On that same plantation, there was the field negro. The field negro, those were the masses... The field negro was beaten, from morning til night. He lived in a shack, in a hut. He wore cast-off clothes. He hated his master. I say, he hated his master. He was intelligent. That house negro loved his master. But that field negro, remember, they were in the majority, and they hated their master. When the house caught on fire, he didn't try to put it out, that field negro prayed for a wind. For a breeze. When the master got sick, the field negro prayed that he died. If someone come to the field negro and said 'Let's separate, let's run.' He didn't say 'Where we going?' He said, 'Any place is better than here'..."

- Kenneth K. Mwenda

70

CHAPTER

7

WORKING FOR A LOUSY BOSS

WHEN some employees quit work, many leave not because they do not like the company. By contrast, they leave because of bad bosses. Indeed, it is the bad decisions of some bosses that force many employees to leave work or to quit the company. Often times, lousy bosses help in festering a lousy work-culture and bad work ethics in the workplace. As Greg Smith argues in an Online op-ed for the *New York Times*, dated March 14, 2012, and titled, 'Why I Am Leaving Goldman Sachs':

"TODAY is my last day at Goldman Sachs. After almost 12 years at the firm — first as a summer intern while at Stanford, then in New York for 10 years, and now in London — I believe I have worked here long enough to understand the trajectory of its culture, its people and its identity. And I can honestly say that the environment now is as toxic and destructive as I have ever seen it. To put the problem in the simplest terms, the interests of the client continue to be sidelined in the way the firm operates and thinks about making money. Goldman Sachs is one of the world's largest and most important investment banks and it is too integral to global finance to continue to act this way. The firm has veered so far from the place I joined right out of college that I can no longer in good conscience say that I identify with what it stands for."

Smith, a white South African, continues: "It might sound surprising to a skeptical public, but culture was always a vital part of Goldman Sachs's success. It revolved around teamwork, integrity, a spirit of humility, and always doing right by our clients. The culture was the secret sauce that made this place great and allowed us to earn our clients' trust for 143 years. It wasn't just about making money; this alone will not sustain a firm for so long. It had something to do with pride and belief in the organization. I am sad to say that I look around today and see virtually no trace of the culture that made me love working for this firm for many years."

In concluding, Smith laments: "When the history books are written about Goldman Sachs, they may reflect that the current chief executive officer, Lloyd C. Blankfein, and the president, Gary D. Cohn, lost hold of the firm's culture on their watch. I truly believe that this decline in the firm's moral fiber represents the single most serious threat to its long-run survival... How did we get here? The firm changed the way it thought about leadership. Leadership used to be about ideas, setting an example and doing the right thing. Today, if you make enough money for the firm (and are not currently an ax murderer) you will be promoted into a position of influence... It makes me ill how callously people talk about ripping their clients off. Over the last 12 months I have seen five different managing directors refer to their own clients as 'muppets,' sometimes over internal e-mail."

As can be seen from the example of Greg Smith above, there is a correlation between good corporate executive leadership and the motivation of employees. This nexus lies at the fulcrum of strategic human resources management (HRM). And so, where there is a bad manager – that is, a manager who performs poorly in his or her management function – the situation can be seen as a recipe for attrition or high turnover of employees.

Have you ever found yourself working under a hopeless and incompetent boss? You could be feeling as though I know you or that I am talking about your situation. Or, you could have felt at some point like punching your boss in the face. Yes, some bosses are quite a pain in the back. Others are plain insecure and will try to make life so difficult for whoever they deem to be a potential threat, especially those employees who appear to be more competent or better skilled than the manager himself or herself. And you do not have to do anything to upset such a manager or to spark-off a conflict.

As Miyanda Maimbo writes in a media article titled, "Managers who make employee work life miserable," published in *Zambia's Post newspaper* on February

20, 2013: "IN the many years that I have been conducting recruitment on behalf of companies and the many years that I have sat across job seekers, I have marveled at the number of employees who quit their jobs not because they are unhappy with the company they are working for but with their immediate supervisor or manager... Two weeks ago a young man came to our office to see whether we could assist him find a job. Looking at his CV, he had good experience and qualifications and was in fact working for a reasonably good organisation so I was a little surprised as to why he would want to leave a company that many jobs seekers approach me wanting to join. He looked at me, looked to the ground and broke down, crying uncontrollably. It took me by surprise, as you don't see men cry easily and so I let him cry for a while and after a few minutes he composed himself and started to tell his story."

Miyanda notes further: "He had been working for the company for about five years. He loved the company and looked forward to going to work each morning for the first three years. A few of those times he was asked to act in the position of the manager whenever the manager was on leave or away on company business. In his fifth year, his manager was promoted and a colleague in the same department as him was appointed to the position of manager and that is when his nightmare began. His former workmate now manager would shout, insult and put him down in front of his workmates. When he was dealing with a customer and made any slight mistake, the manager would reprimand him and threaten to fire him right in front of the customer. When everyone had knocked off work, the manager would wait for the time he was just about to leave and prevent him from leaving and would give him assignments that took no less than three hours to complete, meaning that he arrived home after 21:00hours (9pm) every day."

As Miyanda observes, the situation that this young man was going through was beginning to affect his relationship with his wife. Indeed, his wife started to suspect that he was having an extra-marital affair. Every day, he would get home late in the night, finding his children fast asleep. According to Miyanda, in the three months since the young man's new manager took up his office, the young man got moved out of the company's headquarters to one of its tiny branches in the outskirts of the city. There, he had no access to proper working tools such as a basic computer. Yet, every day his new boss would shout at him for failing to send in a typed weekly report. The young man tried to seek recourse from the human resource department but that, unfortunately, yielded no positive results as the human resource manager was a very good friend of the young man's new manager.

Further, in addition to being moved to a small branch, the young man was informed that his salary would be reduced by 50 per cent because of the 'supposed' demotion. However, he could not quit his job since his now meagre income helped to supplement his wife's salary. But the whole experience had a dent on his self-esteem especially that his wife was now making more money than him. The young man also complained that whenever he sought leave from work for, say, a day only, his new manager would not grant him that leave. And nothing that he did was said to be good enough. His written reports would be over-scrutinized, with deliberate witch-hunting and hair-splitting criticisms, and sent back to him for substantial revisions. His contributions in meetings would be shot down. It reached a point where he had no choice but to start looking for a job elsewhere.

By now, you are probably thinking that this sounds very familiar with what you have experienced or what you are currently experiencing at your workplace. Just know that you are not alone. There are many silent voices out there that continue to suffer quietly in workplaces. And working for a lousy boss can at times affect your health and well-being. So, what to do now? Sadly, due to lack of transparency in many corrupt institutions, the right hand (*i.e.* the Chief Executive) will not always know what the left hand (*i.e.* the line-mangers or supervisors) is up to or has been doing. If anything, the left hand will try to conceal from the right hand all manner of impropriety and prejudice.

BLAME
In many cases, where you have an insecure manager or supervisor be assured that he or she might come out heavy on you with the hammer even if you are minding your own business. Insecure bosses are the worst people you can ever work for. They will do everything to eliminate what they perceive to be a

threat. They will blame you even for things you have not done, so as to make you appear as a non-performer in the eyes of the unsuspecting crowd. And many lousy managers tend to surround themselves with their cronies and bootlickers, promoting an adverse culture of patronage.

Have you ever worked for a boss who promotes or appoints only people that belong to his or her own tribe, nationality or race? Does that sound familiar? Some bosses will by-pass their immediate subordinate and ask someone else much junior to act for them when they are travelling or are on leave. Have you ever been by-passed or overlooked like that? How did it feel?

MICRO-MANAGING

There are also those bosses who are obsessed with micro-managing people or making a mountain out of a mole whenever an employee makes a mistake. Some bosses even use abusive language, screaming at their employees or comparing them to worst performers ever. Other bosses will avoid talking to people they do not like, or those from a different tribe, nationality or race, focusing much of their attention instead on their cronies. Have you ever worked with such a boss? Ask yourself: why does my boss behave the way he or she does?

In many cases, you will find that your boss is quite insecure. He or she could have risen into management not on merit but through patronage or cronyism. And the latter two are nothing but insidious forms of corruption. When you are dealing with such corrupt people, you need to understand that they often lack moral and ethical leadership. Theirs is a crooked life. If it means sleeping their way to the top, they can easily do that without any shame. And if it means taking a bribe, they can do so very easily. Corrupt bosses come in many forms and shapes.

ADVANCES
If you are a lady, have you ever had a male boss at work trying to make a pass at you? How did you handle the situation? And if you are married, did you tell your husband about your boss's unwelcome advances? If not, why? Notwithstanding that many companies now have policies prohibiting sexual harassment, there are still some male bosses out there who will attempt to sleep or flirt with some of their female subordinates.

And if, for some reason, you end up dating your boss and then later decide to halt the affair, how did your boss react? Was your boss vindictive? Or, did he or she come out hard on you, looking for faults in your work or witch-hunting for mistakes in order to make your life so miserable? Did your boss attempt to spread false rumours about you or eventually try to kick you out of the company? And if you declined his or her sexual advances at the very outset, did he or she decide to by-pass you for career development opportunities, offering these opportunities instead to less deserving colleagues? And are there any workmates at the office who could have compromised their morals and slept with your boss? What advice did such colleagues give you: to sleep with your boss or to report his or her unwelcome sexual advances? And what if your boss is the owner of the business entity, rendering ineffective or futile any attempt to report him or her to the human resources manager?

CONTRACT

A young widowed mother of three once mentioned that her fixed-term employment contract was coming to an end, and that her male boss suggested to her that he would consider renewing the contract if she could give him "some". The poor lady noted that the man was married, and that he had been making sexual advances at her for some time, insisting that 'she should not be stingy with her body'. What to do now, as they would say in Russia? In the meantime, she needed the job to support her family and to pay for her children's school fees. She tried to talk to other managers at the workplace for some advice, but many were also into the same vice of illicit sexual affairs at the workplace.

Some bosses have a tendency of giving bad testimonials and references about their subordinates, especially if the latter is seeking employment elsewhere. What do you do when you find out this? Should you punch your boss in the face? Other bosses have a tendency of denying their subordinates entitlement to some incentives provided by the company. For example, X wants to go back to school for further education, and the company does provide for such educational benefits. But X's boss turns down X's application for study-leave on the ground that there would be nobody to act on behalf of X should X go back to school. Based on his or her last performance review, X is aware that senior management indicated that it will consider promoting him or her to the level of his or her manager should X successfully complete an appropriate Masters degree. And, apart from the full-time Masters degree programme that X wants to pursue, there are no alternative distance-learning, Online or part-time Masters programmes. What to do now?

DECISIONS

Sometimes, you will have situations where a manager bases his decisions or actions solely on what his personal assistant tells him, especially if the two enjoy a relationship that goes beyond the office. If your boss is sleeping with his personal assistant, then that personal assistant is, de facto, your boss too. That is the price of working for a lousy boss. He or she can make your life miserable. And you have to stomach such crap. Some bosses will even write bad performance reviews just to keep you from getting promoted. Others will deliberately write glowing performance reviews and excellent reference letters so that you can easily get a job elsewhere and leave their unit. It is a way of getting rid of you quickly.

RACISM

Closely related to the foregoing, institutional racism, like tribalism and nepotism, can encourage bad behaviour of some bosses. A boss who is racist will pretend to be nice and all. But you will notice from the way he or she interacts with people from other races, especially the minorities, that he or she is a racist. Time and again, such bosses will pass remarks that are either stereotypes or demeaning and judgemental of some minorities. And people that are racist often want to justify their behaviour as though it is not personal against the person that they are targeting or have targeted. They will try to use all sorts of lame excuses to try and make themselves look smart and decent. But the bottom-line is that they are racist and are feeding from a racist dominant culture of the institution. Citing a recent scientific study undertaken in Canada regarding the low levels of IQ of many racists, the Huffington Post, in an article titled, "Intelligence Study Links Low I.Q. To Prejudice, Racism, Conservatism," published on February 1, 2012, reports: "Are racists dumb? Do conservatives tend to be less intelligent than liberals? A provocative new study from Brock University in Ontario suggests the answer to both questions may be a qualified yes.The study, published in *Psychological Science*, showed that people who score low on IQ tests in childhood are more likely to develop prejudiced beliefs and socially conservative politics in adulthood."

"IQ, or intelligence quotient," the Huffington Post observes, "is a score determined by standardized tests, but whether the tests truly reveal intelligence remains a topic of hot debate among psychologists." According to the Huffington Post, "Dr. Gordon Hodson, a professor of psychology at the university and the study's lead author, said the finding represented evidence of a vicious cycle: People of low intelligence gravitate toward socially conservative ideologies, which stress resistance to change and, in turn, prejudice, he told LiveScience. Why might less intelligent people be drawn to conservative ideologies? Because such ideologies feature 'structure and order' that make it easier to comprehend a complicated world, Dodson said. 'Unfortunately, many of these features can also contribute to prejudice,' he added. Dr. Brian Nosek, a University of Virginia psychologist, echoed those sentiments. 'Reality is complicated and messy,' he told *The Huffington Post* in an email. 'Ideologies get rid of the messiness and impose a simpler solution. So, it may not be surprising that people with less cognitive capacity will be attracted to simplifying ideologies.'…"

Generally, institutional racism does not appreciate diversity and inclusion. Have you ever worked in a place where everyone else, but you, is either a Caucasian, Indian, Chinese or Hispanic person; that is, meaning that you are the only black person there? Or, have you ever been in a high-level meeting where all the senior managers are from one dominant race, and they are all speaking with one voice? Yet, deep down your heart, and from an objective point of view, you did not agree with much of what they were saying. Did you muster enough courage to tell them so? In such places, if the company has to let go of anyone, you may be the first one on the food chain to be sacrificed on the altar of institutional racism or to be fed to the hungry lions.

EXCUSES

Such folks would rather take care of their own kind, and then throw you instead under the bus, notwithstanding that you are a minority, well-qualified and a good performer. They will use all sorts of excuses like, "Oh, we need people that can speak more than one international language", when all along that has not been an issue. As noted above, racist people have no sense of diversity or inclusion. They simply lack integrity, honesty and sincerity. And they can be mediocre and shameless liars in order to protect themselves. If you ask such people, for example, why they seem not to be hiring black people into management, they will tell you that they cannot find well-qualified black people. Yet it is all veiled bigotry.

PATRONAGE

As we noted at the beginning of this paper, when employees quit work, many leave not because they do not like the company. They leave because of bad bosses who keep making bad decisions. And sometimes, these bad bosses are even rewarded with promotions, especially in organisations with a corrupt culture of cronyism and patronage. All it takes is for them to bootlick the powers-that-be or to belong to the 'right' tribe, nationality, race or ethnic group. What to do now? Punch them in the face?

CHAPTER

8

DOES INTERNATIONAL LAW PERMIT THE SEARCHING OF A DIPLOMAT?

As the DJ kept spinning some smooth mellow R&B at the nightclub, Big Joe, a career diplomat, danced the night away with his new-found love, Sweet Sherry. Clad in black skin-tight jeans, Big Joe held Sweet Sherry jealously and possessively tight as the couple danced away to some romantic ballads. A pulsating bulge began to swell in Big Joe's crotch area. Overcome by lustful passions, Big Joe opted to shift the party to his residence. As Big Joe and Sweet Sherry walked out of the nightclub, the doorman at the entrance stopped them. The doorman pointed Big Joe to a signpost on the wall which read: "It is an offence to take beer-bottles out of this nightclub!" Indeed, Big Joe's perineum area appeared overloaded with what looked like a hidden lunch-box or beer-bottle.

The doorman turned his eyes to the menacingly intimidating bulge in the crotch area of Big Joe's pair of trousers. Undoubtedly, the doorman had every right to be concerned that perhaps Big Joe had hidden a bottle of Mosi in his pants. So, the doorman insisted that Big Joe removes from his pair of trousers the 'hidden' bottle of beer. But Big Joe declined, and appeared offended. It was only when the doorman tried to pat Big Joe in the crotch area to detect the supposedly stolen bottle that he realised that the bulge was actually Big Joe's erect manhood. The whole saga turned into an overwhelmingly embarrassing situation. Against this background, does the law permit the searching of a diplomat, say, at security check-points at international airports or at other immigrant facilities? Or, are diplomats immune and protected from such searches?

Article 29 of the Vienna Convention on Diplomatic Relations 1961 codifies customary international law on the principle of inviolability of a diplomatic agent. Article 29 provides that: "The person of a diplomatic agent shall be inviolable. He shall not be liable to any form of arrest or detention. The receiving State shall treat him with due respect and shall take all appropriate steps to prevent any attack on his person, freedom or dignity."

Now, did the searching of Big Joe constitute an affront to the principle of inviolability of a diplomatic agent? It is evident from the facts that Big Joe was not arrested or detained. Rather, he was merely searched. Article 29 of the Vienna Convention on Diplomatic Relations 1961 refers only to 'any form of arrest or detention', but not to any form of 'search'.

In that sense, and unless the municipal law of the host State, regarding the inviolability of a diplomatic agent, includes a prohibition against such searches, there was (is) no breach of international law. Unlike article 22(3) of the Vienna Convention on Diplomatic Relations 1961 which prohibits the 'searching' of premises of a diplomatic mission, their furnishings and other property thereon, including the means of transport of the diplomatic mission (*i.e.* both the registered vehicles of the diplomats and the diplomatic mission), as well as article 30(1) of that same treaty which extends such restrictions to the private residence of a diplomatic agent, article 29 prohibits only the arrest and detention of a diplomatic agent.

Be that as it may, an important caveat to observe is Article 41(1) of the Vienna Convention on Diplomatic Relations 1961 which requires diplomats: (a) to respect the laws and regulations of the receiving State; and (b) not to interfere in the internal affairs of the receiving State. This means that where the immigration laws or the security laws of a host State require that individuals traveling through or departing from any airport of the host State submit themselves to a routine security search, such a requirement will not necessarily be a violation of the principle of inviolability of the diplomatic agent. Here, the diplomat is not being arrested, detained or prosecuted. Rather, he or she is simply being asked to submit himself or herself to a routine security check. The matter will, however, be different where the diplomat is reported to have been arrested or detained.

Not too long ago, I was flying from London to the US. At the airport's security-check point in London, there was a well-dressed and seemingly well-groomed gentleman that kept resisting immigration calls to take off his shoes before he could walk through the security scanner. He argued spiritedly that calls by the immigration folks were a violation of the people's right to privacy. The man sounded very learned. And I could see that the security folks at the check-point were getting intimidated by his eloquence and confidence. But one tenacious immigration officer insisted that the man takes off his shoes. I stood right behind this immigration officer. After all efforts failed to get the gallant human rights protagonist to take off his shoes, the security folks told him that he could not board the plane. It was only then that the man succumbed. He had no choice but to take off his shoes.

Lo and behold, as the man took off his shoes, it was only then that it dawned on everyone around that the man was wearing a pitifully worn out and torn pair of old socks! The socks had gigantic holes. And they emitted a strong odour characteristic of socks that have not been washed for years. A smelly stench and some apparent sweaty spots on the socks attracted the attention of many onlookers. Here was a claim for the 'violation of human rights'! Indeed, it was a very embarrassing moment to see a well-dressed and handsome man wearing old, worn out and torn socks – that is, 'finished' socks, as we say in Zambian English.

Like in the case of Big Joe, the insistence by the London immigration officers that the human rights protagonist takes off his shoes was not a violation of the man's right to privacy. There is often a debate in the human rights discourse between protecting private interests, on the one hand, and upholding the common good, on the other. Indeed, which of the two should prevail over the other? And where do human rights begin and end? Can private rights of individuals trump or supersede matters of national security, especially where the latter represents mainly the safety of the public as well as mounting public interest values?

CHAPTER

9

CAN A CHRISTIAN DIVORCE AND REMARRY?

At the outset, it should be noted that this paper is not a Law School lecture on Family Law. Neither is it a sermon on the mountain. Rather, it is an intellectual dialogue that tries to draw from some pertinent aspects of Christian theology and secular viewpoints on the issue of marriage, divorce and remarrying. The emphasis, however, is on the Christian dimension of the debate given that the paper asks the question whether or not a married Christian can divorce and remarry.

In Zambia, like in many other Common Law jurisdictions, the law on marriage and divorce falls under a branch of law known as "Family Law". And in Zambia, the institution of marriage is governed primarily by two parallel legal traditions, namely, (a) the English common law and any applicable legislation; and (b) African customary law. Let us take a more reasoned look on how this works.

As a general rule, Christian marriages solemnised in Church as well as those marriages registered at the Civic Centre are taken as statutory marriages. And they are both guided by the English common law and any applicable Zambian or British legislation. In particular, Zambia's Marriage Act 1918, as amended through to 1994, and Zambia's Matrimonial Causes Act 2007 provide examples of local pieces of legislation that govern statutory marriages. The Marriage Act 1918, it should be stressed, provides for the solemnisation of marriages as well as for the validation of marriages that have already been solemnized, and it also deals with any matter incidental to or connected with the foregoing. Incidentally, the High Court for the Republic of Zambia has original jurisdiction in matters pertaining to statutory marriages.

By contrast, where you have "icombela ng'anda", or where a couple marries via a traditional African wedding ceremony that does not involve church or Civic Centre proceedings, or where a couple simply obtains a Local Court endorsement of the marriage, that marriage will be deemed a customary marriage and will be guided mainly by African customary law. Let it be known that customary marriages, unlike statutory marriages, are potentially polygamous. By contrast, it is a legal requirement that all statutory marriages, including any customary marriage that has now been converted validly into a statutory marriage, should remain monogamous. Any attempt to grow or convert a monogamous statutory marriage into a polygamous arrangement can attract criminal sanctions on the culpable party under the offence of bigamy in the Penal Code.

Whereas the Zambian High Court has original jurisdiction in matters pertaining to statutory marriages, the Local Courts in Zambia can hear matters pertaining to customary marriages. Although the High Court often applies the common law and applicable legislation in disputes pertaining to statutory marriages, it also has jurisdiction to apply African customary law wherever applicable. The Local Courts, on the other hand, deal mainly with matrimonial issues under African customary law. Also, the rules of evidence and substantive law in proceedings that follow the English common law are somewhat different from those in proceedings that follow African customary law. For example, adultery is not a crime under the English common law as well as under Zambian legislation. Thus, contesting parties under a statutory marriage can only divorce on one ground only – that is, that their marriage has broken down irretrievably, but not because of adultery *simpliciter*!

By contrast, in disputes pertaining to customary marriages before the Local Courts, the grounds of divorce can depend on a host of factors that range from acts of adultery to spousal neglect. For example, in a *Zambia Daily Mail* article titled, **"Girlfriend's shaving skills earn man divorce," published on** November 4, 2012, Prisca Jangazya reports that: "THE Kanyama local court has granted divorce to a 37-year-old woman of Lusaka's Garden Township who sued her husband for allowing another woman to shave his pubic hair. This is in a case in which Priscilla Ng'uni, 37, sued her husband, Charles Chalwe, 38, for divorce because she believed that Chalwe's girlfriend had shaved his pubic hair."

Another case pertaining to a claim in African customary law which might appear contrary to the English common law was reported in the same *Zambia Daily Mail* of Novemberr 4, 2012, under the title, "Man to pay wife K3.5m for sexless nine years". Prisca Jangazya reports that: "THE Kanyama Local Court has ordered a 48-year-old man of John Laing Township in Lusaka to pay his wife K3.5 million for denying her sex for nine years. This is in a case in which Christine Mwale, 44, sued her husband, Christopher Chotah for divorce saying he had deprived her of sex for nine years, the same period during which he stayed with another woman."

Whereas it is a dictate of the English common law that he who alleges must prove, it is sufficient under African customary law to find someone guilty of, say, adultery if he was seen coming from another woman's house at an awkward hour of the night. In the latter case, the onus is on the accused person to disprove or rebut the accusation of adultery (*i.e.* some form of 'strict liability'), otherwise he will be presumed guilty of the 'wrong' if he fails to give a satisfactory answer.

Against this background, can a Christian divorce and then remarry? Although both the two legal traditions cited above – that is, the English common law and any applicable legislation, on the one hand,

and African customary law, on the other – do not bar or stop a divorced man or woman from remarrying, the Christian interpretation of marriage, divorce and remarrying is somewhat different. What to do now? Should Christians follow secular laws on marriage, divorce and remarrying, or should they obey the Bible? And should Christians pretend that they do not know what the Bible says about divorcing and remarrying? What about the Church, should it allow or accept a couple to remarry, knowing fully well that one of the parties to the proposed marriage is a divorcee?

The Bible, in Malachi 2:16, provides that: "I hate divorce, says the LORD God of Israel." In a sense, the institution of marriage for Christians should be, and is expected to be, a lifetime commitment. There is no wavering, shuffling or turning back. In Matthew 19:6, the institution of marriage is interpreted as follows: "So they are no longer two, but one. Therefore what God has joined together, let man not separate." But others may be quick to argue that the Old Testament, in particular, in Deuteronomy 24:1-4 provides for some flexibility for a divorced woman to remarry. To that, Jesus responds in Matthew 19:8: "Because of your hardness of heart Moses allowed you to divorce your wives, but from the beginning it was not so. And I say to you: whoever divorces his wife, except for sexual immorality, and marries another, commits adultery."

According to GotQuestions.org, the controversy over whether divorce and remarriage is allowed in the

Bible revolves primarily around Jesus' words in Matthew 5:32 and 19:9. The phrase "except for marital unfaithfulness", GotQuestions.org contends, is the only thing in Scripture that possibly gives God's permission for divorce and remarriage, and that many interpreters understand this "exception clause" as referring to "marital unfaithfulness" during the "betrothal" period. GotQuestions.org adds that in Jewish custom, a man and a woman were considered married even while they were still engaged or "betrothed", and that according to this view immorality during this "betrothal" period would then be the only valid reason for a divorce.

However, in 1 Corinthians 7:15, we are told that: "...if the unbelieving partner separates, let it be so. In such cases the brother or sister is not enslaved. God has called you to peace. For how do you know, wife, whether you will save your husband? Or how do you know, husband, whether you will save your wife?" This Biblical verse should not be misconstrued or misinterpreted as encouraging Christians to divorce or to remarry. Indeed, the verse does not mention the words 'divorce' or 'remarry'. It only says a believer cannot stop or prevent an unbelieving spouse from leaving the marriage. Could it be, then, that God desires Christians that have gone through a divorce to remain single after the divorce?

In response to this question, Jesus teaches us in Matthew 5:32, 19:8, as well as in Mark 10:11-12 and in Luke 16:18, that divorcing for any reason causes the other person to commit adultery if he or she remarries. And that argument is really the kernel underpinning this debate. In 1 Corinthians 7:10-16, Paul, like Jesus, preaches that a man and woman should not get divorced, and that if they do, they should remain unmarried or be reconciled. From a secular standpoint, even our courts of law are not expected to be quick at ordering married couples to divorce. Divorce should be the last thing in the line of proceedings, especially as it militates against familial social values. And where reconciliation is proving difficult, a separation order is usually the initial step for the court to rule. But, reconciliation of parties remains the cardinal fulcrum for handling marital disputes. Contesting parties are expected or called to forgive one another. But, then, someone might say: Lord, how many times can I, or should I, forgive this horrible sinner who keeps repeating his or her same old sins again and again?

In John 4:16-18, Jesus says: "...'Go, call your husband, and come here.' The woman answered and said, 'I have no husband.' Jesus said to her, 'You have well said, "I have no husband," for you have had five husbands, and the one whom you now have is not your husband; in that you spoke truly.'...". Yet, some critics might say: "Ahh, Prof, naimwe, fya kale ifyo (i.e. those are old Jewish traditions under the Mosaic law, and that we live in different times)!" But, don't we all believe in the same God of Abraham, Moses and Elijah? If so, one could argue that we are inextricably linked and tied to those same teachings that we now want to call 'fya kale' (i.e. what some claim to be 'outdated' traditions). Every Christian, therefore, must understand that, notwithstanding what the common law, legislation or African customary law may say, the Bible in Matthew 5:32 is very clear: "But I say to you that whoever divorces his wife for any reason except sexual immorality causes her to commit adultery; and whoever marries a woman who is divorced commits adultery." In essence, there is little room for a committed Christian to divorce and remarry. In Christian theology, the institution of marriage enjoys inviolable sanctity. From that angle, decisions or acts of divorce and remarrying are often times seen as tantamount to committing adultery.

CHAPTER

10

CAN A DIVORCED AND REMARRIED CATHOLIC CHRISTIAN RECEIVE HOLY COMMUNION?

This article is a sequel to an earlier article that I wrote, titled, "Can a Christian Divorce and Remarry," published in the *Zambia Daily Mail* on November 8, 2012. In that article, I argued, among other things, that every Christian must understand that, notwithstanding what the common law, legislation or African customary law may say, the Bible in Matthew 5:32 is very clear: "But I say to you that whoever divorces his wife for any reason except sexual immorality causes her to commit adultery; and whoever marries a woman who is divorced commits adultery." In essence, there is little room for a committed Christian to divorce and remarry. From that angle, decisions or acts of divorcing and remarrying are often times seen as tantamount to committing adultery.

As we prepare for Christmas in 2012, many people

are excited at prospects for Christmas celebrations. Some understand Christmas, and rightly so, to be a quest for the rebirth in our lives of the Lord Jesus Christ. Others would rather thunder: "I am tired of these seemingly holier than thou chaps who want to talk Godly things all the time. Let me just enjoy my life, and some beer, plus some prostitutes, if possible. After all, this is Christmas time! We need to enjoy! Let he who has not sinned be the first to cast a stone!"

At the outset, it should be pointed out that the purpose of this paper is not to cause anyone problems. Rather, the paper aims at stimulating debate for critical reflection as we near Christmas. It is Christmas time, and not time to offend people. Admittedly, we are all sinners. And we carry bucket loads of sins that we have to empty every day before they weigh us down. Therefore, nobody is trying to stand on a pedestal of morality, pretending to be a merchant of morals. And the argument in this paper is not about whether or not the other person has also sinned. Each one of us will be accountable individually before God. Neither is the argument about comparing how well off as a sinner one is compared to the other guy next door. By contrast, the argument is about our individual, personal and private relationship with God. As Matthew 10:26 instructs: "...There is nothing concealed that will not be disclosed, or hidden that will not be made known." Indeed, that relationship will expose us completely. We cannot hide from God. And the last thing that anyone would wish for is to die from fright when the Son of Man returns. In Luke 21:26, we are told: "Men will faint from terror, apprehensive of what is coming on the world, for the heavenly bodies will be shaken."

Coming to the question before us – that is, whether a divorced and remarried Catholic Christian can receive Holy Communion – the Holy Bible instructs us in 1 Corinthians 11:27 that: "Therefore, whoever eats the bread or drinks the cup of the Lord in an unworthy manner will be guilty of sinning against the body and blood of the Lord." Let us take a more reasoned look at this scripture verse. What does the expression '...*in an unworthy manner*...' mean? Does it relate only to remarrying after divorce? Arguably, it points generally to all manner of sin, including theft, telling lies, masturbation, pornography, lustful thoughts, fornication, adultery, envy, culpable homicide, jealousy, and so forth.

While the Holy Bible can be likened to the Constitution of a country, or some kind of grund norm or supreme law of the land, religious instruments such as the *Catechism of the Catholic Church*, cannon laws, or pastoral and clerical letters, are subsidiary to the grund norm. Their validity should be inspired by the Word of God, and they can only attain and retain such validity where they are not repugnant to the spirit and intendment of the Holy Bible. Admittedly, every church or religion has its traditions. So, we must understand that Church teachings must not depart from the Holy Bible since the latter is sacrosanct. It, therefore, begs the question: should a celebrant Priest or Bishop at mass or elsewhere refuse to give Holy Communion to an individual who is divorced and remarried, especially where the Priest or Bishop is aware of these facts? Expectedly, the common reaction from some readers will be: "Let he who is without sin be the first to cast a stone!" But that type of reasoning simply deflects our attention from the real issue. The issue here is not about what others are doing in their lives. Rather, the issue is whether or not a divorced and remarried Catholic Christian should be receiving Holy Communion. That, indeed, is the issue.

Colin B. Donovan, STL, in an undated Online article titled, **"Communion of Divorced and Remarried,"** observes that, in 'Concerning the Reception of Holy Communion by Divorced-and-Remarried Members of the Faithful', the Congregation for the Doctrine of the Faith in a letter to the world's bishops on October 14, 1994 postulated as follows: "The mistaken conviction of a divorced-and-remarried person that he may receive holy communion normally presupposes that personal conscience is considered in the final analysis to be able, on the basis of one's own convictions, to come to a decision about the existence or absence of a previous marriage and the value of the new union. However, such a position is inadmissible. Marriage, in fact, both because it is the image of the spousal relationship between Christ and his church as well as the fundamental core and an important factor in the life of civil society, is essentially a public reality."

Donovan also makes reference to the *Catechism of the Catholic Church, contending that* God hates divorce. He cites *Catechisms* 2382 to 2386, *highlighting the Church's teachings, traditions and doctrines on the institution and sanctity of marriage. In particular, Donovan stresses that Catechism* 2382 posits that a ratified and consummated Christian marriage is indissoluble. *Closely related to this view, Catechism* 2386 posits that: "It can happen that one of the spouses is the innocent victim of a divorce decreed by civil law; this spouse therefore has not contravened the moral law. There is a considerable difference between a spouse who has sincerely tried to be faithful to the sacrament of marriage and is unjustly abandoned, and one who through his own grave fault destroys a canonically valid marriage." While *Catechism* 2386 distinguishes between innocent breach and culpable breach of marriage, it does not decree or endorse remarrying. As Donovan observes, "...the innocent spouse in a marital break-up has the same possibility to receive Communion as other Catholics, with the usual conditions (being free from mortal sin in other areas of life, going to Confession if not, Eucharistic fast and so on)".

The policy basis underlying Catechism 2382 of the *Catechism of the Catholic Church* is that no power on earth can declare a valid Christian marriage to be null, or that the parties are now free to remarry. In essence, any divorce proceedings brought before a competent court of law are not recognised as valid means of dissolving a marriage under the Christian faith. Rather, a person who decides to divorce and remarry will be deemed to be lost in the desert of adultery. The question then follows: should such a person receive Holy Communion, knowing full well that he or she is living in an adulterous union outside the original marriage, despite the court of law purporting to have dissolved such a marriage?

In exceptional cases, the Catholic Church makes provision for the issuance of a Decree of Nullity where a marriage is said to be void *ab initio* from inception. However, it could be argued that the issuance of a Decree of Nullity could at times be political where, for example, the Church is trying to justify what is seemingly a divorce (claiming that it is an annulment instead) by one of its influential members. Furthermore, such a Decree is only Church tradition and dogma. It is not a Biblical dictate. And to a non-Catholic, the issuance of a Decree of Nullity, as espoused under Catholic teachings, can present itself as a departure from the Word of God.

In concluding, would it be considered a sin on the part of a Priest or Bishop to give Holy Communion to someone who is divorced and remarried where the Priest or Bishop is fully aware that the concerned individual is divorced and remarried? In short, can a Priest or Bishop be seen to be colluding or abating the commission of the sin of adultery where he does not stop or exclude a divorced and remarried individual from receiving Holy Communion? Is there a moral or ethical duty on the Priest or Bishop to deny such an individual the sacrament of Holy Communion? What say ye?

One correspondent observes that: "I personally believe that, when one professes to be a Christian, the onus is on him or her to live by the rules of Christianity, though they are not free from human error. However, to impose observance or adherence to Christian tenets may be seen to be unethical, more like the Sanhedrins in the days of the Lord. So, a divorced and remarried Catholic needs to search within himself or herself, and consult the clergy for solutions. Arguably, the reasons for divorce will now come into play; that is, was it because of adultery or not? If, for arguments sake, hubby commits adultery and wife sues for divorce, can society blame wife for receiving Holy Communion if she remarries? Or vice versa, can society blame hubby?"

The correspondent continues: "The modern Christian way of life should not be based on the New Testament alone but also on the Old Testament – that is, the Laws of Moses. However, the teachings on marriage as a sacrament from the Catholic point of view are very clear on divorce. Adultery, though common a cause, can and is overtaken by forgiving the other more than 77 times. It emphasises forgiving one another in that union, however it does not spell out situations when to forgive and when not to forgive. One may divorce and still forgive the partner; that is, hold no grudge. Today, however, we see many Priests ruled by earthly things where they appease the socialites but neglect to correct the wrongs that these people do. For example, a particular Catholic parish in Lusaka, Zambia, patronised mainly by the elite and well-to-do, has come under fire for this kind of attitude. Someone even has a permanent seat in that church where he

- Kenneth K. Mwenda

sits, and no one dares take that seat. And the priest is actually aware of this…"

As plausible as the above views may seem, many religious people today, Christians or otherwise, hardly ever stop to examine their conscience. They would rather pretend that all is well. Maybe such people ought to be reminded by 'someone'. And perhaps that someone could be a priest who is aware of some helpful background information, but not a fellow congregant. Indeed, they may not listen to or heed advice from the latter. But they may listen to a priest even where the priest is of questionable moral character.

Yes, in ideal situations where people are honest with themselves, self-censure works fine. But in situations where dishonesty thrives, folks don't stop to check themselves. They can even tell lies in broad daylight like nothing is wrong with that. So, what to do? Leave them to their own devices? There is no such thing as a white lie or a blue lie. Even some proponents of Interpersonal Deception Theory (IDT), who try to explain the manner in which individuals deal with actual or perceived deception on the conscious and subconscious levels when engaged in face-to-face communication, contending that communication is not static and that it is influenced not only by one's own goals, but also by the context of the interaction as it unfolds, agree that lies don't have colours.

The problem with telling lies is that the liar often forgets the lies that he or she told a while back, and thus often gets entangled in a web of contradictions! To tell a good lie, you must remember everything as well as be consistent with all your lies. A single lapse in memory can expose a person as a liar. That is why in economic terms, telling a lie is sometimes known as being 'economical with the truth' because lies can be 'costly'. Many people tell lies in workplaces, churches, social-settiings and families because of 'insecurity'. They would rather hold out or pretend that nabo bali paja olo ati nabo ni Bantu (*i.e.* that they also matter in society). For example, if a workmate is narrating to her colleagues at the office about how she went for holidays or vacation with her boyfriend to the UK, one of the listeners may pretend or be compelled to say things like "Oh, my husband and I actually had our honeymoon there..." or "I am going to the USA with my husband and children this Christmas since one of my sibblings is based there. In fact, he is now a US citizen..." It is all about social spice and pretence! Even a simple comment of appreciation such as "I like your shoes" can attract an inflated and egoistic response, especially if there are people nearby. Responses such as "Oh, my boyfriend/husband got them for me when he was in Paris or Italy..." are not uncommon when in actual fact the shoes could have come from nearby South Africa (smile)!

CHAPTER

11

AN EMERGING CULTURE OF CONSUMPTION AND ACCUMULATION

In a recent media article dated November 21, 2012, published in Zambia's *Post* newspaper, Mukosha Funga reports: "CHARLOTTE Scott says she is worried that Zambians have become too materialistic. Charlotte, who is Vice-President Dr Guy Scott's wife, said in an interview recently that there was a problem of materialism in Zambia." It is this very issue of materialism that we endeavour to examine in this paper.

Quoting Dr. Charlotte Scott further, Mukosha Funga writes: "...'I think there is a problem of materialism in Zambia. Materialism is a culture that is not only in Zambia but in Africa as a whole,' she said. Charlotte added that materialism led to dissatisfaction as people desire to identify themselves with what they own. 'The problem with it is that ultimately it is not satisfactory because materialism is the desire to show yourself through what you own as compared to what others own and therefore what happens is you will always be dissatisfied,' she said."

There is no doubt that Dr. Charlotte Scott is on firm ground. We are living in very troubled times culturally, intellectually and materially. As she rightly observes, there is need to derive pleasure or satisfaction from human relations and not material possessions. The *Post* newspaper quotes her further: "...'Human relations are very important and they are expressed through people and not through objects. It is not always about fancy things and fancy places'..."

Closely related to Dr. Charlotte Scott's observations, the *Post* newspaper of November 23, 2012, reports that: "ALEXANDER Chikwanda says most Zambians serving in the public sector spend a lot of their time wandering about and showing pomposity instead of addressing real issues... Chikwanda who is the Minister of Finance said un-bankable development ideas end up not bearing any fruits... Chikwanda said Africa's misery and poverty has more of its origins in intellectual bankruptcy."

The issue of consumption is closely tied to that of accumulation. And many cultures that have stronger dispositions toward consumption and accumulation often exhibit compromised moral and ethical bases, unless such consumption and accumulation is accompanied by sustained production. Indeed, you cannot consume or accumulate where there is no corresponding production, notwithstanding the exports and imports argument. Where will you get the things from that you are consuming or accumulating if there is no corresponding production? And reckless consumption and accumulation deprives many individuals of the ability to make valuable savings and worthwhile investments. Even the townships have not been spared. Some township dwellers would rather drink from expensive shopping malls in the more uptown part of the city, abandoning the taverns in their local neighbourhoods. Others would want to accumulate as much property as those in the more affluent neighbourhoods.

When I visited Zambia sometime this year, I met an old childhood friend at Arcades Shopping Mall. We sat down to a drink. I asked him about another old childhood friend of ours, and if he had heard from him. My friend responded: "Me and him, we don't hang out in the same circles." I struggled to connect the dots regarding my question and the response that I got. Later, I shared this story with one of my cousins, a local Lusaka dweller, who then explained to me as follows: "Ba mdala, ni pa Lusaka pano. You have been away from Zambia for too long. Some of these people will only associate with you if they know that you are coming from abroad, or if they see that a person is rich, or when they notice that you have been appointed, say, by the President to a top position of power. Then, they will quickly claim you as their friend or relative!"

I could not believe what I was hearing. What has become of us? Growing up as a child, I was taught by my dear parents not to look down on people and not to discriminate against others based on such grounds as whether they are 'haves' or 'have-nots', 'been to' or 'never been to', or by looking first at what they own, where they live, or who their parents are. Those parameters are still very alien to me. But where you find materialistic individuals, your relationship with them is not based on a genuine friendship but on the material possessions surrounding you.

Many people are obsessed with associating themselves with the rich. Even those that have grown up in very poor environments try very hard to 'mutate' or transform themselves into elites as soon as they move to Lusaka or some other urban cities. They try as much as possible to distance themselves from their poor rural upbringing. In their day-to-day parlance, they will only refer to the good times when they were either visiting or studying, say, in London, Paris, New York, Cape Town, and so forth. They will never mention the village or township where they were born or grew up. Some don't even want people to know that they never wore shoes when growing up until much later in life. All that they would want people to know about them is that they are now aristocrats who smoke cigars and even play golf with the apa-mwambas (*i.e.* elite). One of these people is reported to have choked severely on cigar-smoke at the golf club because he had no clue of how to hold a cigar or how to inhale the smoke from the cigar, yet he was busy trying to score points to impress everyone around. Indeed, we are living in very strange times.

This craziness with obsessing about material things and with accumulation of wealth has contributed, partly, to the rising numbers of divorce cases. If you marry someone for their money, or because they have just come from abroad, what will happen if that person is no longer rich or when they have now settled into the Zambian way of life? In an online article published by *Jezebel.com*, titled, "Materialistic people have shitty marriages," it has been reported that: "The results of a new study may not surprise you much: turns out, being obsessed with money and material things could be bad for your marriage. ABC reports on the study by a BYU professor, who asked married people how much they agreed with statements like 'I like to own things to impress people' and 'money can buy happiness.' Couples in which both spouses reported a 'strong love of money' (which turned out to be one in five of the couples surveyed) scored worse than others in measures of marital stability, satisfaction, and communication. Those who are least materialistic score significantly better — and the results held true no matter how much actual money the couples had."

Akin to this, what happens if you marry someone just because her father is a prominent name in Zambia, or because her father is a prominent politician, and then that man suddenly becomes broke and bankrupt, or he dies? Will you stay in your marriage or will you leave your wife now that her family 'glory days' are a past tense? Sadly, many people want to live a Hollywood type of lifestyle in the midst of our economically distressed African continent. But, much of the America and Europe that we see on television in Africa is nowhere close to some real life challenges out there. Our people in Africa need to understand this. OK, it is good to dream, but we must be realistic with our dreams instead of just fantasising. Even the issue of human trafficking of women from some developing countries for purposes of prostitution in the West has been fueled partly by the fake impressions and delusional images that many of our people have about lifestyles in the Western world. Look, hardly a year goes by without reading unfortunate incidents in the media of some stowaways from, say, West Africa trying to make it to Europe illegally but only to drown at high sea. It is the same for some Caribbean and Latino folks who try to enter the US illegally by sea using some make-shift water rafts. When is this gonna stop?

Recently, I met a Zambian brother in one of the European major cities. He had a wet-look in his hair, or rather what is commonly known as a Jheri curl (often spelled Jerry curl or Jeri Curl). Now, this hairstyle was common and popular in the African-American community during the 1970s and 1980s. Yet, here we were in the 2000s, and the Zambian brother was kicking it hard in Europe with his Jheri curls and an adopted American accent. When I inquired from the other Zambian brothers around on what was up with this brother, one of them laughed and said: "Mdala, kaili that is what happens usually if you have never lived in Lusaka before, and just come straight from the village to Europe! At least some of us had to go through Lusaka first before coming here. Now, for him, he just came straight from the bundus! Ndiye ma wetlook yamene mu wona yaja..."

The church too has not been spared from the plague of materialistic clerics who mainly attend to the needs of the wealthy, but not those of the poor, as well as pastors who are so obsessed with accumulating wealth. The latter often justify their material greed by saying that nowhere in the Bible does it say Christians should be poor. God forbid! In Hebrews 13:5, we are told: "Keep your life free from love of money, and be content with what you have, for he has said, 'I will never leave you nor forsake you.'..." In 1 John 2:16, we are instructed: "For all that is in the world—the desires of the flesh and the desires of the eyes and pride in possessions—is not from the Father but is from the world." In 1 Timothy 6:9-10, we learn that: "But those who desire to be rich fall into temptation, into a snare, into many senseless and harmful desires that plunge people into ruin and destruction. For the love of money is a root of all kinds of evils. It is through this craving that some have wandered away from the faith and pierced themselves with many pangs." And Luke 12:15 posits: "And he said to them, 'Take care, and be on your guard against all covetousness, for one's life does not consist in the abundance of his possessions.'." Then, Ecclesiastes 5:10 sums it up: "He who loves money will not be satisfied with money, nor he who loves wealth with his income; this also is vanity."

Many eyebrows may be rising, as you look at the person right next to you, asking yourself: how many more pair of shoes and outfits does she need? And how many times does she need to change her hairstyle, nails or make-up? Likewise, others may be asking: just how many more women or ladies will he go out with, and how many latest cars, smartphones or big mansions does he need for his ego?

117

CHAPTER

12

DECONSTRUCTING THE MYTH OF
SELF-IMAGINED ARISTOCRACIES

In the English vocabulary, the word 'aristocracy' means: (a) a hereditary ruling class or nobility; (b) a Government by a ruling class or a state or country having such a form of government; or (c) a group or class considered superior to others. But, do we have a hereditary ruling class or nobility in Zambia? Or, is there a group or class considered superior to others?

Over the years, we have had different governments in Zambia ushered in through a democratic electoral process. At no time has Zambia been ruled, or subjected to a government, by an established or permanent ruling class. We do not have such a thing in Zambia, albeit the indirect forms of aristocracy that exist when it comes to ascendancy to chieftaincy in many tribal regions and villages.

As a postgraduate student in England many years back, I recall certain friends of mine from some parts

of West Africa who were in the habbit of claiming
that their dad was a chief in their home country. It
was as if they were sons and daughters of chiefs.
One of them, for example, would say: "My brada,
when our currency, the Naira, was very strong, we
would play cards using the Naira." And another one
would say: "As for me, my fada is a chief, and my
junior uncle is a millionaire while my senior uncle
has shares in many top companies in America. This
England of theirs, I have nothing to gain from it.
Besides, de weather here is too cold. As soon as I
finish my course, I am going back!" But, as I
understand, the guy is still in England to this day.

There are many people who tend to have an illusory
or false sense of aristocracy. Such notions of self-
importance are common, for example, where one
makes a bit of money or where one is appointed to a
political position. It is as if that individual has
transformed into a new being. Suddenly, he has
henchmen. But these so-called "friends" will only
stick around when things are fine or when you are
up there. When the chips are down, you will be lucky
to get a visit from one of them. Such is life. Why
then are some people so obsessed with wanting to be
seen as aristocrats?

Sometimes you will find some folks who will brag
that they are actually dating a chic that is based is
in the UK or who has just come from the UK. Others
will tell you that their wife's father is Mr XYZ, a
famous politician. And some will tell you that they
are looking after their Old Man, say, a former
Cabinet Minister, at the farm, yet in actual fact it is

the Old Man who is looking after them. Others will raise their voices conspicuously when indulging in an altercation, "Don't mess with me!!! Do you know who I am? I can make your life miserable!" Some of these individuals rely on past glory as a means of social mobility. Granted that they could have been "somebody" at some point, but that is all now history. It is like water that has gone beneath the bridge. You cannot step in the same water twice. It's already gone.

Others will introduce themselves as follows: "I am the friend to the President's son." While such machinations may cow some people, they may not succeed with everybody. I have also heard stories of some conmen who, when calling some business company to solicit business, will introduce themselves over the phone, or at the company's security checkpoint, as: "I am the friend to the Managing Director, don't you know me?" Some will give themselves military titles, so as to appear important, when they never even served in the army. Then there are also those that claim esteemed academic titles such as "Professor" when they are no longer associated with academia, or those that want to be addressed as "Dr", especially some clerics, politicians and businessmen, based primarily on their honorary doctorate or "PhD" from a diploma mill.

I once met a childhood friend on the streets of Lusaka, and he wanted to introduce me to his business associate. My friend pontificated spiritedly and enthusiastically, "Prof, meet Mr. XYZ, the former Managing Director of ABC Company." Politely, I extended a handshake to Mr. XYZ. We chatted a bit before Mr. XYZ took a phone call. I then took the opportunity to draw my friend to the side and asked him what Mr XYZ currently does in life. "Oh, he does this and that, a bit of some consultancy here and there", said my friend. I smiled and explained to my friend, "But that is what you should have said in the first place instead of saying, 'Meet Mr. XYZ, the former Managing Director'. That is past and gone. He is no longer a Managing Director. You should have simply said, 'Meet XYZ. He does this and that, a bit of consultancy here and there.'."

Often times, people with an illusory and false sense of self-imagined aristocracy tend to dwell on figments of their own misconception. Although I am not a psychologist, I do know that if one suffers from such misconceptions of reality they are less likely to be objective and honest in making their own self-evaluations. People that suffer from such inferiority complex tend to overrate themselves, sometimes even trying to talk down on others that are better endowed with the appropriate and relevant resources and skills. The idea of an illusory and false sense of self-imagined aristocracy can also be found in individuals that are just too ambitious for nothing. Some of them would like to ascend to positions that they are not even qualified to hold. Others feel that the world owes them something because they are the son or daughter to XYZ. But the real world is not like that. You have to earn your respect to make a mark. You cannot ride on other people's successes. And neither can you be condemned for other people's failures. You are accountable only for your actions alone.

Over the years, I have mentored many young people that have been inspired by my writing and intellectual leadership. Some have asked me where I get the drive and motivation to do what I do. It is not something that I can explain in simple words. I have been inspired by so many different people at different levels of my life. When I was in Zambia recently, someone shared some light humour with me on a radio-talk show, asking why I, unlike many others in the Diaspora, had not changed my accent after having lived abroad for so many years. Yes, I have spent much of my adulthood in the UK and the US. But, when you are true to yourself, you do not have to wear a blonde wig to earn respect. Neither do you have to change the way you speak for someone to notice you. I have been away from Zambia for almost twenty (20) years now. But I still love my nsima even here in the US. Yes, I love my nsima. It's not a secret or something over which I would feel shy or ashamed. Of course, I do eat other foodstuffs too, but nsima remains the main deal.

I have heard stories of some Africans who pretend to have forgotten their mother tongue the moment they step foot on European or American soil. But how can that be? A test in knowing if someone has genuinely forgotten his or her mother tongue lies in uttering to that person some profound profanity. If he or she gets upset, simply tell them: "Oh, so you speak Bemba, I thought you said you have forgotten!"

- Kenneth K. Mwenda

Some people's obsession with presenting themselves as aristocrats causes them to claim to know only relatives that are financially comfortable, but not those that are of limited means. Such people will quote all the famous names in town and tell you that they are related to them when, in actual fact, it is just that their parents happen to have come from the same village. People that are obsessed with a false sense of aristocracy often choose who to associate with and who to befriend based on all sorts of distorted notions of social class. And such people only get to accept and recognize their poor relatives when the latter make it in life.

I have heard stories of how some young poor lads would struggle through school and life, with nobody to lend a hand. But no sooner do they make it in life, do relatives suddenly start showing up. Even some irresponsible male parent that could have denied paternity of a child, and eventually abandoned the child and her mother, will suddenly pitch up and claim that he is the father to the now successful child. Because of the changing culture and the evolving trends in the process of socialization, driven primarily by economic hardship, many people would rather focus their attention on wealthy relatives to avoid the poor relatives who are often seen as nothing but troublesome beggars. But when there is crisis involving African traditional issues, the same urban snobs will rush to their poor relatives in the township to ask for counsel and guidance, especially if it has to do with matters of marriage. Then, and only then, does that old poor uncle or auntie in the village or township become important.

A young man once told me how his then college girlfriend decided to end their relationship because, as he explained to me, she was of the view that he would not be accepted into her family since he came from a not so well to do family and that his parents were not that well known in her family circles. She obviously had a serious inferiority complex and an obsession with self-imagined aristocracy. At the time when the young man was pouring out his heart, he was visibly heart-broken. I ordered a few more beers for him as we sat in a pub in London. As they say in Bemba, "Ubwa-lwa ni'nsokolola twebo" (*i.e.* people often open up easily when they are drunk). I comforted him that that was not the end of the world. To calm him down, I referred to some old Bemba adage which many feminists may not, however, agree with, that the Bemba language says, "Aba nakashi mafi ya mpombo!" (*i.e.* there are so many other pretty women out there. Do not worry, young man. You will be OK. I can even introduce you to some).

Many years later when I met that same young man again, he told me that he is now happily married to another lady and that the chic that diss'ed him is now divorced from the seemingly successful man that she quickly married. I smiled as before, looked him in the eye and said: "Son, you have to be happy in life. We all have preferences. That's fine. But you have to make sure that the preference that you go for is one that does not fade away or depreciate easily. In short, marriage is not about just names or marrying names. With time, names can fade and depreciate. Names come and go. That young lady should have thought about making her own name instead of talking about her father much of the time. It's now too late. Besides, not everyone gets excited about names. Only cheap guys do, but not solid and self-made men. And, in Bemba, we say, 'Eko sulile, e-kopa noko' (*i.e.* Never look down upon anyone for you do not know what great things the future holds for them)."

I pushed on further: "Young man, you made a wise decision to let that lady go. It would have been hell. Many of us, including that same young lady that we are talking about, our parents were born in the village or in some poor parts of the city in the colonial days. So, where does she get that distorted notion that she is some kind of elite or that she comes from some aristocratic family? Look, there was no rich Zambian when we got independence. Most of our parents or grandparents were the first generation to come out the so-called darkness of the village into modern civilization. So, where do some people get this notion that they are aristocrats? It's not like Prince Charles whose family dynasty is marked with royal wealth over the centuries. Our situation in Africa is different. We are only a generation or two away from the village. It was only a few years back that our forefathers came from the village into town. And there were no super rich Zambians at independence. It was a white man's world."

The young man sighed and stared me straight in the

eyes, and said: "Big man, that's why I like you. You are so real. Noti aba ba ngwele aba fake! Just the other day, I was having drinks with this other Zambian guy. His dad was a Cabinet Minister in the UNIP days, and the guy still talks about it to this day. Can you imagine? It is as if that is the only thing on his CV. The guy is about fifty (50) years old now, but he still talks about his dad who was a Cabinet Minister in the Kaunda days." I just smiled and told the young man that such pretentions are known as: "Ubu-limi bwa kale tabutalalika mwana" (*i.e.* the other guy's claims of past glory will not stop a child from crying. The child is hungry and cannot feed from past accomplishments. The question is: what can he offer the child today to stop him from crying?).

The young man then continued: "But he is always drinking beers on me, and he has never ever bought me a beer, not even once! But he wants to talk about how well connected his family is, and how they lived abroad when he was young. But are we not all living abroad now? Does that really make sense? We are all here in the UK, not so? But he keeps talking about how his family lived abroad as if we are still in Zambia. Are we not all abroad?" I smiled and nodded. The young man then continued: "You know, Big Man, I decided to tell off this guy and to put him in his place, right where he belongs. I don't beg from anyone. I feed myself. By contrast, he is always begging beers from me. My parents may not have been that rich, but I have integrity and have earned my place in society. So, I told him off the other day. He has since stopped talking to me and he keeps telling people that I am very rude and arrogant." To that, I smiled again and told the young man, "When people say you are rude and arrogant, it's better that way. I say so because then they will not bother you. But deep down your heart you know that you are not rude and arrogant but are merely uncompromisingly honest and frank. Many people do not like to hear the truth. And the truth, as they say, often hurts. So, you must understand your friend's predicament. He has nothing to offer for himself. So, all he can do now is talk about his Old Man."

Generally, whereas genuine aristocracy does often entail and entitle one to inherit some class status from his or her parents, self-imagined aristocracy never does so. This is just a fact. The bottom line is that in life you can be born of parents that are rich or are politicians but you may not be in a position to replicate their successes. You must make your own mark. Whilst children are permitted to bask in the successes of their parents, it is shameful for an adult to do so. By parity of reasoning, an individual can be born of parents that are struggling financially but may end up as the president of a country or as the chief executive officer of a leading organization. The bottom line is that we do not have aristocracies, in the real sense, in Zambia. For what is there to inherit other than a few household furniture or property which any Dick, Tom and Harry can also inherit? Understand this: as a result of the illusory notion of aristocracy, some individuals tend to rate their ability as above average, or as much higher than it actually is. Sadly, some sections of the audience do buy into this. And these pretentious and self-conceited individuals are then able to intimidate the poor fainthearted listeners and observers until they meet folks that are well-grounded and not easily cowed.

Often a time, you will find that while the really learned and highly skilled, for example, underrate their own abilities due to a complex manifested through what seems like the lack of self-confidence, the average minds get confident given that the intelligent ones doubt themselves. In psychology, it is called the Dunning-Kruger effect. Charles Darwin once said: "Ignorance more frequently begets confidence than does knowledge." And Bertrand Russell made a closely related remark, observing that: "One of the painful things about our time is that those who feel certainty are stupid, and those with any imagination and understanding are filled with doubt and indecision."

128

CHAPTER

13

SHOULD WORK EXPERIENCE MATTER SO MUCH IN HIRING SOMEONE?

In many parts of the world, it is not uncommon to hear young university and college graduates complain about certain requirements pertaining to some job adverts, asking for candidates with a certain number of years of work experience. Many a young folk seeking employment often complain that: "OK, given that we don't have those years of work experience, how do they expect us to compete for some of these jobs for which we have been trained if all they keep asking for is work experience?" In short, is work experience the only thing that matters in life? Increasingly, we are beginning to see more young Chief Executive Officers (CEOs) of large corporations as well as young Heads of State. In the past, for example, there were very few, if any, ladies that were heading such financial institutions as banks and insurance companies in Zambia. But here we are today. The world is changing. Likewise, with time, the right mix of skills requirements may shift

130

from emphasis on work experience *simpliciter* to additional competences such as multi-skills in an employee to cover for many jobs, thereby cutting down the costs of the company hiring extra people to do the other jobs being covered by that one person.

Let us ask ourselves the following question: should it be mandatory to subject all university and college graduates with no work experience to stringent requirements of 'work experience', especially that the job market in Zambia does not provide them with much room for internships whilst they are studying so that they gain some modest work experience? There is an unfortunate generalization out there that many young graduates without work experience can't make the cut (*i.e.* that they can't perform or deliver). Do such generalisations always hold true? Let us take a more reasoned look.

A young lawyer attending a job interview is asked by the interviewing panel about her work experience, and she responds by saying: "Well, although I have never practiced law for a law firm, I did pass the Bar at first attempt as the best graduating student. And shortly thereafter, I was appointed as a magistrate in my home town. So, I have been guiding many lawyers that work for law firms in my court. And I hand down judgments which they respect and adhere to. So, I am not sure that I need to work for a law firm or to carry out litigation for me to have what is called 'experience'..." What would you say to this? Of course, it would be different if the skills being sought are clinical or practice-based skills such as those of a neurosurgeon. To be a neurosurgeon, a person must have undertaken the relevant pedagogical and clinical training in neurosurgery. By contrast, if a person is getting married, say, under a monogamous Christian marriage, the person does not need to have prior experience with marriage. Indeed, a monogamous Christian marriage is perhaps one of the few institutions or 'occupations' where parties are not expected by the court of public opinion to have any prior experience, notwithstanding that some divorced or widowed individuals may later opt to remarry. Yet, marriages, generally, are expected to last. And many marriages do, in fact, last and prosper. So, how important then is the issue of prior experience?

In the western world, the requirement that a candidate should have some prior work experience is often applied more stringently to minorities. If, say, a black person, with the same qualifications as a white person, applies for a job, he or she is likely to be expected to demonstrate evidence of additional competences drawn from his or her prior work experience whereas the white counterpart could be evaluated simply on the strength of his or her potential. So, the formula is 'evidence of solid prior experience for blacks' versus 'potential for whites'. Indeed, if a Mr. White went to Harvard or Sorbonne, it would entail that he is good enough, and that he does have the potential to perform. But if a Mr. Black also went to Harvard or Sorbonne, the court of public opinion is still not convinced. Mr. Black must show proof of evidence that he is that good. It would entail that the court of public opinion has to check thoroughly all of Mr. Black's references, including scrutinising him carefully during and after the interviews. Ever wondered why President Obama's well-earned Harvard education became an issue to some people during the election campaign for his second term of office, yet the same critics never once questioned the Harvard qualifications of Obama's presidential opponent?

Closely related to the foregoing, let us assume that the President of a particular country is looking for an economic advisor, and that he is eager to appoint a certain renowned economics professor at a local university. But some people that claim to be 'close' to the President are trying to dissuade him from doing so. They contend that: "The professor is just an academician! He has never worked anywhere else other than in the university. He lacks practical experience, sir." Would you agree with this line of thought? Is it true that only those that have been out there in the so-called 'real world' have the ability to carry out such work? And what about all the economic research and intellectual thinking underlying policy formulation and implementation, does it not benefit from academic work and the contributions of think-tank institutions? These are some of the questions that we should be asking ourselves.

And what lessons can we learn from some developed countries such as the US? Are their experiences not helpful in any way to our condition in Africa, or should we continue to seek only what we deem as 'afro-centric' solutions just for the sake of soothing our own egos? Economic pundits such as Professor Joseph Stiglitz and Professor Larry Summers have both served as senior advisors to respective US Presidents, yet they are primarily from the academic world. And they have both held senior positions at the World Bank. Surely, to argue that those from academia can't make the cut elsewhere is being too simplistic. Until recently, for example, it was customary for many individuals that held a PhD (and occasionally some university teaching experience as well, albeit with few publications) to join the Bank of Zambia (BOZ) or the Zambia Revenue Authority (ZRA) as full Director. Likewise, many individuals with a PhD and some university teaching experience who got appointed to the civil service would start at no less than Permanent Secretary. And where such an individual was being posted as a diplomat to the foreign service, he or she would be appointed as an Ambassador, and nothing less! Indeed, that has been the tradition and practice for our country. But you might be wondering how these examples help to explain the plight of young university graduates with no work experience. Let me push.

What I am trying to say is that while relevant experience can be helpful, it is not the only determining factor for an individual to be proficient in his or her work. Indeed, some skills are not born out of either books or out of experience alone. Transferable skills can arise out of many different contexts. And not every form of experience is relevant and useful in the carrying out of particular tasks. In the sojourns of international development practice that I have traversed over the last fifteen (15) years, as well as in my close association with academia over the last twenty (20) years, covering Africa, Europe and North America, I have come to understand that nothing is as practical as a good theory. Often a time, a good theory is reflective of, and a culmination of, evidence of best practice. As such, there is no substitute for research when it comes to seeking the truth. And that is why successful companies fully understand the importance of 'Research and Development (R&D)'.

It is therefore utopian to argue that, without experience, many young graduates cannot perform. If this were true, where would we all be today? We all had to start from somewhere. And that is why companies should have training programmes as well as mentoring systems to support young graduates. Relying solely on old and tired people that often hide behind the rubric, 'experience is the best teacher', can deny the company of prospects for innovation and creativity. Many young folks are still energetic, and they have the zeal and enthusiasm to bring about progressive change. They just have to be managed properly. The good thing, though, is that many young folks are not yet tainted with the bad habbits and lethargy that could have been going on in the company for years.

However, an anonymous commentator from Zambia writes: "How about the argument that tertiary qualifications, especially university education is not necessary in improved work performance?" While this view does hold in some cases, it is equally possible that the provision of training and education to employees can contribute to improved work performance. Overall, the workforce can also benefit from effective leadership, thereby maintaining the desired levels of employee motivation. A motivated team tends to perform better than one that is not motivated. But the commentator from Zambia agues further:

"We had an assignment at the University of Zambia (UNZA) in Business Ethics... If one had a company, what would be the ethical mode or best practice of remunerating and promoting employees; is it according to qualifications or performance? And should a certificate holder who performs better earn higher than a masters degree holder who is said to be performing at a lower level? Also, should this be the case when it comes to promotions?"

It is important to observe that for many new hires the yardstick for determining their starting salary and grade is their respective levels of educational attainment. However, as individuals progress in their careers, other factors come into play when it comes to promotions. At that point, qualifications alone do not matter much. Ideally, as many companies would want to argue, promotions should be based on good performance. But in reality, that is not always the case. Sometimes issues such as tribalism, sexual favours, institutional racism, cronyism, patronage and corporate hustling, despite all of them being unethical, do influence promotions. Indeed, there is a lot of dirty stuff that goes on in the real world. It's just that the dirt is often swept underneath the carpet.

Finally, the commentator from Zambia posits: "In Zambia, apart from Lawyers who form their own Law firms, most graduates/academics, say, in Journalism/Media Studies and Education cannot establish and successfully run a news-media organisation or a school/college or university (Apart from the minds behind the University of Lusaka (UNILUS), Zambian Open University, and one or two more...). In the business world, it is also said that academicians do not do well; that is, millionnaires in Zambia and elsewhere are said to have not gone far in education. And how about politics? In Zambia, it also said that academics in the field of political science and related fields do not make good politicians. Do you agree? What explains this?"

Again, as already established above, books alone are not enough. Neither is experience on its own (without sound intellect) sufficient. Some people may be book-smart but not street-smart. Others may be street-smart, but not book-smart. It is important to strike a balance between the two extremes. Also, the environment in which one gets to learn can have a telling effect on the processes and outcomes of the learning. For example, to acquire a degree transcript per se does not confirm that one has acquired the relevant skills for the job. We have to go back into issues of pedagogy and training to find out if the education to which the individual was or has been exposed did give him or her the relevant skills for the market. That then begs the question: what is effective learning? And what is effective teaching?

Generally, there is a strong nexus between sound intellect, on the one hand, and best practice, on the other. For example, for a development practitioner or policy-maker to articulate or lead policy dialogue proficiently, it would be too costly to rely solely on some long-held dogmatic practice. Such dogmas or articles of faith do not often benefit from circumspection to determine the validity of the underlying theoretical or ideological premise. Yet, there are some people who claim, and proudly too, to have many years of practical experience in doing the same thing over and over again, forgetting that they may have been doing that same thing wrongly much of their life. Such human failings, predicated on robotic and dogmatic intuitions, are often a result of treating lightly, or paying insufficient attention to, valuable and useful theories or ideas in a relevant discipline. Indeed, practice devoid of enlightenment is a good recipe for failure, as much as the carrying out of unintelligent repetitive tasks does not make one a genius. There can be no substitute for erudition.

By parity of reasoning, many theoretical and ideological constructs are developed on the basis of systematically and repeatedly observed facts. Therefore, a theory that subsists in the abstract only, without much relevance to concrete reality, is of less value to socio-economic and political inquiry. In this vein, intellectual leadership should not be understood as confined solely to the congenial habitats of classroom pedagogy. Ideally, this form of leadership should extend also to the practical implementation of policies, projects and programmes, as it often points to evidence of best practice. It is, therefore, a fallacy for some apologists, not having the necessary appetite or intellectual capacity to pursue knowledge fully, to argue that practical experience in the 'real world' is entirely different from academia. To argue that theory and practice are totally de-linked, or that there is no correlation between the two, is a shortsighted sanctuary of laziness or simply the economical treatment of the truth. The two, academia and the so-called 'real world', do feed into each other like a hand and a matching glove, or like the blossoming love between a bride and a groom. And that particular cross-breed is a path that some of us have chosen to travel. We can only profess best that which we have put to test or practiced, as much as we can only practice diligently that which is grounded in sound and scientific theory.

CHAPTER

14

CAN WE BE THERE FOR THEM?

Bana Kambwili and her sisters do not get along with their brother's wife, Bana Chisha. Bana Kambwili is married to a blue colour worker, Bashi Kambwili, who does not earn much. He is a spanner-boy at some car service garage. However, Bana Kambili's brother, Bashi Chisha, is a successful businessman. Bashi Chisha used to support all of his sibblings financially, including Bana Kambwili and her husband, until he married Bana Chisha. But before he married Bana Chisha, he was married to Bana Lombe. At the time, Bana Lombe and Bana Chisha were best of friends. In fact, Bana Chisha would often spend weekends at Bana Lombe's place without the latter suspecting that something was going on between her husband and her best friend.

Bana Kambwili and her sisters, including Bashi Kambili who is simply a brother-in-marriage to Bashi Chisha, claim that Bana Chisha actually 'stole' or 'grabbed' her best friend's marriage; that is, Bana Lombe's marriage! And Bana Lombe has now

teamed up with Bana Kambwili, Bashi Kambwili
and Bana Kambwili's sisters against Bana Chisha.
In the meantime, Bana Chisha and Bana Lombe do
not see eye to eye. When asked why she dislikes or
hates her sister-in-law, Bana Kambwili responded:
"She grabbed her best friend's marriage from my
brother. And she has now confused my brother with
all sorts of love-potions. He no longer helps our
family. If you go to his house, it is full of her
relatives. You will not find a single one of my
relatives there. It's all about her family and her
relatives!"

How often do we come across such situations where
a family is inundated with dependants, family visits
or frequent financial requests from relatives of one
spouse only? The story of Bashi Chisha is very
common in many Zambian households today. Indeed,
if Bana Chisha keeps packing her home full of/with
her sibblings and relatives, showing little kindness
and generosity to her in-laws, it may come as no
surprise that Bashi Chisha's sisters and mother may
not take kindly to such an arrangement. It will be
particularly disheartening for Bashi Chisha's mother
who is not only old, but also quietly suffering from
economic hardship in the village while her son,
Bashi Chisha, is busy scoring points with his father-
in-law, mother-in-law and sisters-in-law, buying
them a house and some mini-buses or trucks for
business. Does that sound familiar? Don't panic, just
stay with me.

In our part of the world, it is not unusual to find a
fella who is seemingly accomplished and wealthy,

yet does not show much care for his aging parents. The guy will be living in a mansion, flying places, talking big, and all that comes with ama wala (*i.e.* pomp) yapa Zambia, yet his own father and mother are living in a shack in the village. If you ask people who know the guy whether there is a problem or dispute between the guy and his family for him to abandon his old folks just like that, you will find that there is hardly any justification for such uncalled for behaviour. By contrast, you will find that such guys are very eager to impress their in-laws, trying to score points unnecessarily. But, as they say, blood is thicker than water. And when cooking nshima, it is always best to measure the right amount of water before mixing it with mealie-meal. Otherwise, the nshima will be messed up!

Someone told me a story of a fella that would only connect with relatives that are allegedly successful or well-off. He was raised in a snobbish family where his parents only encouraged their children to know wealthy relatives, while hiding the children from poor relatives for fear of exposing them to such malevolent factors associated with poverty as superstition and endless begging. So, the guy never wanted to know any of his poor relatives. Even at his house, he only used to keep nieces or nephews that appeared to have promising career or future prospects. He would not even keep, for example, his own siblings just because they lived in the townships and never made it to university. Does that sound familiar?

Further, it is not uncommon in Zambia to find

people who are raised in matrilineal cultures. Very often, though not always, such individuals grow up knowing mainly their mother's relatives. It is not really their fault. But, as we all grow older, we should be able to detect this bias, and try to work our way towards objectivity. However, where such biases persist, many family relatives that tend to visit the parents' home are the mother's relatives. Yet, it is also not uncommon in some cultures that have strong inclinations towards extended family and polygamy to find men that will channel much of their earnings and resources towards educating and supporting their own siblings at the expense of supporting their own nuclear family. From such cultures, you often find men that are in the habit of crowding their home with siblings or their relatives. Such behaviour tends to make the Madame of the house feel uncomfortable, as she is likely to feel a stranger among 'strangers' in her own home. Of course, one could counter-argue that such views are mere stereotypes. I will not contest that argument, but will leave it to history and experience to teach us the way forward.

But why do some people exhibit such unfairness in the way they treat others? Recently, I called up a friend of mine in one of the neighbouring African countries. He is a former Cabinet Minister in his country. We both took our postgraduate studies in the UK at the same university. I asked him about a mutual friend of ours who is also from his native country. My friend responded: "Oh, he hardly calls me nowadays. In fact, you happen to call me more often than he does. He used to call me every other day when I was a Cabinet Minister, asking me for this and that favour. I would always reach out and try to help him with whatever he wanted. But now that I am no longer a Cabinet Minister, he has stopped calling me. He sees no need in contacting me. That is how our people are. They just want to use you. The moment you are no longer in power, it is as if they do not know you."

I was dumbfounded, and asked: "By why should it be like that? You and I have maintained our friendship from the time we were both students in the UK. Look, you never became big-headed or grew wings just because you had become a Cabinet Minister. You remained the same down-to-earth person that I have always known. But I am not surprised with our friend. Even when we were at university together in England, he had a bit of those unpleasant dispositions of pretence, fake accents and trying to be what he is not. So, it does not come as a surprise. I could see it through him even back then." From the discussion, I could sense that my friend was not too pleased with the behaviour of the other guy. But such is life. You will come across people like that – that is, those that only show up or call when they want something from you!

I went on to explain to my friend: "Do not be surprised. Your phone will not ring the moment that they feel you are of no use to them. And that is when you know who your true friends are. Hypocrites are quick at abandoning even the people that helped them or who have been there for them. In fact, do not be surprised if these same people jump on the bandwagon of a powerful person that you once introduced them to or whom they knew through your efforts, claiming now to be closer to that person than you are. Hypocrites and opportunists are like that, my brother. They choose who to associate with and who to mix with, depending on where they stand to gain. Personally, I find it very hard to deal with such people. My friends will always be my friends through thick and thin. You do not abandon people just because you feel that they are no longer doing well or are of no material gain to you. You should always look back at the past and where you are coming from. Those people could have made a difference to your life. And do not belittle their support when, in actual fact, you were desperate for their help just the other day."

After listening in quietly and attentively, my friend said: "That is why in some cultures people love animals more than human beings. A dog, for example, will always be loyal to its owner, irrespective of whether or not the boss is still rich." To that, I smiled calmly and said: "But even better, know ye that God's love will never let you down. He will always be there for you, no matter what season or reason." Thereafter, I concluded by sharing an insightful Bible verse for my friend to meditate on. Luke 17:11-19 captures what he was going through, and it reads as follows: "Now on his way to Jerusalem, Jesus traveled along the border between Samaria and Galilee. As he was going into a village, ten men who had leprosy met him. They stood at a distance and called out in a loud voice, 'Jesus, Master, have pity on us!' When he saw them, he said, 'Go, show yourselves to the priests.' And as they went, they were cleansed. One of them, when he saw he was healed, came back, praising God in a loud voice. He threw himself at Jesus' feet and thanked him—and he was a Samaritan. Jesus asked, 'Were not all ten cleansed? Where are the other nine? Has no one returned to give praise to God except this foreigner?'…"

And so, can we be there for those who have been there for us, or even stop-by to say: "Thank you"? Or, are we too proud to acknowledge the help that we get from others, and would rather turn around, pretend and belittle their help by saying offensively: "Just because you gave me a little help here and there does not mean that you now have to start singing about it to the whole world day and night!" Yet, as we say in Bemba, a person's life finds safety in the attentiveness of his or her ears: that is, for those with ears not only to hear, but also to listen, life teaches us that: "Uwushi tasha patu nono, napa fingi pene taka-tashe!" (i.e. a person who hardly shows gratitude when presented with small but meaningful and kind gestures cannot be expected to show gratitude over greater gestures). Indeed, if we can't be appreciative of the help that we get from others, then how can we claim to have a heart to help the less fortunate that could be in need of our help? As they say, charity begins at home.

- *Kenneth K. Mwenda*

CHAPTER
15

DEALING WITH CHANGING TIMES
AND PARADIGM SHIFTS

The emergence of global warming can be compared to a rising tsunami, sweeping across the world as it ushers in disturbing climatic changes. But, we are all not used to such changes. Yet, change is inevitable at some point. There is a closely related tsunami that has been sweeping across the globe. From a world dominated by masculinity in the corridors of power to an emerging ideology of gender empowerment of women, the world is increasingly seeing a shift from the traditional patriarchical structures of society. For example, in many workplaces, schools, governments, homes, churches, and many other institutions, the call for gender empowerment of women continues to be relentless. While this tsunami is still riding high, there is also a decline in how far matters of religion can be discussed or expressed in workplaces or schools. Many schools and workplaces have deliberate policies that prohibit the expression of religious views, perhaps fearing that religious extremism

- Kenneth K. Mwenda

could find its way into such civic institutions.

Yet, in many countries that have not criminalised homosexuality, gay rights are widely protected in workplaces and schools, whilst there is less talk about the protection of religious minorities or the prevention and curbing of racism and bigotry in schools, workplaces, churches and other institutions. It is as if racism and bigotry do not exist, or religious minorities are not real minorities, in contrast to the excessive zeal to protect gay and lesbian rights. In the corporate world, for example, the situation is exacerbated when some of those in power have a softer heart for homosexual tendencies. Their social class interests will be projected as corporate policy, thus deliberately shifting away attention from equally pressing matters such as institutional racism and bigotry. But then, would it be right to allow a gay man who claims to be a "female" to use the ladies' bathroom or toilets at the office? And how would the ladies react when they see such an individual in the ladies' restroom (although "he" maybe wearing women's clothes), especially if they know that the concerned individual is biologically a man? Would it make a difference if "he" were to argue that "he" has had surgical operation to change "his" sex? And can the concerned individual claim that the company is discriminating against "him" should "he" be told not to use the ladies' restroom? We are living in very difficult times.

In many families, the old paradigm of the father or husband being the main breadwinner is slowly withering away. Some mothers or wives are now the main breadwinners. Also, the old notion of a housewife is evolving steadily into that of a househusband. Many unemployed men find themselves staying at home, and even cooking or looking after the children, whilst their wives are at work. It is not unusual to come across such arrangements. However, some househusbands will tell you that they are businessmen or self-employed, just to ward off some negative perception from the public. We are living in trying times. Indeed, there are a number of men who are being looked after by women today. And if you were to inspect the title deeds of some of these homes, you will find that the house is registered in the wife's name, although the man will be busy telling his friends that he has just bought a house for his wife and family. We are living in interesting times.

That said, with the evolving and changing culture of our time, it will soon be no longer humiliating or embarrassing for a man to stay at home, or even to live off a woman. The male chauvinistic view of life is increasingly dying out. There is a paradigm shift against certain conservative attitudes engrained in male chauvinism. Increasingly, we are seeing more female bosses in workplaces, as well as more educated women. Although Zambia, like the US and many other great nations, is yet to have a female Head of State, the new tsunami of gender empowerment may sooner or later usher in a paradigm shift. Who thought that Liberia or Malawi would have a female Head of State? By contrast, for the British, the Germans and others in the Western hemisphere, we can understand. Theirs are much more advanced democracies. Yet, today, Malawi and Liberia both have female presidents.

Closely related to the foregoing, there are many more women out there that have become billionaires. Others are highly accomplished in their careers and professional fields. Even in academia, we are now seeing more and more female scholars that have attained high scholarly recognition internationally. The Nobel Prizes, too, cannot ignore the hard work of some distinguished women. Times are changing fast. It no longer matters who wears the pants in the home. By contrast, the wallet and intellect, and not the pants, are providing some new leadership. Likewise, the good old times when a man would pay for dinner when out on a date are changing gradually. Times are getting tough. Dutch treatment at dinner outings is now not unusual. And Dutch treatment helps to stop the man from demanding lustfully a 'quid pro quo' from the lady after incurring heavy dinner expenses. Indeed, nothing is for free in this world. And Charity cannot sit at the bedroom table.

Similarly, in the olden days, it was rare to find a lady sponsoring her own wedding. The groom and his family would shoulder most of the expenses. Today, with the weakening links of material support under the extended family arrangement, as well as that there are few eligible bachelors out there, it may not be uncommon for a lady to sponsor her own wedding. It is not even surprising to hear of stories where the bride secretly gives the groom money for the latter to pay the bridal price. We are living in tough times – it no longer matters who is wearing the pants! As noted above, a number of men today, including single ones, are being kept by women. In the case of some men, there is nothing wrong with that, as long as there are morally acceptable and genuine reasons for such an arrangement. By contrast, in the case of other men, there is everything wrong with living off a woman, especially if the man is just a conman, hustler and chancer! Such unscrupulous fellas often proudly drive their girlfriend's car, although sometimes ungratefully abusing that privilege to take detours unto other "uncalled for adventures". At times, even the other female party where the detour leads to will know that the main financier of her "boyfriend" is the man's wife. We are living in strange times.

Today, both women and men can wear a pair of trousers at work. Some women hardly even wear dresses or skirts now, leaving such clothes to and for the gay men and elderly women. However, an anonymous female commentator observes that: "Sadly, the issue of sex orientation in many Zambian circles   seems   to be linked with poverty. Many conmen seek gay partners to cushion off their economic hardship – that is, they have steady women on the side, and some are even married. To allow such a block in the ladies' bathroom would mean disaster; that is, he may end up raping some of the women! As for modern ladies preferring to wear slacks, the joke making rounds is that our legs are very stiff – that is, "Uu-kuma" as they say in Bemba – unlike our mothers' who had coca-cola shaped structures, with well-formed legs..."

And when ladies go out swimming, or are working out in the gym, unlike men, they are not expected to expose their bare chests. Some female gender activists claim that this is discrimination. But whether such restrictions are an infringement of women's rights, your guess is as good as mine. Sooner or later, we may start seeing some female boxers showing up in the ring with no upper clothing, like men do. What to do now? Is this not all part of "equal rights" and "gender empowerment"?

The pulpit, too, has not been spared. Many women are preaching the Gospel today. There is a wave of gender empowerment in the church, although some traditional churches have shown resistance to admitting female clerics. But it may not be too far-fetched to envisage in the near future a female pope, female cardinal, female archbishop, female bishop or female priest. We are living in tumultuous times. Who thought that the US would have a black person for a Head of State or for a First Lady? And who thought that the African Union would ever be headed by a lady? But, here we are today. Sooner or later, even Western European countries such as England and France will have to smell the coffee. It is not far-fetched that England will one day have a black person for a Prime Minister. Likewise, France and the other European powers may not be spared. Much as the conservative and right wing pockets of society may not like this song, the music is playing.

No doubt, we are living in fascinating times. Sooner

or later, we will begin to see many more happy marriages between, say, a young black Zambian man and a young Asian lady in Zambia. For a long time, much of the Zambian public has been conditioned to accept situations where some old Asian or Arab man is dating some young black Zambian lady. By contrast, much of our public rarely raises issues on why it is extremely rare in our part of the world for a black Zambian man to date a young Arab or Asian lady. Now understand this: I am not trying to incite any public discord, but merely provoking some critical reflection on major social issues. You only have to watch the movie "Mississippi Masala", starring Denzel Washington, to understand what I am talking about. We are living in changing times when some neighbourhoods such as Madras in Lusaka can no longer be a preserve of certain ethnic groups. Even Thornpark in Lusaka had to give way to others. Look, the world is moving towards more racial integration and harmony. Who thought that apartheid would end in South Africa? But, here we are today. Times are changing, and they are changing fast.

154

CHAPTER

16

ENFORCING THE LAW AGAINST UNAUTHORISED SEXUAL STIMULANTS

In a recent media article titled, "Sex drug kills man", dated October 4, 2012, the *Zambia Daily Mail* reported that a Zambian man died after taking a sexual stimulant locally known as 'mutototo'. The man is suspected by police to have taken an overdose. The deceased is said to have received a 'prescription' to take the mutototo from a local herbalist. But, a leading urologist in Zambia, Dr Francis Manda, quoted by the *Zambia Daily Mail*, said that the actual mutototo found in villages does not kill. Dr. Manda pointed out that many of the herbal medicines being administered in urban areas are a concoction of some leaves and western sexual enhancing drugs. According to Dr. Manda, "It's a fact that in the villages, mutototo exists and it is administered to young men who have come of age or are sexually weak, while in the cities, fake herbalists do it for money." He added further that a lot of people have died due to an overdose of fake stimulants, resulting in the prolonged hardening of the manhood. What a way to die!

In yet another *Zambia Daily Mail* article, "Libido potion lands man in court for murder," published on November 8, 2012, Caroline Kalombe reports that: "A BRICKLAYER of Lusaka has appeared in the Lusaka Magistrates Court for allegedly causing the death of a man whom he gave a libido concoction that went wrong. John Banda, 52, of Libala South is charged with murder... According to court documents, it is alleged that Banda was approached by Abitone Phiri who was looking for a herbal treatment for his low libido. Banda is said to have offered the herbal concoction which was in a form of a powder and was administered using a tangy soft drink which Mr Phiri took. Mr Phiri experienced dizziness, diarrhoea, frequent urination and abdominal pains which worsened with time. He was taken to a clinic by his relatives and later was referred to the University Teaching Hospital. At the hospital, Mr Phiri revealed to his relatives what concoction he had taken and who gave it to him. A post-mortem revealed that Mr Phiri died of poisoning. Particulars of the offence are that Banda on September 30, 2012 in Lusaka did murder Abitone Phiri."

In Zambia, there is now an increasing a call from some sections of the public and the media for the Government to regulate the peddling of unauthorised sexual stimulants. But, Zambia already has a modern piece of legislation to regulate medicines such as herbal sexual stimulants. The

Pharmaceutical Act 2004 provides for the establishment of the Pharmaceutical Regulatory Authority and the regulation and registration of pharmacies, as well as for the regulation of medicines intended for human use and for animal use. Section 47(1) of that statute stipulates that 'a person shall not manufacture, export, import, distribute or sell herbal medicines unless that person has a licence issued by the Authority.' The term 'herbal medicine' is then defined in section 2 as 'any medicinal product that contains, as active ingredients, aerial or underground parts of plants, other plant materials or combinations thereof, whether in a crude state or as plant preparations and includes herbal medicines which contain natural, organic or inorganic active ingredients and are processed or packaged in such manner that they appear like medicines under the western system but does not include medicines containing plant material combined with chemically defined active substances, or chemically defined isolated constituents of plants.' It is evident from this broad definition of 'herbal medicine' that it includes herbal sexual stimulants that are often sold in the form of herbs or herbal extracts. So, the issue here has to do more with the implementation and enforcement of the existing law rather than the need to enact a new law.

Apparently, some traditional healers, despite the existence of the Traditional Health Practitioners Association of Zambia, are reported to be the worst culprits when it comes to the indiscriminate supply of unauthorised sex drugs. But the enactment of laws and the setting up of a practitioners association are not an end in and of themselves. People must learn to exercise self-restraint with or without the enactment of laws. In short, if someone does not require sexual stimulants to 'perform', why in the world would they take such stimulants? Besides, it is only prudent and advisable to seek proper medical advice before taking any sexual stimulants. In a *Zambia Daily Mail* article titled, "A call to regulate sex drug business," dated October 18, 2012, Emelda Shonga reports that 'the booming sale of sexual stimulants in the cities is a matter of grave concern – streets, markets, bus stations, chemists...are freely dispensing these herbs and drugs to anyone, anyhow and anywhere. Herbalists and quack doctors purporting to have intimate knowledge of herbs have given rise to the sale of sexual stimulants; business that pose danger to the lives of potential users.'

As Shonga rightly observes, there are so many men who have been taken ill to hospital for liver and kidney complications after serial consumption of self or street-prescribed sexual stimulants. Shonga adds: "You find that people who are physically and mentally fit, with no reason to enhance their sex drive jump on the bandwagon to have a feel of abnormal 'strength'." But even more worrying are instances where a single man without a wife, or, for lack of a better word, someone who is not entitled to conjugal rights, takes these sexual stimulants in the hope that he will work his way around the neighbourhood to find a prostitute. But, as fate would have it, the prostitute may not show up that day! Others have taken sexual stimulants whilst expecting a visit from a girlfriend who later calls to say that she cannot make it due to some unforeseen family matter. What to do now? Many women's movement bodies have raised concern that the rampant cases of sexual offences in the country are influenced partly by substance abuse, including the abuse of such substances as sexual stimulants.

In Russia, as a leading British newspaper, *The Sun*, reports in an article dated February 26, 2009, and titled, "Viagra orgy man collapses," a sex-mad Russian died after guzzling a bottle of Viagra pills to keep him going for a 12-hour orgy with two women pals. According to *The Sun*, "The women had bet mechanic Sergey Tuganov £3,000 that he wouldn't be able to satisfy them both non-stop for the half-day sex marathon. But minutes after winning the wager, the randy 28-year-old dropped dead with a heart attack, revealed Moscow police. One of the women, named only as Alina, said: 'We called emergency services but it was too late, there was nothing they could do.'..."

Some people might say that the Russian guy died a happy man! However, incidences of this nature are becoming all too common nowadays. Another article in *The Sun*, titled "Viagra turned my eyesight blue," published on October 22, 2012, posits that: "SEX-STARVED John Pettigrew took too many Viagras — and now lives his life in a constant blue movie. Plumber John, 58, sees everything in shades of blue after the sex pills damaged his vision. The dad of two said: 'I admit I ignored the advice on the packet — I was having too much fun — but I'd give up all the sex in the world to be able to see a red letterbox again.' Divorced John turned to Viagra when he had trouble rising to the occasion after a year without sex. He topped up his GP's prescription with pills bought over the internet. He said: 'I didn't have any side-effects, so I didn't see any harm in increasing the dose. But I have been seeing the world in blue for more than a fortnight now and it's doing my head in.'..."

John Pettigrew is said to be undergoing some tests to see if the damage to his eyesight is permanent. And John maintains, according to *The Sun*, "At least, I'm a Chelsea fan..."! But, Pfizer Inc, the manufacturer of Viagra, *The Sun* reports, say some men may experience a blue tint to their sight after taking Viagra, warning users not to exceed the recommended dose. Thus, men are best advised to seek professional guidance from a qualified medical doctor before taking any sexual stimulants. It might just be that a healthy man does not need to take any sexual stimulant in order for him to rise to the occasion. Sometimes, sexual performance challenges could result from psychological or environmental factors. Typical among such cases are those involving work-related stress, inkongole (*i.e.* financial debts), ubwikalo (*i.e.* economic hardship), fear of being discovered over an extra-marital affair, or some other underlying marital problems. However, a qualified medical doctor is in a better position to give reliable professional advice.

As for mutototo and other such herbal sexual stimulants, it is doubtful that there is a standard dosage. It would appear that, depending on what the indulging man views as the task at hand, he may be tempted to increase the dosage so as to deliver a potentially explosive act! There are stories, for example, of how some African Head of State died after taking an overdose of Viagra. Faced with a number of female sexual clients, it is said that the Head of State took an overdose of Viagra in an effort to conquer a sexual milestone akin to that of the Russian man noted above. Like the Russian man, the president died too.

Writing from Malawi, a Malawian friend of mine told me a story of his male cousin who had gone to see an African herbalist in order to help him grow his manhood to a larger and denser size. But, why in the world would someone try to do such a thing? Your guess is as good as mine! Anyhow, the herbalist gave the guy a small tree to go and plant at his house. Also, the herbalist informed his client that as the tree begins to grow the client's manhood would also begin to grow proportionately. The guy was told to cut the tree as soon as he was satisfied with the size, girth and denseness of his manhood. But before long, the guy got a scholarship to go abroad. He left Malawi hurriedly, without cutting the tree! He was too excited with the prospects of going to Europe, and thus forgot about the tree. But, when he got to Europe, it was then that it dawned upon him that he had not cut the 'miracle' tree back home in Malawi.

The tree had now reached the size of a big potentially expansive Baobab tree. He started panicking, making frantic phone-calls to his relatives in Malawi to cut down the tree. But, he was shy and embarrassed to tell the relatives why they had to cut the tree down. And by then, an expatriate whiteman had moved into the house where this guy used to stay. And the whiteman kept vicious dogs. Just how were the guy's relatives going to explain to the whiteman that they wanted to cut down the tree at the whiteman's house, especially that there was even a lovely hammock tied to that tree? Indeed, what to do now? That's the problem with ifya kunwa-nwa ne fya kwi-kata-ikata (*i.e.* that's the problem with drinking and meddling in all kinds of stuff)!

CHAPTER
17

GROWING UP AND MOVING OUT OF YOUR PARENT'S HOME

Not too long ago, while on vacation in Zambia, I visited a friend of mine in some affluent suburb of Lusaka. He was very delighted to see me. He asked his wife, Bana Mulenga, to get us some cold beers from the fridge. Before we knew it, Bana Mulenga was back from where the beers should have been. She lamented: "Ala aba-sungwa ba pano pa ng'anda naba mpesha amano (*i.e.* these dependants that we keep at this house really amaze me)! They've drank all the beers!"

My friend turned to me to apologise. I smiled warmly, saying it was all fine. I then asked for a glass of water. As the conversation went on, Bana Mulenga joined us. She picked an appropriate moment to chip in, asking: "Ayini ba Professor, at what stage should a person move out of his parents' or guardians' home? I have been telling Bashi Mulenga that these dependants that we keep here should move out and find a place of their own. They should take all their nonsense elsewhere instead of bringing it here!"

It was a tough question. First, there is nothing wrong with a child or student being a dependant. Different people are faced with different hardships, including being orphaned at a young age. Secondly, it is how someone uses that experience of being a dependant that matters. I explained to my hosts that at some African funerals, for example, it is the adult dependants that mourn and wail the loudest. That is often the case because such people feel pity upon themselves, as they do not know where to go or where the next meal will come from! Indeed, section 169 of Zambia's Penal Code protects only children, but not adult dependants. The said statutory provision stipulates that: "Any person who being the – (a) parent; (b) guardian; or (c) person in charge; of a child that is unable to provide for itself, refuses or willfully neglects to provide, being able to do so, sufficient food, clothes, bedding or other necessities for such child, and thereby injures the health of such child, commits an offence and is liable, on conviction, to a fine...or to imprisonment ...". Then, section 131A defines a 'child' as a person below the age of sixteen years.

In many cases, children born out-of-wedlock or through adulterous relationships or fornication are abandoned by their biological fathers even where their mothers have not re-married, or where the custody and support of the child has not been granted to some other man by, say, a court order. The poor woman is often left to fend for the child alone. In a way, this explains the increasing number of street kids in Zambia today. Yet, section 168 of the Penal Code provides clearly that 'any person who being the parent, guardian or other person having the lawful care *or charge* of a child being able to maintain such child, willfully and without lawful or reasonable cause deserts the child and leaves it without means of support commits an offence and is liable, upon conviction,...to imprisonment.' What to do now? Section 169 adds in the offence of neglecting to provide, among other things, food for the children.

Some of these street kids have relatively wealthy or financially comfortable fathers who, upon impregnating the kid's mother through, say, an adulterous relationship, will dispute paternity so as to avoid parental responsibility. Usually, these men do not want their wives to know about such adulterous affairs or the illegitimate child born out of the illicit sexual relationship. So, what to do now, as a Christian nation? And closely related to the above is the issue of adult dependants and relatives who also want a share of the man's earnings. Should the man support his children first, including any child born out of wedlock, before he can support any adult dependant, uncle or auntie? Where should his priorities lie? Indeed, who comes first, adults or children? Some relatives will be quick to say that they come first, arguing that it is so because they have children to support. But what about the provider's own children, are they not children as well? I went on to explain that once someone is done with college or university, or for those adult dependants with no proper game plan after high school, they should be given a short grace period to prepare themselves to move out. Otherwise, if they stay on, they will be taking up the space meant for the children of the house. The last thing you want to see is children sleeping on the floor or on the sofa because some stranded uncle or auntie has taken over their bed!

I could see that Bana Mulenga was in full agreement with my views. But Bashi Mulenga seemed rather uneasy with my strong views, especially because one of the dependants was his nephew. So, he interjected, and addressed his question to his wife: "Why is it that whenever my relatives come to this house, whether as dependants or not, you always want them to leave? Look, your elder sister, along with her two children, came to stay with us when her husband chased her from their marriage, but you did not complain or ask her to leave! Why?"

There was some silence. I looked at my friend, Shi Mulenga, but he continued: "Md'ala, ba mlamu bobe aba, ba kapatulula sana (*i.e.* your sister-in-law here, she is not fair)." I asked him why he thought like that. And he went on to say: "The other day after I came back from work, I found my nephew at home. So, I asked him to get me some cold beers and to join me for a light drink since Bana Mulenga was still at church attending an evening prayer meeting. When the boy got drunk, that is when 'he started talking' (meaning that that is when the boy openned up), as he sobbed while tears fell uncontrollably down his cheeks, lamenting that, 'Ba Yama, mwaliba fye bwino. Nomba fye ba Madame, eba shaba bwino! Nobwali bala ntana nga ta mulipo! (*i.e.* Uncle, you are a nice man. However, Auntie is very cruel. She hardly ever leaves food for me when you are not around)."

I turned to look at Bana Mulenga to see if what her husband was saying was true. She kept quiet for a while, and then went on: "OK, lekeni fye ndande (*i.e.* let me tell you the truth). We used to have maids at this house, but Bashi Mulenga, aba, would turn them into his second wives! He would always sneak in from work when the maid is alone at home. One of my neighbours tipped me, and that is how I quietly came back home one day unannounced only to find him entangled with the maid!" Shi Mulenga tried to clear his throat to stop his wife from talking, but it was too late. Bana Mulenga went on: "It's a long story, my brother. That is why we only have male dependants at this house, and no female maids anymore. Pantu cali cilamo fye, shi Mulenga, uyu! (*i.e.* It became too much of shi Mulenga's infidelity)".

Anyhow, I tactfully steered Bana Mulenga away from the issue of her husband's infidelity so as to bring everyone back to the main issue of when a dependant should move out of the house. I posited that there is no rule of thumb on this issue. However, I went on to add that: (a) umu-sungwa afwile uku kwata akatina elo noku icefya no mucinshi, and that tafwile kula linganya ama-puli na bene ba ng'anda (*i.e.* dependants should be humble and respectful, with good manners, and not competing with the owner of the house); (b) dependants, however, should be well-looked after by the guardian and should not be mistreated or exploited; (c) dependants should be hardworking and not lazing around while the owner of the house is up early doing house chores; (d) the parent or guardian has no right to abuse children or dependants, but that that does not mean that dependants can now do as they please; (e) dependants who have a child or children should not be kept as dependants, but should be asked instead to leave because anyone who feels that he or she is ready or old enough to have sex is presumably an adult – the logic here is that children, unlike adults in marriage, are not supposed to have sex or to bear fellow children; and, (f) dependants should not enter the master-bedroom anyhow nor try on the Madame's or Master's clothes or perfumes without the owner's permission.

At the end of the conversation, I added that Bana Mulenga should also be fair in her dealings with her in-laws. Marriage is like a seesaw or a scale of justice, I implored. You don't put too much weight on one side of the seesaw. It will lose its balance, tilt to one side and you will fall off. The seesaw or scale of justice must remain balanced fairly on both ends. She agreed, but cautioned Shi Mulenga with a kitchen knife that she would not hesitate to cut-off the unspeakables should he misbehave again.

CHAPTER

18

UNDERSTANDING AFRICAN 'SOCIAL SECURITY'

While the concept of African social security is premised mainly on the ideology of collectivism, it is a truism that globalization has dealt an affront to many traditional practices of collectivism, promoting instead a heightened sense of individualism in many parts of the developing world, including Asia, Eastern Europe and Latin America. Could the increasing levels of individualism signal an end to collectivism? In much of the capitalist world, there is not much room for collectivism. Rather, it is each for his or her own.

The American Heritage Dictionary defines the term 'social security' as 'a government program that provides economic assistance to persons faced with unemployment, disability, or agedness, financed by assessment of employers and employees.' Let us take a more reasoned look at this term. Whilst ordinary parlance often refers to State-funded programmes of social security, such a definition is not the concern of

- Kenneth K. Mwenda

this paper. Rather, we will look at the term social security in a broader sense that refers to being secure in society generally from want, and the various systems that help to ensure such security. We will not look at such State-funded programmes as some pension schemes in Zambia. By contrast, our concern is with the non-traditional forms of social security that we often do not even realise are forms of social security in our part of the world. And this is what is referred to in the article as "African social security"! You can, however, find different versions of such "non-traditional" social security in many other parts of the world, too. But what are some examples of African social security?

Due to high levels of poverty in many developing countries, it has often been the norm and practice of many couples to have large families. Now, you may be wondering what I am getting at. You may have heard of funny stories that since "ba Katolika (i.e. Catholics) bali kanya ama condoms nama contraceptive pills", they tend to have many children. But that is not true. I am Catholic myself, and I don't have a large family. Anyhow, that aside, in our part of the world, having many children has often been a good example of a parent investing in social security even if that parent cannot afford to look after all the many children. The idea is that when one gets old, you need someone to look after you since the State has no effective or meaningful programmes of social security. Ever wondered why some irresponsible men who once denied paternity of a child born out of wedlock suddenly show up, claiming to be the father to the child after realizing that the child has grown up into a successful professional or star? It is very common to have such irresponsible absentee fathers show up when they know that their days are now numbered, and that the child they once denied has made it in life. Quite often, in such cases, the crooked and irresponsible man will just be after social security as well as an association with success and fame. Sadly though, such characters are often embraced by the unsuspecting grown-up child and her mother, but only to realize that a conman hardly ever ceases to be a conman. Neither does a tiger change its spots in old age.

Another example of African social security is the extended family concept. How many of you remember growing up in situations of some relatives travelling all the way from the village to come and get some money from your parents in the urban areas? We all have relatives of one kind or another in the village, no matter how sophisticated we may pretend to be. A friend of mine from East Africa once told me of a funny story. He got a letter from a female cousin of his in Kenya who had dropped out of school to get married to some disco-freak. The lady was asking for financial help to pay for her children's school fees. So, my friend asked why she could not get money from her husband instead. And she replied: "That is why God gave us someone like you in the family, who is very intelligent...so that you can help us and look after us!" And referring to her children, my friend's nieces and nephews, she continued: "These are your children. You cannot abandon them just like that!" Now, perhaps you understand why many Heads of State in Africa, including Zambia, find it hard not to give jobs to relatives. Even those in the opposition would do the same if given a chance to rule. It is different for someone like Obama, although he has paternal African roots. He has never appointed any of his relatives from Kenya or elsewhere to a US Government job! Do you see what I mean?

In Africa, some relatives will ask that they keep up at your place for a short while they look for a place of their own to stay. Believe you me, they may never leave! Others will borrow money from you, promising to pay back as soon as 'the cheque clears in the bank.' But, believe you me, they might not pay you back. You will be very lucky if they ever pay back. In short, you are for them a source of social security. As one anonymous Zambian professional based in Botswana observes: "It's just very true that issues of social security still affect us. The problem is that in Africa there is this culture of 'entitlement' where one feels that their brother's or sister's achievements are theirs too. One wonders which generation will champion and change this. This mentality has even affected the occurrence of development in a broad sense."

Closely related to that, another anonymous Zambian professional observes that: "The extended family concept is a good one; only that with the high poverty levels in Africa, people have tended to take advantage of their relatives who happen to be well off. I say it's a good concept because it brings people together and where there's no abuse, we all can benefit from it. It can and does foster cooperation among relations – at funerals and weddings, for example. Each family member can lend a hand by helping with a financial contribution, or even with giving of their time to do some work at the function."

The said Zambian writer continues: "Of course, nowadays, we have more parasitic extended family relations than symbiotic ones, as you correctly postulated. There's also the 'neighbourhood' social security group which comprises those who stay within one's precincts and are always ready to show up at the slightest sign of a bereavement at one's home. They purport to come to help with mourning when in actual fact all they want is 'free' food to fill their stomachs! Well, I think the cure for these African social security problems lies in eliminating poverty more than it does in enlightening people. For as long as they are hungry, they will continue to perpetrate even the abhorrent practice of property-grabbing when their distant relatives pass away."

You can also have some friends and workmates who behave in the same way as some troublesome extended family members when it comes to African social security. Some of these friends and/or workmates will borrow your nice car if they want to go and 'shine' somewhere, and then return the vehicle with almost no fuel left in the tank. What do you do? For them, you are a form of social security. Others will visit your home at strategic times when they know that you are about to have dinner or lunch. And when you ask them to join you at the dinner table, they will first politely and shyly decline the invitation hoping that you will press on so that it appears as though you forced them to join you for the meal. Even some Christians pull such stunts on Sundays, especially after church service when the sun is so strong and they are damn hungry! They will stop-by a family member's home after church with a view of nourishing their tummies.

And you probably have had a member of the extended family who, for some strange reason best known to himself or herself, decided to have a wedding when he or she could not afford to finance the wedding. If you asked such a person where the money would come from for the wedding, he or she must have said something like this: "Kaili, ba Yama bali kwata ama business. Elo naba m'lamu nabo baka twafwilisha ko, pamo naba kalamba bandi…" (i.e. My uncle has money and is a businessman. And my brother-in-law, together with my elder brother, will also chip in financially. So, we are OK). But, surely, why have a wedding when you cannot afford one? Why not just have "icombela ng'anda" (i.e. African traditional marriage) if you cannot afford a wedding? We live in a world of pretence. Many people are no longer humble. You cannot be planning a wedding on the basis of other people financing your wedding. It does not work like that. The two of you, the bride and the groom, must bear the main expenses. Other members of the family or friends can only come in as invited guests to get you some gifts, if they so wish. Even then, it is not polite for the bride, for example, to be demanding expensive wedding gifts from some guests. And it does not matter that such guests have been assigned privileged and visible roles for the wedding ceremony! I have heard crazy stories where a bride demands outrageous gifts from her in-laws or family members. Again, in situations of this nature, it has nothing to do with culture. It's all about poverty. I do not know of any culture that encourages people to demand expensive gifts from others. Indeed, a beggar is not a chooser. And as they say in Swahili, "he who lives by relatives dies poor".

Culturally, when a man decides to marry, between him and the bride, he should be the one providing leadership in gathering the main resources for the wedding. Here, notwithstanding any gender-empowered arguments of equal rights, it is the man who should show more leadership in handling the finances of the wedding because, after all, he is the one who proposed to marry the lady! Now, let me push a bit before you jump in. I am awake to the fact that nowadays some women do propose marriage to men, especially with the ever shrinking numbers of eligible bachelors out there. And this brings me to the next example of African social security.

Haven't you heard of people who marry for money? And, if you look at statistics regarding many divorce cases worldwide, money is one of the top reasons why many couples divorce, followed by infidelity. With money, even some really ugly-looking illiterate man can afford to get himself an educated, pretty and fine lady. She will have found herself some good social security in the ugly-looking man, notwithstanding his weird looks and low intellectual disposition. Likewise, some destitute men, with

limited financial means, tend to live-off single
women that have good jobs or good incomes. Again,
it comes back to issues of poverty and our sense of
African social security. Now, do not get me wrong.
Even in the developed world like the USA, UK, and
other parts of Europe, there are a lot of such conmen
who live-off women. In fact, it is actually worse in
the Western world! People even sign pre-nuptial
agreements before getting married to protect their
assets in case of a divorce. But, why do they sign
such agreements? Because they know that money
can be a major attracting factor for some people to
get into a supposedly "lucrative" marriage. So, it's
not entirely an African thing. It applies elsewhere
too. Admittedly, the term "African social security"
can be seen from such a perspective as somewhat a
misnomer. But, we are using the term loosely here
since we are looking at our African society, and not
other societies.

Marriage can also be a good form of African social
security if you marry off your son or daughter to
someone who is supposedly wealthy, rich and
generous. Back in the days, some Zambian parents
were eager to marry off their youthful daughters on
the Copperbelt to some elderly French-speaking
West African men that were illegal emerald dealers.
And some of these men were polygamists, and came
from very troubled backgrounds in their native West
African countries. It would only dawn on the young
Zambian brides that they had gotten themselves into
trouble after going with their West African husbands
to live in the latter's country of origin. And that is
the problem with African social security. It is not

always stable and reliable. In the diasporas, for example, you will find many interracial marriages that are predicated on African or non-traditional social security, especially where one party is, say, an African, Middle East or Caribbean immigrant. Some get into these interracial marriages just to get "papers" (i.e. immigration and residency documents). Others do so mainly due to an inferiority complex, thinking that they will now look more sophisticated in the eyes of their fellow people of colour. Whereas some pockets of the Middle East, Africa or the Caribbean aspire towards values of self-esteem and a dignified conscience, there are also some opportunistic pockets from these societies that suffer from the inferiority complex of race.

It is no different for Latino immigrants who marry whites for reasons akin to those of the African, Middle East and Caribbean folks noted above. The majority are in search of non-traditional social security. Also, it is not uncommon to find, say, an Asian or Oriental man or woman who crosses their race, with a premeditated motive, just to marry a white person in a developed country. The motives are still the same; that is, either a search for non-traditional social security, the person of colour involved has an inferiority complex, or it is one of those rare but possible cases of genuine love. But one might ask: what about the whites themselves, what attracts them to such marriages? There are many reasons that help to explain such issues, including some form of curiosity regarding different skin pigmentation as well as some myths about the sexuality of certain races, but few of these are predicated on non-traditional social security. It is usually some notorious folks from some poorer countries that are driven by motives of non-traditional social security. That said, the practice of "mail order" brides, as one anonymous commentator observes, "…is now big in the US and many parts of Europe; that is, where some white man places an 'order', via some dating website, for the 'importation' of an oriental or Asian woman as a spouse, notwithstanding that the woman hardly speaks any English." It is often said that many oriental women are well-cultured and are much more submissive to their husbands than many women from the West. Thus, some western men see the potential of a good wife in many of these oriental women. Indeed, due to the increasing levels of feminism in the West, a good number of western men are reluctant to deal with (assertive???) aggressive feminism by some western women, opting instead for "mail order" brides from, say, the Far East or Central Asia. That said, like some people of colour, some white people, too, do fall in love genuinely and for good reasons with individuals of colour. Yes, it is possible, and it does happen.

Among the whites themselves, some whites from the poorer parts of Europe (e.g. those from the former socialist and communist States) or from the Pacific regions tend to look up to their brothers and sisters from, say, the US, the UK, Canada, France, Italy, Germany, Belgium or the Netherlands, as somewhat a better kind. And many of these white folks from the poorer parts of Europe envy the lifestyles in the aforementioned western countries. Because of this, those from the poorer parts of Europe will not hesitate to marry their counterparts from the western world as a means to migrate and live in the much craved for western world. Thus, it is not uncommon for some women from the former socialist states of Eastern Europe to go after white men from Western Europe or North America. Much of it is simply opportunistic behaviour of rent seeking. We live in a crazy world. As noted above, there are very few of these folks who do things for genuine love.

CHAPTER

19

CLOSING THE KNOWLEDGE GAP FACING AFRICA THROUGH THE DIASPORANS

It is now widely recognised by many pundits that the knowledge gap that exists between the developed world and the developing world explains much of the challenges to development in such places as Sub-Sahara Africa. Going forward, we need to close the chasm of this knowledge divide. Many commentators have been crying for an improved culture of reading in Zambia. But for many people to read there must be books to read. Here, the type of books that we are referring to are not certain types of novels, biographies, autobiographies, consultancy reports or conference proceedings that are less intellectually stimulating. Such publications are less helpful in closing the knowledge gap. Rather, we need to put in place deliberate policies that promote scientific research and scholarship. Researchers need to be given the appropriate space and incentives to carry out meaningful and valuable research. In cultures that do not value scholarship and research, it is hard

- Kenneth K. Mwenda

for economies to take-off. Look, even countries that are known for breaching intellectual property laws by copying other people's technology tend to invest somehow in research for copying that foreign technology. For some time now, our universities in Africa have been neglected badly. Yet, that is where much of the thinking should be taking place. And some of our own intellectuals tend to look down on our local universities, not even wanting to give credit to the intellectual fountain that gave birth to their careers.

This past summer, I travelled with my family on vacation to Cape Town, South Africa, for a week before connecting to Zambia for another week. In Cape Town, apart from vacationing, I was also delivering some postgraduate lectures on a Master of Laws (LLM) degree programme in International Trade and Investment Law at the University of Western Cape. The said LLM programme alternates between the University of Western Cape and the University of Pretoria every other year. Last year, I was lecturing at the University of Pretoria. That is how I often spend my vacation time.

When I arrived in Zambia, my schedule was very tight. I had to fly to the Copperbelt to attend to a family bereavement before flying back to Lusaka to give lectures at the University of Lusaka. All in all, I had two weeks scheduled for my annual leave. In the US, I have also been teaching recently at American University in Washington DC. But I can only carry out these on-the side professional engagements outside of my office hours. In short, I have very little idle time. Drawn between different demanding schedules, including my full-time work at the World Bank, which often involves a lot of international travel, I have continued to engage in intellectual leadership. This multi-pronged approach has kept my professional life active and busy, and it enriches my intellectual well-being, too.

While visiting Zambia, I was set to launch officially my twenty-second book at Pamodzi Hotel. Over the years, I have written a good twenty-two (22) scholarly books, in addition to over eighty (80) peer-reviewed articles in leading international journals and law reviews worldwide. Some of my scholarly publications have been cited not only in academia, but also by the courts of law as well as in some studies by the IMF and the World Bank. I must sincerely thank the sponsors of this Pamodzi Hotel book launch, namely, Meanwood Group of Companies, Bankers Association of Zambia, the Institute of Finance and Economics and the University of Lusaka, for their kind and most generous support. Without them, it would not have been easy for me to pull it together. Also, I am most grateful to all the colleagues and friends that attended the event.

Many people often ask me where I get the energy, time and zeal to write. One thing that is certain: I am not a dogmatic and routine type of person. I often think outside the box, and thus have held, in addition, a number of esteemed Professorial appointments at many leading universities. I started my academic career in 1991 as a Staff Development

Fellow (SDF) at the University of Zambia (UNZA) before proceeding on a Rhodes Scholarship to the University of Oxford. After my postgraduate studies in the UK, I took up a full-time Law Lectureship at one of the top British universities, the University of Warwick. At the time, I was only 26 years old. And I had no academic mentor to guide me on how to get into academia in the UK, as this was the first time that a Zambian lawyer was being appointed as a Law Lecturer at a top British university. Thus, I found myself unexpectedly as a Zambian legal academic pioneer in the UK, despite my young age. At Warwick, I taught both on the undergraduate and postgraduate law degree programmes, as well as supervised and examined several postgraduate law degree dissertations.

While teaching at Warwick, I won a competitive fellowship at Yale University Law School in the US. At the same time, I had just been selected to join the World Bank's Young Professionals Program. I weighed the two options, and went for the latter option. It was a difficult choice to make given that Yale Law School is consistently ranked as the best law school in the US, ranking ahead of even Harvard Law School. And so, the book that I was launching in Lusaka recently is somewhat part of this story. It focusses on banking regulation and supervision in Zambia, drawing comparatives from parallel common law jurisdictions.

Our African intellectuals in the diaspora must begin to make a difference by transferring the knowledge and experience that they have gained from wherever they are to the African continent. My twenty years both in the UK and US is very richly informed by the many great lessons of experience that I have captured over the years. Also, I have worked in and on many other different countries in Europe, Central Asia, Latin America, South America, East Asia, South Asia, the Middle East, and the Pacific, interacting and leading policy dialogue with several senior government officials. Thus, I am able to write books and journal articles that often bring together these international and global experiences. And the scholar in me tends to complement my development practitioner experience. Indeed, I have purposely kept it that way. If one has a talent that God has given him or her, it is wise not to waste or throw it away. You must find a way in which that talent should or can enhance and complement your work life. The often-cited argument about lack of time to do other things is simply a lame excuse. Everyone has time outside their work to do other things no matter how busy they are. Some have time to handle several girlfriends or extra-marital affairs. Others have time to play golf or to go clubbing or partying. Then, there are also people that have more than enough time to go drinking beers daily, or to attend all the posh weddings and kitchen parties in town. Others spend their free time shopping, loitering around the shopping malls, or gossiping. It just depends on how an individual manages his or her time outside their work hours. Indeed, much of the time, we are either asleep or cannot even account for how we spent the day.

Thus, the launching of my book on banking

regulation at Pamodzi Hotel was not an exercise in futility or an egoistic trip of self-fulfillment. That is far from it. Rather, our children and grandchildren, especially those focussed on legal scholarship or academia, must have a story to tell of where they come from. They must have role models that they can easily relate to as one of their own, as opposed to just reading about foreign scholars that they may never even meet. It gives the young ones self-reassurance that they too can be like the person standing in front of them. On March 28, 2008, when I stepped forward to receive the Higher Doctorate Degree of Doctor of Laws (LLD) at Rhodes University in South Africa, awarded in recognition of my significant and substantial contribution to legal scholarship over the years, I could see the immense pride in the eyes of many African students and graduands at the ceremony. It was the first and only time in the rich history of Rhodes University – that is, Rhodes University is arguably one of the top five universities on the African continent – that a Higher Doctorate in Law was being awarded. And that remains so for Zambia as well. This Higher Doctorate came through almost ten years after my PhD. And there are only as few as eight to ten individuals with such an award from the entire African continent. As always, I think of my country first. When I walked up to receive this prestigious award, I could see the writing of "Zambia" on the global intellectual map. And the inspiring applause from the large gathering of parents, professors, lecturers, graduands, students and friends continued for ends on. Many asked later: "Where are you from to come and receive such an esteemed and prestigious award?" And I would reply calmly: "I am from Zambia", although I flew into South Africa directly from the US.

188

CHAPTER

20

FIGHTING-OFF THE SIN OF ENVY IN MAN

Some people worry a lot and they don't like it when others are supposedly doing better than them. Then, there are those that don't like it when others have too much of what everyone else wants. I once overheard a young lady badmouthing a friend of hers who was about to get married, saying: "After all, kali huule fye (i.e. that the bride is of loose morals). Kwati pali na kaume ka ku yumfwila po (i.e. the groom, too, is just a jerk)." I could tell that the badmouthing lady was envious of the friend getting married.

I am one person who knows no envy, nor gets intimidated or bothered by what others are doing. I set my own goals and agenda. That's just me. Many young people that I have mentored know how much I will try to help others, without fearing that if I help them they will later on do better than me. God has given each one of us different talents. We all can't have everything at the same time. What a rich man has, I may not have. By parity of reasoning, what God has blessed me with, a rich man will never have. You can't have it all. Once you grasp that concept, you will stop worrying and panicking unnecessarily.

In the Old Testament, the Bible teaches us that one of the earliest sins to be committed by mankind was predicated on the sin of envy. Satan was envious of God. Yes, he was envious and jealousy of God. So, to try and wrestle back God's infinite goodness, Satan tempted Adam and Eve to commit sin against God, the Creator and Almighty. Next, Cain killed his brother Abel because Cain was jealousy and envious of Abel's successes. Even our Lord Jesus Christ was crucified, notwithstanding God's divine plan, partly because someone somewhere on this earth was envious of Jesus. But, why should it be like that?

The morning before Jesus appeared before Pilate, Pilate's wife warned Pilate that he should have nothing to do with that innocent man. But because Pilate was consumed with his love of political power, he was instead concerned with how Rome would view him should the people rebel at the release of Jesus. So, Pilate, like many of us, opted to throw Jesus underneath the bus. For Pilate, it was all about securing his own political fortunes. In short, Pilate sacrificed Jesus to keep his political power! How many times do we come across people who are willing to sacrifice the truth on the altar of political expediency? The parable of the Good Samaritan, as told by our Lord Jesus Christ in the Gospel of Luke 10:29-37, talks of a traveller, possibly a Jewish man, who is beaten, robbed, and left half dead along the road. First, a priest and then a Levite come by, but both ignore the man. Finally, a Samaritan comes by. At the time, Samaritans and Jews generally despised each other. But it was the Samaritan who helped the injured man. In short, while the priest and the Levite thought only of their own safety, and did not want to risk anything by helping the injured man, the Samaritan, by contrast, worried about what would happen to the injured man should he ignore him. Through this parable, we can see that our character can at times be shaped by our own insecurities as well as our insatiable love of self-preservation, especially where we lack moral conviction to do right.

In today's world, one would have thought that the stories referred to above are all of the past, and that we now live in a modern world where a knowledge economy is all that matters. But history has a tendency of repeating itself. And so, we, writers and intellectuals, like musicians, clerics, artists and griots (i.e. a griot is a West African historian, a repository of oral tradition and a storyteller, praise singer, poet and/or musician), have a moral responsibility to engage in erudite and edifying thought-leadership. We cannot, as thought-leaders, afford to compromise our moral responsibility for the sake of winning acceptability in the eyes of those from whom we often seek political favours. An intellectual, like a priest or pastor, should not owe political allegiances to anyone. Neither is he or she required to seek public or political approval. He or she should remain apolitical.

- Kenneth K. Mwenda

Referring to the sin of envy, the Bible, in James 3:14, postulates that: "But if you have **bitter envy** and self-seeking in your hearts, do not boast and lie against the truth." Recently, a friend of my family visited us here in the USA. That Sunday morning, she joined us at church. When we got back from church, I kindly asked my wife to prepare me a rich African dish while they all enjoyed their American and European food. On special and rare occasions such as this, I often love to eat "ifi-sashi" (i.e. cassava leaves cooked with peanut butter) and "ubwali bwa tute" (i.e. nsima made from cassava mealie-meal), with "isabi lya koca" (i.e. smoked tilapia fish), a side-dish of "ci sense" (i.e. kapenta or sardines), some well roasted African peanuts and nicely smoked cassava. Now, some readers might be wondering how and why in the world would a man who has lived abroad for so long (both in Europe and America for over twenty (20) years) be eating African food out there instead of eating American and European food? To be honest, I have had enough of the latter two. Besides, I am a man of eclectic taste in my appreciation of food, drink, dressing, music and culture.

Also, it is good to know that most of our African food is not genetically modified (GMO). It comes as organic as it can be. When my Dad and Mum visited me in the UK in the summer of 1996 – I was then lecturing at the University of Warwick – I insisted that they bring me some African food which I dearly missed, despite having studied at a top elite British school; that is, as a Rhodes Scholar at Oxford. To this day, I have never lost my roots. I speak my Zambian languages as fresh as you can imagine. That is who I am. I have no apologies to make to anyone for my love of Africa and for my Afro-centricity. There are many Africans both in Africa and the diaspora who don't want to have anything to do with Africa. Yet they can't shed off that visible polio vaccination mark on their upper arm which gives them away easily!

Anyhow, that Sunday, our visitor wore a nice dress. My wife and I complimented her, saying: "You look great! That's a very lovely outfit!" She smiled and said, "Thank you!" Then, she continued: "You are the only ones who have said I look good in this dress. None of my friends at work or at church in Zambia ever compliment me. Many will just look elsewhere, and pretend not to have noticed." I smiled and said to her: "It's called envy. Who wouldn't want to look good and nice, anyhow?" Indeed, how many times do we come across people that are like that; that is, people that hardly say good things about us or about others? How many times do we come across people that are constantly trying to put us down, peddling falsehoods and innuendos? Yet, the Bible, in Hebrews 12:15, teaches us that: "Looking diligently lest anyone fall short of the grace of God; lest any root of bitterness springing up cause trouble, and by this many become defiled." Indeed, envy often matures into bitterness inside of man or woman. It then springs up and grows to a proportion where man or woman can no longer control it. And it is the *bitterness* that results from *envy* that will ultimately defile and destroy mankind, if we are not careful. It is a sin to be envious of others. We all have different possessions, abilities and talents. We are reminded in James 3:16 that: "For where *envy* and self-seeking exist, confusion and every evil thing will be there."

Friendships have been lost and families broken over envy and jealousy. Many people have committed evil all because of envy. Envy comes in many forms. For example, some will deliberately choose not to say congratulations to a friend when their friend does better than them in school. Others will try to belittle or downplay the accomplishments of someone. Yet, some will try to flex their small muscles, contending that they too are deserving, or that they are better than the other person when they can't even measure up. **Envy, it is said,** removes you from the will of God. It places you outside of the will of God, into a place frequented by all types of evil. And once you are placed outside the will of God, you become extremely vulnerable. In fighting-off the sin of envy, a major defence lies in Matthew 26:41 where Jesus says: "Watch and pray so that you will not fall into temptation. The spirit is willing, but the flesh is weak."

CHAPTER

21

UNDERSTANDING THE NEXUS BETWEEN TRADITIONS AND CULTURE

It is a widely accepted practice that you do not answer your phone when you are in the toilet to avoid telling lies to the caller that you are busy in a meeting. On the one hand, the Merriam-Webster dictionary defines a custom as a practice common to many or a particular place or class. Tradition, on the other hand, is defined as an inherited, established or customary pattern of thought, action or behavior, such as a religious practice or a social custom. In essence, a tradition tends to be representative of a person's culture. Also, a tradition can be widely practiced, and will usually be passed down through generations, families or other institutions.

A critical distinction, however, between traditions and culture lies in the fact that whereas culture, as a way of life, evolves with time, and does get modified or adapted to changing technologies, traditions, by contrast, seem to remain static. Often times, traditions try to defy changing technologies, resisting societal or individual efforts at modification. Unlike some progressive cultures, many traditions are very slow to change or to adapt. To that extent, certain elements of our culture that represent traditions tend to resist change.

However, mindful that studies on matters of 'culture and tradition' are often a preserve of the disciplines of anthropology and sociology, it would be helpful here to stray into some pertinent aspects of these disciplines. Very often, we hear people using phrases such as 'Kaili, it's the kacha...' (i.e. It is the culture) or 'kacha yali cinja pa Zambia' (i.e. Culture has changed in Zambia). Let us take the following examples to get a better sense of what we are talking about. Why do men often wear suits when they are going out on a dinner date? Is there a law that requires them to wear suits for such occassions? Or, does this have to do with culture or tradition? And what about those young ladies that like to expose their bare waist with African beads stringed around the waist? Is that a new kacha or what? Have African traditions on discreet wearing of beads now evolved or what? Besides, do traditions change that easily?

Many years ago, I had dinner with a vice-chancellor of a certain leading university in Europe. As we were enjoying our dinner, the man asked me if I knew of a certain famous academician. I responded that I knew the academician very well. And the vice-chancellor continued: "I like that guy. When he applied for a professorial chair at this university, I asked our university registrar to contact him to arrange for an interview. But when the registrar contacted him to ask for his availability, the man told the registrar that he thought that he had applied for the job and not for the interviews!" We all burst out laughing, knowing the great sense of humour of the academician that the vice-chancellor was talking about.

Then, the vice-chancellor added: "Of course, he came for the interviews, and that is how we got him to join us here." Now, understand this: it is correct to say that the man had applied for the job, and not the interviews. Unless the job advert had specified that only suitable candidates would be invited for interviews, why should he be asked to attend interviews when he had applied for the job? One would easily imagine that only a confident candidate who truly knows what he or she is worth can have such guts! You can only make such jokes if you know full well how good you are. Yet, tradition requires us all to conform, submitting ourselves humbly to the authorities. I can only imagine that someone else would have thought of the famous professor in the example above as arrogant and not worthy considering any further. But he was damn good at what he does, and could thus afford to pull such a light-hearted joke that could have been easily misunderstood by many.

Closely related to the foregoing, is there a law that requires people to wear suits when they show up for a job interview? If the job advert does not specify the dress code for the interviewees, why do we still want to show up in a suit? What is it that has conditioned us to think that job interviews are partly about impressive clothes? I recall sitting on an interview panel, and one of the interviewees showed up in jeans, T-shirt and sneakers. But he was damn good at the interviews, and he knew his field of expertise very well. The other panelists voted him down simply because they all felt he was inappropriately dressed for the interviews. I then asked them if they had specified in the job advert the preferred dress code for the interviewees. They all responded: "Come on...it is obvious! He should know." But we can't be making such assumptions. People come from different cultural backgrounds. What is considered formal dress code in some culture may not be acceptable in another culture.

Likewise, in some cultures, it aint a taboo for an elderly person to break the wind loudly and audibly in the presence young people. They all will laugh about it lightly, and life continues. Yet, in some cultures, such as where many of us come from, if someone elderly fouls the air silently it is the young ones who will be blamed. And they are not expected to deny. Again, is this about tradition or culture?

A Caucasian friend of mine married to a Zambian lady in Norway could not understand why his Zambian in-laws would not sit with him at the dinner table when having dinner. And one day, he woke up in the morning with only his underwear on. He went to sit on the patio to enjoy the rising summer sun. Unknowingly, his mother-in-law was also headed for the balcony when she found him seated outside with underwear only. She collapsed! They had to call medical emergency to resuscitate her from the shock. It was then that I had to explain to my Caucasian friend some pertinent aspects about culture, customs and traditions. I had to offer him a crush-course in Anthropology 101.

Even in some churches, some of the things that we practice or follow have very little to do with the Word of God. We are often overburdened with traditions! And these traditions are created by fellow human mortals. Traditions are not divine wisdom. They are simply church traditions established by fellow human mortals. Period! We must distinguish church traditions from the actual Word of God. The Pharisees, for example, were experts primarily in church traditions. But their understanding of the Word of God was arguably exposed at times by our Lord Jesus Christ. And they hated Him for that!

A nephew of mine once asked me: "Uncle, why is it that elderly people have to wash their hands first before everyone else at the dinner table? Why can't it just be democracy that whoever arrives first can wash his or her hands, and then start eating?" Before I could answer, the boy's father, who was seated nearby, interjected: "It's kacha and good table manners for you to let elders wash their hands first!!!" The boy looked at me quietly, and we both went silent. The boy then asked me again: "Uncle, OK, let us assume that Dad is right by saying young people should allow the elders to wash their hands first, can I still be allowed to start eating if I can run and overtake the elders before they get to the dinner table?"

I looked at my nephew, and smiled: "No, son, you cannot do that. There is another rule to follow. You must first wait for the elders to get seated at the dinner table and to take their meal potion before you can make any attempt at the food..." My nephew was quick to respond: "But is that not selfish? At school, they teach us that young people should eat more healthy food in order to grow up. What if the elders get all the good pieces of chicken, as they often do, and they leave for the children an ugly foot of a chicken or a chicken wing with only large gallons of soup?" Before I could answer, the boy's father cleared his throat, and put down his newspaper. He ordered my nephew to go outside and play with his friends. I kept wondering to myself: the boy had a point! But why did his father chase him away? The reason is simple: the boy was challenging traditions! It is called marshalling a paradigm shift.

Even in corporate organisations, as an employee, you are not expected to challenge traditions. You will not get away easily with that. Serious consequences and repercussions can follow. And so it is with certain churches and other institutions. There is no sitting on the fence. In the end, we find that human beings become enslaved with traditions, constantly seeking to be accepted by society and institutions. But some traditions and cultures can rob you of your happiness! What to do now? Rebel, and face the consequences?

CHAPTER

22

ONLY GOD IS GOOD ENOUGH

Someone asked me recently why I like to write and contribute to literature. I smiled and responded calmly: "Instead of spending hours and hours talking about people, I would rather be addressing issues. Look, we can fix issues, but we can't fix people...certainly not by gossiping about them. Only God is good enough to fix people, through, say, the professional work of medical doctors who cure the sick. So, stop trying to fix each other when there are more than enough issues to fix out there in society. When I write, I endeavour to fix issues, as opposed to fixing people. There is a difference there."

Against this background, why do some individuals like judging others? You will hear allegations such as XYZ is so full of himself. And that ABC is so arrogant. Or, she is such a difficult person to work with. Yet, we are very slow, and reluctant too, to congratulate others when they do better than us. We would rather celebrate their failures than their successes. Why? Wouldn't it be nice if people could also gossip about other people's successes and accomplishments as opposed to just talking about people's hardships and failures?

In some cases, you will hear a relative or some family member say: "Ba lya bali-yafya..." (i.e. He is such a difficult person). In our culture, a common allegation of 'ukwafya' (i.e. being difficult) is when a financially sound relative does not share his or her wealth with relatives, or where he or she does not keep or look after dependants in his or her home. In short, ukwafya is often associated with, although not always, of course, hopes for economic redemption by the distressed complainants.

Likewise, when you hear that ba boss bali-yafya (i.e. he is such a difficult boss), quite often, although not always, of course, it means that the boss is a disciplinarian, and does not tolerate laziness from his or her subordinates. We are mindful, however, that there is also ukwafya kwa genuine where an individual is truly difficult to work with or to get along with. But that is not the concern of this article. Rather, we are concerned with the situation of unfounded allegations of ukwafya.

Closely related to that, why are some individuals so quick and eager to share any slightest bit of bad or sad news concerning others (e.g. 'friends', neighbours, or relatives)? Some individuals will even opine and make statements about something or someone that they hardly know. Why is it like that kanshi? Whether it is in politics or at the office, home, the club, or church, rumours and gossip are the order of the day. Many want to come out as though they are the good ones, while busy condemning others. Even Christians are in the habit of doing this. We live in a strange world full of prejudices, and presided over by the courts of public opinion. But why should it be like this? What do people gain from judging others unfairly or spreading false rumours? It certainly does not make us better people by gossiping or judging XYZ as a bad or difficult person. Indeed, how good are we ourselves?

Let us assume, for example, that X is poor. Will X become rich by talking ill of Y? Even if we were to assume that Y is a flamboyant diva of Lusaka who competed, albeit unsuccessfully, for the Miss World Beauty contest, will X, an envious lady, by laughing and gossiping about Y's predicament at the contest, now become the Miss World? The Holy Bible, in Luke 18:19, provides some interesting philosophical insights into ethical and moral dimensions of good character. "Why do you call me good?" Jesus asked him. "Only God is truly good." In Mark 10:18, Jesus goes on to say: "There is none Good but One, that is, God." So, why are human beings so obsessed with passing unfounded opinions on or about each other every other day, especially when there is no legal basis or moral ground for doing so?

The picture below helps to demonstrate this moral travesty (i.e. the picture below has been doing rounds via email, although the source of the said picture remains unknown). Who could have thought that the pastor, after preaching against sin, would be indulging in the same himself? And you do not have to understand the language in order to get the gist of what is going on at this supposedly Friday night prayer-meeting. *As the pastor pretends to pray, while shouting in tongues and exploring with impropriety the forbidden fruit of the young lady: "Phuma Satane..!!! phuma Satane!!! Phuma tempeleni ka Jehova..!!!! phuma Satane!"*

In an Online article of August 3, 2003, titled, 'Only God is Good', Tom Stewart makes the following compelling argument on what our Lord Jesus Christ means in Luke 18:19: "Did He mean that both angels in Heaven and Saints living and departed could not also be Good? Apparently not, for Jesus also spoke of a 'Good man out of the Good treasure of the heart [bringing] forth Good things' (Matthew 12:35). Further, the Son of Man will commend the appropriate people, 'Well done, thou Good and

Faithful servant: thou hast been faithful over a few things, I will make thee ruler over many things: enter thou into the joy of thy LORD' (25:21, 23). You may ask, 'But, did not Jesus plainly label us as evil?' 'If ye then, being evil, know how to give good gifts unto your children: how much more shall your Heavenly Father give the Holy Spirit to them that ask Him?' (Luke 11:13)."

Tom Stewart continues: "True. We have all undoubtedly been and too often are evil, so the shoe fits. But, as a rule, we should also be able to say as the Apostle Paul said, 'By the Grace of God I am what I am: and His Grace which was bestowed upon me was not in vain' (1Corinthians 15:10)." Now, you might be wondering whether this article is a sermon. It is not. Neither is this author a preacher. Further, unlike the Pharisees of the time, I am not a scholar of Christian legal traditions. Rather, I am a scholar of modern law. Christianity is, however, about some kind of law; that is, the Law of God. Therefore, legal theory cannot divorce itself entirely from the study of law and religion.

Mindful that the secular approach to philosophical discourse on morality and ethics may be quick to dismiss some well-known religious dictates as simply subjective, we endeavour in this article to raise some critical questions that can help the reader to get back to the academic debate of what is 'good' versus what is 'bad', or what is 'wrong' versus what is 'right'. Legend has it that the great philosopher, Socrates, once confronted the issues of rumour-mongering and ukwafya in the following manner.

One day, Socrates met an acquaintance who ran up to him excitedly and said: "Socrates, do you know what I just heard about one of your students...?"

"Wait a moment," Socrates replied. "Before you tell me, I'd like you to pass a little test. It's called the Test of Three."

"Test of Three?" asked Socrates' acquaintance.

"That's correct," Socrates continued. "Before you talk to me about my student let's take a moment to test what you're going to say. The first test is *Truth*. Have you made absolutely sure that what you are about to tell me is true?"

"No," the man replied, "actually I just heard about it."

"All right," said Socrates. "So you don't really know if it's true or not. Now let's try the second test, the test of *Goodness*. Is what you are about to tell me about my student something good?"

"No, on the contrary..."

"So," Socrates continued, "you want to tell me something bad about him even though you're not certain it's true?"

The man shrugged, a little embarrassed.

Socrates continued, "You may still pass though because there is a third test – the filter of *Usefulness*. Is what you want to tell me about my student going to be useful to me?"

"No, not really..."

"Well," concluded Socrates, "if what you want to tell me is neither *True* nor *Good* nor even *Useful*, why tell it to me at all?"

The man was defeated, felt ashamed and said no more. How many times are we confronted with such acquaintances or friends? Look, if, for example, I had once taught a law student many years ago who now thinks or feels that he or she is so accomplished to acknowledge me as his or her former professor, the fact still remains that that individual was my student, whether or not they like it. It is a fact. It is not an opinion. And I will be the first to congratulate that individual for his or her accomplishments, whether or not they go around saying this or that. That is what Socrates is teaching us here. Indeed, we must ask ourselves: what can we learn from Socrates?

CHAPTER

23

DISTORTED NOTIONS OF POWER

Many management gurus, industrial psychologists and other social scientists argue that there are generally five types of power in management, and that these are: (i) reward power; (ii) coercive power; (iii) legitimate power; (iv) referent power; and, (v) expert power (see for example: Stojkovic, S., Kalinich, D., and Klofas, J., *Criminal justice organizations: Administration and management,* (2003:247)). In this article, we will endeavour to think outside the box, drawing on some useful analogies from our everyday life, as opposed to using only examples from the corporate world.

Reward power, it has been argued, refers to situations where an employee believes he or she is going to get some type of reward for doing his or her job. By contrast, coercive power occurs in situations where a supervisor intimidates employees to do their work or risk being fired or demoted. Then, legitimate power is found in situations where an employee believes that the orders being given are authoritatively genuine even if they are coming from a higher power that does not normally give out such orders. Contrastingly, referent power refers to cases where a subordinate has an attraction somehow to the person who wields or exudes power. As a result, the subordinate will basically do whatever the supervisor or manager says. Then, expert power is based on a subordinate believing that a manager or supervisor has so much expertise in the relevant area that the employee believes everything that the manager or supervisor says. Now, let us put this discussion in context by looking at some examples in the real world of how some people exploit or respond to the different types of power referenced above.

Hardly a day passes by without Ba Mulenga, a resident of Kabwata township, Lusaka, explaining to his neighbours and friends about his good old days in the UK. His audience is now tired of these same rhetorical tales about the UK. But, Ba Mulenga never seems to notice. And he likes to throw in punch-lines of famous Zambians that he used to hang out with in the UK. Interestingly, Ba Mulenga has been back in Zambia since 1986. It has been a while, although he still maintains faithfully, and proudly too, his British cockney accent, as if he goes for accent-rehearsals every day. Sometimes, when Ba Mulenga is drunk, especially after drinking off some beers from a good Samaritan, he switches gears from his British accent into an American accent, although he has never been to the US. It appears that Ba Mulenga does this to attract more people that easily get fascinated with his fake mannerisms and accents to buy him more 'free' beers. So, what type of power is Ba Mulenga using here?

Old Lungu got 6 points for his Cambridge O'Levels back in the days. But he has not done much after that. So, he keeps drumming noise about his 6 points at O'Levels. Pastor Holiwell has now changed the prefix to his name after obtaining an Honorary Doctorate from some unaccredited Christian college. He insists on being addressed as 'Dr. Bishop Holiwell'. To pass the final professional exams, Gladys is reported to have given in to the sexual demands of one of her lecturers. Mr. Mubita is off to study for his PhD because his neighbour has just obtained one. Mr. Hang'ombe has five Masters degrees, and keeps arguing down his friend, Mwansa, who has a PhD. Mwansa gets upset and responds rudely: "Even a hundred Masters degrees are not equivalent to one PhD!" What type of power is involved in these scenarios?

Jack-boy arrives in Lusaka from a year's graduate studies in Finland, but cannot recognise the lady with an orange-bleached face that is part of the family entourage waiting for him at the airport. The lady's name is Sherry-Babe, and she and Jack-boy are first cousins. They also grew up together. But how can Jack-boy forget his cousin after having been abroad for nine months only? Indeed, a typical Masters degree takes only nine to twelve months. So, is it because Jack-boy has now been abroad, and thus feels some sophistry around himself, or what?

Jack-boy was not able to recognise Sherry-Babe

because of the extensive bleaching on Sherry-Babe's face. Sherry-Babe's facial complexion now looks like a glowing fire place. One can easily mistake her for a witch. Only Sherry-Babe's ankles, elbows and knuckles have resisted the effect of the bleaching detergents, leaving these body parts as dark as her knees and bums. Also, you can easily tell that Sherry-Babe has accumulated quite heavy 'social mileage' through the nightlife of Lusaka as well as possibly from the streets of Lusaka. But, before Jack-boy can even settle down, Sherry-Babe is quick to implore: "So, Jack, have you found me a white man from Europe to marry me?" Sherry-Babe would often pester Jack-boy on the phone to find her a white man in Europe to marry her, as she believed that that was the easiest way to get out of her African poverty. Sherry-Babe had no clue that there are also poor white people in and from Europe. A few months ago, Sherry-Babe's closest friend from Chimwemwe in Kitwe, Rose "Big-bokosi", who also has a bleached orange face, got married to a white Frenchman that she met at some nightclub in Lusaka. So, Sherry-Babe wants to replicate that model. What type of power does Sherry-Babe see in marrying a white man?

Uncle Businga is an affluent businessman by local Zambian standards. He often tells people that he has an MBA degree from Harvard University when, in fact, he only attended a short three-months Executive Management Program at Harvard. Closely related to that, Faidess, a female business consultant in Lusaka, talks highly of having been to the reputable Oxford University in the UK when, in fact, at Oxford, she never attended a degree programme, but attended only a short three months Executive Management programme. Then, Uwamawala, a PhD student, often offers unsolicited public commentary on various contemporary issues. She is regularly quoted as an 'expert' by a local tabloid. Uwamawala makes no effort to correct this grave error. What type of power are Uncle Businga, Faidess and Uwamawala trying to push?

Bana Chisha is usually bragging about her son who she claims is now doing a PhD in the US when, in fact, the young man is at a polytechnic or community college, struggling to complete his Associate Degree (*i.e.* in Zambia, the equivalent of an Associate Degree is a College Diploma). Inonge sells some human hair to some affluent ladies in Lusaka, claiming that she often goes to England to buy the human hair. Yet, Inonge has only been to the UK once, and relies instead on her cousin who goes for business to South Africa regularly to buy her the same. Closely related to that, Ba Kawilo is avoiding calling his chic on her birthday, pantu (because) he is very broke and, thus, fears that she may be expecting some expensive birthday gifts. So, Ba Kawilo conveniently switches off his phone, and later tells her that he tried to reach her instead, but her phone was not ringing throughout the day. What type of power are Bana Chisha, Inonge and Ba Kawilo trying to push?

Kelenka is well-known for borrowing money from friends and relatives, but he hardly ever pays back. Kelenka often talks big, and is an expert at name-dropping. You would think that he is a sophisticated guy, but he is just a cheap conman! Ba Muletekanya is known for wanting to dominate discussions on any topic or subject, whether at home, the pub, or internet forums, as well as elsewhere too. He just never stops. He wants to sound knowledgeable even over things he hardly understands that well. And his pretentious and charlatan stunts do, however, succeed at impressing some people. But others can read through him easily. What type of power are Kelenka and Ba Muletekanya trying to push?

Shorty, a pretty young lady, likes to wear very tight and short mini-skirts at work, leaving most men with racing thoughts and increased heart palpitations. She is often flirting with, and sexually teasing, her male bosses so as to get work-related favours such as promotions and international trips, yet she contends that she cannot date or sleep with anyone of them because she is married. By contrast, Ushayafya, another pretty young lady at the same workplace, is known for having slept her way to the top. What type of power are Shorty and Ushayafya using?

Uwafiloto, an educated and pretty Zambian lady, feels that she should get married to a guy that comes from some well-known aristocratic family in Zambia, or at least a wealthy man, even though age is now showing on her face. She, however, remains hopeful that even as a single mother she can beat the competition from the younger ladies in town. Her friend, Naumbi-uwafiloto, also an educated beauty and single mother of two, feels strongly that she deserves marrying a Mr Right just because she is the daughter to a famous Mr. XYZ. What type of power are the two ladies trying to push here?

CHAPTER

24

UNDERSTANDING WHISTLE-SWALLOWING IN THE FIGHT AGAINST CORRUPTION

All too often, many countries are preoccupied with enacting or enforcing legislation, or promulgating regulations, to protect whistleblowers in the fight against such white collar crimes as corruption, insider dealing and money laundering. A whistleblower is someone who reports to the authorities that some alleged misconduct by someone else in a public or private institution has taken place or is taking place. And depending on the categories of persons permitted under the law (or regulations) to blow the whistle, a whistleblower can be an insider or an outsider.

Other incidences where the protection of whistleblowers is often stressed include cases involving the fight against drug-trafficking. And that is a hot one. You don't wanna go there! Indeed, in many countries, there are laws to protect the rights of individuals to blow the whistle on wrongful conduct. In the US, for example, Joe Davidson, reporting for the Washington Post (September 28, 2012), observes that: "The Whistleblower Protection Enhancement Act, which has been bouncing around Congress for a decade, took an important step toward becoming law with House approval... The bill would strengthen protections for federal employees who report waste, fraud and abuse. The measure closes loopholes created by court interpretations of an earlier whistleblower law. The loopholes had the effect of restricting whistleblower protections."

According to Davidson, "Under the current legislation, for example, whistleblowers don't have to be the first to report misconduct to be covered, according to the Government Accountability Project (GAP), an advocacy group that supports the legislation." In this paper, however, we examine not the concept of whistleblowing, but the related concept of whistle-swallowing. What is whistle-swallowing, or, as we would say in Bemba, 'Uku-mina pinto', in the context of combatting corruption?

Whistle-swallowing can occur in any one or more of the following circumstances: (1) where there is negligent or reckless failure to warn the authorities of reasonably suspicious activities or transactions; (2) where there is negligent or reckless failure to conduct due diligence of reasonably suspicious activities or transactions when the law requires an individual to do so; or, (3) where an individual willfully, deliberately or recklessly shuts his or her eyes to the truth or to the facts. Now, let us take a more reasoned look.

In jurisdictions such as the UK, it is a criminal offence under the UK Proceeds of Crime Act 2002 not to report suspicious transactions of money laundering (see also the UK Money Laundering Regulations 2007) to the investigative authorities. Also, tipping-off a suspected money launderer, like failing to disclose knowledge or suspicion of money laundering, is a criminal offence. By comparison, what would happen in Zambia if, say, Mulenga, a civil servant in one of the Government Ministries, armed with valuable information about the corrupt or collusive practices of the Minister and some senior Government officials in the Ministry, decides not to report the matter to the Anti-Corruption Commission? Does the law place a statutory obligation on Mulenga to blow the whistle? Indeed, how loud should Mulenga blow the whistle? And what does the Anti-Corruption Act 2012 say?

Notwithstanding the enactment of Zambia's Public Interest Disclosure (Protection of Whistleblowers) Act 2010, it is doubtful that Mulenga would feel safe to snitch on the Minister. Indeed, how safe or protected would Mulenga's job be should he snitch on the Minister, knowing that the prospects for retaliation and reprisals are quite high? Although section 46 of the Public Interest Disclosure (Protection of Whistleblowers) Act 2010 posits that 'a person shall not engage, or attempt or conspire to engage, in an unlawful reprisal', and that 'any person who contravenes subsection (1) commits an offence...', how certain are we that, in accordance with section 44 of the said Public Interest Disclosure

(Protection of Whistleblowers) Act 2010, the investigating authority to whom Mulenga could make a protected disclosure will not disclose the information to the 'powers-that-be', identifying Mulenga as the person who made the protected disclosure? Fearing for his life and job, Mulenga might end up swallowing the whistle by remaining mute.

However, where the law places a mandatory obligation on anyone who has reasonable knowledge and suspicion of corrupt activities of a public officer (or any other individual) to report such activities to the investigative wings, whistle-swallowing can be minimised. That said, we are mindful of the higher standard of proof required in criminal law cases to show that an individual like Mulenga had knowledge or reasonable of suspicion of the things that the Minister was up to. But then, is the law alone enough?

The enactment of good laws is not a self-fulfilling exercise. It should be accompanied by effective law enforcement and a strong culture of compliance. Also, to have an effective mandatory disclosure regime, the public must be availed easily accessible training and public awareness programmes to educate and inform them of their obligations under the law. Such training programmes should be mandatory in schools, workplaces and other related institutions. Furthermore, as a corollary to the efficacy of the law, the political culture in a given country should support the fight against corruption. The argument that in countries where you have strong and efficient institutions such efforts can help to overcome and stop corruption is only a fraction of the bigger picture. You can have strong and efficient institutions, including a well-designed complaints handling system, as well as excellent procedures for preventing and fighting corruption and for promoting good governance, but if the political will of the State to fight corruption is missing, then the whole exercise might not succeed.

In jurisdictions that have political cultures that tend to favour or promote reprisals or retaliations against whistleblowers, many potential witnesses, complainants or whistleblowers would rather swallow the whistle and avoid rocking the boat. The fear of retaliation, especially where a notable suspect has already demonstrated his or her uncompromising wrath by inflicting excruciating pain on other whistleblowers, can have the effect of muting out all whistles. And no eyebrows will rise. All heads will remain low like nothing has happened. Indeed, it takes courage, character, moral conviction and one's appealing ethical conduct to blow the whistle. Whistleblowing, it must be stressed, should not be about sour-grapes or vendettas. Let us consider the following fable.

Banda has been trying to get a promotion at work for years. He stumbles across information about his boss' corrupt conduct at work. Banda ponders on what to do with the information. Should he report his boss? Wouldn't that jeopardise his chances for a promotion? Finally, Banda musters some courage and approaches his boss to let him know that he,

Banda, has some damaging information about the boss. Banda thinks that that move would cow the boss into promoting him as a way of buying Banda's silence. But, the boss simply clears his throat, while staring Banda straight in the eyes. The boss does not say a word. He simply walks away. And, in an hour's time, Banda receives an anonymous phone-call. The anonymous caller implores: "Mr. Banda, listen carefully. We know who you are and where you stay. And we know where your children go to school, and what time they are picked up and who picks them up. We also know where your wife works, and what time she leaves work and when she gets home. And we know where your mother stays as well as where your in-laws stay. Now, do you love them all? If you do, then stay away from your boss' case! Otherwise, we won't be giving you a second warning when we come for you!"

Banda is so freightened, terrified and shell-shocked. His pants are almost wet. The anonymous caller gave Banda accurate information about Banda's family. So, Banda quickly calls his wife to tell her about the anonymous caller and the circumstances surrounding the same. She quickly advises Banda to stay clear and to remain as far away as possible from the case. And so, Banda has no choice but to swallow the whistle. He has to pretend that he has not seen or heard anything. Later on, the boss notices that Banda is now scared out of his pants. And to reward Banda for swallowing the whistle, the boss promotes him, commending him as a very hardworking young man. In the meantime, the boss' corrupt activities are now soaring. And Banda knows this fully well. What to do now? Should Banda vomit and blow the whistle? Well, the whistle might not blow or sound due to Banda's vomit inside it. Indeed, the whistle is too contaminated with Banda's complicity.

CHAPTER

25

TO WHOM MUCH IS GIVEN, MUCH IS DEMANDED!

I once read an interesting article by a European-Caucasian academic who argued that Black people have small brains compared to White people, and that that is why Black people have not been able to develop Africa. His theory was that Orientals, by contrast, have the largest brains, followed by Caucasians and then Blacks on the lower echelons. Of course, the reaction from many Black scholars was as expected – heated! But then, I simply laughed it off. These are simply veiled prejudices and stereotypes masquerading as science. Projecting similar prejudices, one James Buchanan writes in an Online article of the *US.Altermedia.info*, titled, "Blacks and Whites Differ in Brain Size and Intelligence," dated July 26, 2009:

"Scientists have known for a long, long time that Blacks have smaller brains on average. If you can find a 1959 Encyclopedia Britannica, the section on races will mention that Whites have a larger average brain size than Blacks. The liberals and Jews apparently got this important racial information scrubbed out of most books published after 1959. About every ten years since 1960, some brave White academic will publish a book talking about these significant differences. Just off hand I remember the authors, Carleton Coon, Murray and Herrnstein and Arthur Jensen. The 'Bell Curve' is perhaps the most famous of these racial reality books."

Buchanan continues with his onslaught: "The latest data from J. Philippe Rushton states that Blacks have brains that are 80cc smaller on average. This data may be based on African-American Blacks, who tend to have about 25% White genes mixed in with IQs around 85. Their primitive all-Black cousins in West Africa have IQs down around 70 (with even smaller brains). One source notes 'The black-white gap is 15 points when measured on the Wechsler tests, 18 on the Stanford-Binet. Both tests are, of course, normed so as to produce an average of 100, but the white average is a bit higher. On the Wechsler metric, whites and blacks average 102 and 87, respectively. On both tests, the gap between the races is almost exactly 1 SD (standard deviation). The gap of 1 SD has been observed since the earliest days of intelligence testing."

In contrast to Buchanan's views, the *New York Times*, in an Online article of December 9, 2007, written by Richard E. Nisbett, and titled, "All Brains Are the Same Color," reports that: "JAMES WATSON, the 1962 Nobel laureate, recently asserted that he was 'inherently gloomy about the prospect of Africa' and its citizens because 'all our social policies are based on the fact that their intelligence is the same as ours — whereas all the testing says not really.' Dr. Watson's remarks created a huge stir because they implied that blacks were genetically inferior to whites, and the controversy resulted in his resignation as chancellor of Cold Spring Harbor Laboratory. But was he right? Is there a genetic difference between blacks and whites that condemns blacks in perpetuity to be less intelligent?"

Nisbett observes further that the first notable public airing of the scientific question came in a 1969 article in *The Harvard Educational Review* by Arthur Jensen, a psychologist at the University of California, Berkeley. "Dr. Jensen", Nisbett points out, "maintained that a 15-point difference in I.Q. between blacks and whites was mostly due to a genetic difference between the races that could never be erased. But his argument gave a misleading account of the evidence. And others who later made the same argument — Richard Herrnstein and Charles Murray in 'The Bell Curve,' in 1994, for example, and just recently, William Saletan in a series of articles on Slate — have made the same mistake. In fact, the evidence heavily favors the view that race differences in I.Q. are environmental in origin, not genetic."

Let us take a more reasoned look. When I was a graduate student in the UK many years ago, I recall that some of my Caucasian male colleagues would whisper quietly among themselves to find out if it is true that Black men tend to have the biggest, largest and thickest penis size in town. One of the guys approached me to find out if that was indeed the case. The others were too scared to ask me directly. Well, I opine that life is full of stereotypes. But check this out – a Zimbabwean Online media outlet, *Newsdze Zimbabwe*, in a recent article dated October 2, 2012, and titled, "Congolese men have the largest manhoods in the world," reports that: "Research on average penis size has confirmed racial stereotypes, with Africans coming out on top, Asians at the bottom and Europeans somewhere in between."

According to the *Newsdze Zimbabwe*, which cites reliable British media sources, "Richard Lynn, emeritus professor of psychology at Ulster University carried out the research, which is published in the scientific journal, *Personality and Individual Differences*.113 nationalities were included in a study of average penis lengths. In the penis size league tables the *Daily Mail* reports that men from the Republic of the Congo (DRC) take top position with a porn star like 7.1 inches, with the Ecuadorians, Ghanaians and Columbians not far behind with 7 inches, 6.8 inches and 6.7 inches respectively...The average for the African continent as a whole is a whopping 6.3 inches. The Icelanders come top of the Europeans with 6.5 inches. The Germans are Mr European average with 5.7 inches. The Brits come out above the French, beating the more traditional country of love and romance, by a

229

full 0.2 inches. The Brits also beat the Australians (5.2in), Americans (5.1in) and Irish (5in). Small, at the other end of the table, North and South Korea measure in at 3.8 inches."

The *Newsdze Zimbabwe* article continues: "India and Thailand are only slightly bigger at 4 inches. The overall average for north-east Asians was the lowest at 4.2 inches." One wonders, however, what would be the ideal choice for any reasonable man: (a) a humongous, long and agile penis with much wide girth accompanied by a small brain, or; (b) a big and smart brain accompanied by a tiny and fragile shrimp-like penis? Which of the two would you choose, especially if there is no compromising middle ground or third choice for some moderate average?

Some would argue that size does not matter, and that, besides, you need the right kind of brains to use whatever tool-size you have. Others would argue that brains alone won't get the job done, and that you surely need the right size of tool to get the job done. As someone once remarked, to get the hips of snow out of your driveway in winter, you don't need a teaspoon no matter how smart you are. What you need instead is the actual shovel to haul the snow out! And that, it is argued, does not require much brains to figure out.

Anyhow, to satisfy their curiosity, my Caucasian friends would surf some porn cites with an *a priori* approach to confirm their prejudices about the penises of Black men. Perhaps, they were too scared to inspect mine, and thus opted to check elsewhere. I am not sure, though, that their vain efforts helped to explain Spike Lee's movie in the 1980's, *Jungle Fever*, or what is known as *'renting a dread'* for *some* adventurous white female tourists at the nice sandy beaches of Jamaica.

And so, there is an unconfirmed view out there that while some races, such as whites, tend to have bigger brains than, say, blacks, other races, such as blacks, tend to have bigger and more agile penises than, say, whites. And Orientals, though being credited with the biggest and smartest brains on earth, and hence their ability to revolutionize the IT industry, fall pretty lowest on the penis size index. But, hey, I am not a natural scientist. So, please do not be mad with me here. I am merely regurgitating the perspectives and prejudices that have been floating around out there which many people are too scared to confront.

CHAPTER
26

PHILOSOPHIE YA LA VIE

While the field of philosophy can be understood as the study of the fundamental nature of knowledge, reality, and existence, especially when taken as an academic discipline, a philosophy of life, by contrast, is a philosophical view or vision of the nature or purpose of life, or of the way that life should be lived. A philosophy of life is an overall vision of or attitude towards life and the purpose of life. It often involves a theory or attitude that acts as a guiding principle for behaviour. Indeed, this is what we refer to as 'philosophie ya la vie' in this article. This expression was popularised by the Congo DRC musical legend, Jules Shungu Wembadio Pene Kikumba, alias Papa Wemba, in his song, 'Philosophie ya la vie.'

There is a general principle of law that where an individual holds himself out or professes to be endowed with certain technical skills then he or she will be judged as competent enough to perform such skills at the level at which he or she professes or holds himself or herself out. For example, where someone practices medicine as a neurosurgeon, or pretends to be one, if a case of medical malpractice were to come up against him or her, then he or she will be expected by the court to have discharged his or her professional functions and skills at the level of a neurosurgeon of his or her standing. It is no good excuse for the purported neurosurgeon to argue that: "After all, we all make mistakes as doctors once in a while."

Indeed, the standard of care expected of a neurosurgeon is different from that of an ordinary medical doctor who is, say, a General Practitioner, especially when it comes to neurosurgery. The standard of care expected of a neurosurgeon is far much higher. Now, you may be wondering what I am trying to get at. A day hardly passes by without reading intriguing and shocking incidents in the media of some seemingly 'holy' people committing all manner of deliberate and intentional sin. Sometimes, it is about turf wars and wrangles among church leaders on who should be heading or running the church or parish. These turf wars are no different from those of drug-lords. Then, there is also the common issue of abuse of church funds by some church leaders. Now, I am not trying to put myself on a pedestal of the holier than thou. Indeed, that is not the point.

Like the example of the surgeon provided above, it is no good excuse for a pastor, priest or bishop to counter-argue that: "Let he, who is without sin, be the first to cast a stone"! That is not good enough an excuse. Granted that mankind continues to struggle with sin, when someone holds himself out as a pastor, priest, bishop, prophet and so forth, the standard of care and moral conduct expected of that individual is much higher than that of the congregants at his church. Indeed, it is no good excuse to say: "A pastor is also just as human as everyone else!" Then, why did he become a pastor if he knew that he is not morally or ethically strong? In fact, church leaders, like elders and parents in society, are supposed to be role models that edify those under their charge. To rise to the helm of leadership, a leader must have the right qualities and an inspiring moral character.

Closely related to the foregoing, it has now become fashionable for many clerics to bestow upon each other or upon themselves such grandiose titles as "Bishop", "Dr", "Prophet", "Prophetess", "Saint", "Apostle", and so forth. Many pastors, especially those from some self-styled Pentecostal churches, are busy queuing up for Honorary Doctorates at some suspicious unaccredited Christian colleges. Why? Is it an ego thing or what? Yet, the Lord Jesus Christ never took any earthly titles.

Some pastors have amassed so much wealth, constantly imploring their church members to keep tithing more and more. And the poor congregants keep throwing in more and more money, hoping that that may secure them a place in Heaven. Running a church has now become a lucrative business for some people. But the point is this: you cannot buy your way into Heaven by simply donating heavily to these churches! And there is no hook or crook to get to Heaven. It is only by honesty and truthfulness that you will get there.

Look, a few years ago, I travelled to the Middle East for work. Whilst there, I decided to visit the Holy Site, the Baptism Site, in Jordan. This Holy Site is on the banks of the Jordan River, overlooking Bethlehem in Israel. It is reported be the place where our Lord Jesus Christ was baptised by John the Baptist. I boarded the shuttle that takes you through the desert area where John the Baptist used to live. You also get to see the place where the Prophet Elisha is said to have ascended into Heaven. After a short drive, we all disembarked from the shuttle to walk to the actual Baptism Site. Then, suddenly, the Tour Guide stopped, pointing to a place that we were approaching. I knew there and then, that this is it! And so, as I explained later to my wife: "I stood there quietly, thinking how it could have been back in the days. Spontaneously, a powerful thought quickly ran through my mind. I decided to pull a fast one by looking up to the sky to see if the sky would open, and if I would hear that voice from Heaven, 'This is my Son in whom I am well pleased... Listen to Him!'..." Now, you might be laughing (smile). But, hearken my words: I aint crazy. And, of course, I heard no voice. Neither did the sky open.

To this day, my wife says she cannot believe that I dared to pull such a stunt at the Baptism Site in Jordan. She says that she cannot believe that I could even entertain such a thought. But, I keep telling her: "Ifintu kwesha besha...You just have to have faith, in case it is you that God wants to shower His good favour on that day." Many a reader, if placed in my shoes, could have done the same. Some would even have prayed for money or miracles of amassing wealth. But, at least for me, it was only God's good favour and blessings that I sought. That is all I asked for, and then proceeded to wash my face in the Jordan River. The reason why I have used this example here is to show you that with God, there is neither a shortcut nor hook or crook to get to Heaven. And that, I learned very well when I tried to pull a fast one at the Baptism Site in Jordan. With God, you must earn your place. Indeed, there are no dubious or crafty free-kicks allowed. You must sweat for your place.

Now, in Zambia, until the advent of the 'Ninsanga' Pentecostal and Evangelical Movement in the late 1970s, there were very few denominations of protestant churches. Today, there are so many of them. But do not get me wrong here. I am not saying that there is something or anything wrong with worship. Rather, it is the manner in which some of these unscrupulous church leaders are using the pulpit and the name of God in vain that is very displeasing. And it is not only in some of the Pentecostal or protestant churches that you will find some dubious and fraudulent pastors, even in the Catholic Church you will find some dodgy clerics in sheep's clothing. Many churches today, including the Catholic Church, have been rocked with all manner of sexual scandals by some pastors, priests and bishops. The picture below demonstrates this moral travesty in some factions of church leadership (*i.e.*

the picture below has been doing rounds via email, although the source of the said picture remains unknown). And you do not have to understand the language below in order to get the gist of what is going on at this supposedly Friday night prayer-meeting.

As the pastor pretends to pray, while shouting in tongues and exploring with impropriety the forbidden fruit: "Phuma Satane..!!! phuma Satane!!! Phuma tempeleni ka Jehova..!!!! phuma Satane!"

With such issues now commonplace in some churches, it makes it hard for many religious people to confide in some clerics for the latter's moral guidance or to go for confession before some of these pastors and priests. Likewise, it is hard for many to receive Holy Communion from the hands of some of these pastors and priests. Now, do not get me wrong. There are some good and decent pastors, priests and bishops out there. But as long as the bad ones are not weeded out, the good ones will also suffer reputational risk. Consequently, many people will begin to leave the church. And who do we blame? We cannot pretend any longer.

In fact, we need to be honest with ourselves. When we, as Christians, tithe, that money is not meant to be an entertainment allowance for the pastor. Neither is it meant for the church to use in settling a priest's court cases involving his sexual scandals. Look, we shall all be accountable before God. And there are no earthy titles before God. There is nothing like: "No, me, I am 'Dr Pastor XYZ'..." or "Because, me, I am 'Bishop Prophet ABC'...". There will only be one Heaven and one Lake of Fire, with only one Living God to make the final ruling. And there will be no second chance or right of appeal. It then brings us back to our own Philosophie Ya La Vie.

238

CHAPTER

27

DISCERNING THE MORALITY
OF POLITICKING

Many a time, we hear of contentious arguments on why some politicians often abuse power or why they should not be entrusted with power. Closely related to that, there are commentators who advance various postulates and dictates on why some tribes have not succeeded at producing a Republican President. In some other African countries, I have heard similar debates, albeit focusing more on which tribe has produced the highest number of intellectuals.

While some tribes may not have produced a Republican President yet, they are generally known to be good at building and preserving wealth. But that is an area for the anthropologists to study and confirm. What I do know, though, is that the principle of relativity in life is always a balancing act. After all, life is all about arrivals and departures however way we look at it.

- Kenneth K. Mwenda

This paper focuses on the morality of politicking in Zambia. As President Michael Sata rightly observed during his recent visit to Ethiopia, '…if talking were an industry, Zambia would have already prospered to greater heights than where it is now…' (see Online article: LusakaTimes.com, January 27, 2012). Mindful that the practice of politics is not the same as political science, it is sometimes hard to distinguish in Zambia between who is a politician *simpliciter* and who is a learned political scientist. As a general rule, politicians are constantly engaged in managing some kind of conflict. Indeed, it is conflict that defines politics. For without conflict, we will be dealing with policy instead, knowing that policy derives its pedigree from consensus as opposed to conflict.

In Zambia, like many other countries, we often hear of how some politicians appear so wise and caring for the poor only after they have lost elections or have been voted out of power. What an irony! Does common sense have to wait until you are out power to realize that if you do not fix the mess of our Zambian hospitals that will be the same place where you will be attended to should you fall sick after you have left politics? Does one need to wait until he or she loses political power to realize that, as a country, we need to fix our health and education sectors beyond modest and superficial structural changes? Does one have to wait until he or she can no longer afford medical treatment abroad or can no longer afford to pay university tuition fees for his or her children abroad since he does not have a cabinet post anymore? Why do we only talk much sense when we are hungry?

In some constituencies, many university students have been duped into voting for some politician who made promises to them that all the problems facing their institution of learning will be solved as soon as he or she is voted into power. No sooner does the politician gets into power, does he abandons the students' interests and the promises he made. Likewise, some of those that were in power but have now lost power, and who used to turn a blind eye on the plight of the people whilst in power, will now want to appear as heroic mouthpieces of the downtrodden. But it's too late. Judgment day has already come. And one wonders how sincere such political machinations are.

To get a vote, a good number of our politicians often promise so much even when most of them know full well that they have neither the capacity nor the intention to deliver on all those promises. And others begin to criticize only because they are no longer eating from the national cake. What a life; a life devoid of honesty. Accusations and counter-accusations keep flying from one corner to the other. Those who may have been accomplices or those who colluded with others in looting the national treasury just the other day will today distance themselves from such vices.

Likewise, those that felt politically victimized yesterday will now ensure that the law takes a vindictive course, as opposed to a vindicating role, on the election losers. We live in a world fraught with contradictions. I sometimes wonder, for example, how it could have taken the country so many years and cost us such grand financial resources to conclude those cases of corruption in Zambia. Some of these cases have not even been concluded to this day. Could it be that maybe someone somewhere is benefitting from these delayed court cases? We can only speculate. That said, I have written widely on corruption matters, and this is a subject that I have studied and taught at universities over the years. Whereas we have seen, for example, an excessive reliance on basic criminal law relating to corruption and theft, there is very little to show in the way of civil remedies such as the tracing of stolen assets under equity.

As a general rule, where monies are comingled in a trust account, there are principles of trusts law relating to the tracing of co-mingled funds, as opposed to over-reliance on criminal procedure and evidence. Besides, as we all know, the standard of proof in criminal law cases is much higher than in civil law cases. To overcome this hurdle, you can trace and recover some strategic stolen assets by using civil procedure and trusts law. But I do not want to give a public lecture on this. We have many 'experts' on anti-corruption out there. I will leave this topic for another time. Let us now take a reasoned look at the following fable whose source is not known but that has been doing rounds on emails. The fable appearing hereunder can help us to contextualize the morality of politicking in Zambia.

As it were, Mwamba, a young and overzealous Bemba-speaking houseboy, is in the habit of drinking his boss' Chardonnay wine whenever the boss, Mr. Chirwa Hamaantoyo, a Ngoni-Tonga speaking fellow, is away at work. After drinking from the wine bottle, Mwamba would habitually add some water to the remaining Chardonnay to make it appear as though the bottle is still full and untouched. As he would say in his humble mind, 'Kaili, ta-baise bee shibe... (i.e. How will the boss know? He won't know!)

But the boss, being a seasoned connoisseur, knows full well how a good mild Chardonnay tastes. As such, he becomes suspicious that the quality of his Chardonnay wine tastes different and feels somewhat diluted. He knows it can only be Mwamba who could have helped himself to the wine and then added some water to make it appear as though the wine bottle is still intact. The boss decides to trap Mwamba. He buys some white French wine that changes colour once water is added to it.

The next day, the unsuspecting and somewhat naïve Mwamba, as usual, takes a mouthful of the new French wine and then adds water to replace what he has drunk. As soon as he adds water, the French wine turns milky. Mwamba begins to panic now. What to do now, as one would say in Russian English? When the boss returns home from work, he notices the milky drink. He is sure that he has managed to nail Mwamba this time as the thief who has been drinking his wine. At the same time, Mwamba realizes that he is in deep trouble and thus decides to go to the kitchen to recouperate from fear, panic and anxiety. His stomach begins to rumble and make noise from the fear, but he is not too sure whether to head for the toilet or not, as his legs feel too weak, after seeing that the boss has spotted the milky-looking wine.

The boss proceeds straight to his bedroom and finds that his wife is already at home from work. He tells his wife, "Mary, you will see today, uyu kapuli Mwamba will be obliged to acknowledge ati ewu nwa wine yandi." (Here, the Bemba text is self-explanatory to any foreign language reader). So, the boss walks towards the hallway and calls out Mwamba. The boss shouts: "Mwamba!" And Mwamba answers: "Yes, boss...". The boss continues: "Who drank my wine?" Mwamba suddenly goes quiet, or, rather, mute by malice. There is no answer. One would have thought that perhaps Mwamba had become mute by visitation of God, but certainly not. The boss presses on: "Mwamba, I said, 'Who drank my wine?'..." Mwamba is still mute, and there is now a deafening silence from the kitchen.

Realizing that there is no answer forthcoming from Mwamba, the boss walks over to the kitchen to confront Mwamba, and he storms the kitchen in a rage, imploring: "Are you crazy or what? When I call your name you answer. But when I ask you how has been drinking my wine you don't answer, why?" The fearful Mwamba laments to the boss: "It is just that... boss, when you are in the kitchen there, you don't hear anything at all, except the name." This annoys the boss further, seeing that Mwamba is trying to look smart. So, to prove that Mwamba is telling lies, the boss says to him: "You stay beside Madam here, me I go in the kitchen, and you ask me a question." Mwamba has no choice but to oblige. So, the boss goes to the kitchen and stands where Mwamba had been standing whilst Mwamba remains where the boss was. And Mwamba begins to call out the boss, as instructed. Mwamba calls, "Boss?". And the boss answers: "Yes, Mwamba...". Mwamba continues: "Who goes in the maid's bedroom when the Madam is not here?" Suddenly, there is no answer from the boss. Mwamba presses on: "Boss, I say, who made the maid pregnant?" Still there is no answer from the boss. Mwamba shouts again (a third time): "Boss, I say, who made the maid pregnant?" The boss returns running quickly from the kitchen before Mwamba asks more damaging questions, and says to Mwamba: "Mwamba...it is true, you are right. When one is in the kitchen, one does not hear anything, only the name!"

And so it is with politics. Many of our politicians only hear their name when they are in power. When one is power, one does not hear anything but only the sweetness of power. After all, as one famous politician once said, 'I did not know that power is sweet...'. And when you do not have that power anymore, the loss of power itself can be very sour and bitter. There is usually a nostalgic craving for returning to power again. Some feel disrespected because even those cronies and henchmen that used to run and fall on their feet before these politicians no longer do so. Some former henchmen and cronies will even pretend not to know you. Their allegiances have shifted to the new kids on the bloc. Such is life. You now become an ordinary citizen whose cheques will occasionally bounce at the bank and your business entities or companies will now begin to struggle financially because you can no longer influence big procurement contracts in your favour. What to do now? You begin to shift the goalpost, making accusation after accusation, like Mwamba and his boss, until you can only hear your name.

But even for those that ascend to power, how can we be so sure that they are all clean and free of corruption? Yes, there could be some clean and decent individuals both in the opposition and in government, but corruption is not a vice perpetuated only by those that have lost power. We should remember that corruption, like Mwamba demonstrated to his boss, cuts across many segments of society. Many have stolen, but few have been caught. Just how many businessmen and politicians (past and present) have failed to service their loans, for example, when they acquired some of these loans through somewhat unsound or politically influenced lending decisions? Yet, the law is silent. Perhaps, Mwamba and his boss are right – when you are in the kitchen, you can only hear your name, but not other questions, until you leave political office!

CHAPTER

28

UNDERSTANDING THE LAW AGAINST PORNOGRAPHY

Recently, at a Sunday church service in Maryland, US, a celebrant priest made the following poignant observation during the homily: "If you were to ask any priest today, one of the most commonly confessed sins by many Christians is watching pornography."

In Zambia, the recent outcry against the habitual and pitiful tendency of some youths to be preoccupied regularly with watching pornography on the internet has attracted much public debate. Some critics have gone so far as to contend that the regulatory body responsible for the provision of internet services in Zambia should ensure that young folks have no access to pornographic material. Others contend that charity begins at home and that good family values inculcated in the youths by their parents can help to keep these young folks away from the temptations of pornography. But pornography can be accessed not only through desktop or lap-top computers but also through smart-phones and modern tablets.

In this article, I will endeavour to highlight the salient aspects of the law prohibiting pornography in Zambia. With that, we can ask ourselves: (i) Is the law sound enough? (ii) Or, is enforcement of the law and compliance with the same weak? Let us take a more reasoned look. There are two principal statutes governing the law against pornography in Zambia, and these are: (a) the Penal Code; and (b) the Electronic Communications and Transactions Act 2009.

Section 177(1) of the Penal Code provides that any person who makes, produces or has in his possession obscene writings, drawings, prints, paintings, printed matter, pictures, posters, emblems, photographs, cinematograph films or any other object tending to corrupt morals will be guilty of a misdemeanour and liable to imprisonment or to a fine. The said statutory provision also makes it an offence for a person to import, convey or export, or cause to be imported, conveyed or exported, any such pornographic material, or in any manner whatsoever to put any of these pornographic materials in circulation. Here, the issue of what constitutes 'corrupting morals' or 'circulating pornographic material' can draw inspiration from the jurisprudence of parallel common law jurisdictions such as the United Kingdom and the US.

But to argue that where a journalist takes nude pictures of a naked pregnant woman giving birth should never at all be taken as the production and distribution of 'erotic pictures and their potential to corrupt the morals of those who view them' is somewhat of a red herring. Let me push my argument a bit. While the initial act of the journalist taking the pictures may pass the test of not constituting an offence under section 177 of the Penal Code, what about subsequent transmissions or sharing of such pictures by folks who are imbued with lewd intentions to excite sexual feelings in people who eventually come across the pictures? Sometimes, what could have started off innocently as the practice of good investigative journalism might end up in wrong hands if wrong people were to lay their hands on such controversial pictures. And so, does a journalist owe a duty of care to the naked woman that is being photographed? What about if the photographed woman were to suffer reputational damage as a result of those pictures? Can the aggrieved sue the journalist for negligence? And can we apply the test of reasonable foresight here, contending that the journalist ought to have reasonably foreseen the implications of taking such photographs?

An anonymous commentator from Zambia observes as follows: "Lovely and informative piece. Your citation of a journalist and a woman giving birth conjures memories of a case in Zambia not so long ago. I followed it with keenness, and one thing I observed was that once again legal technicalities were at play. A common question asked to the witnesses was: 'Were you aroused by the picture?' The answer was 'NO!' from every one of them. In fact, it brought more empathy. This means the motive was not to corrupt any one's morals. In such a case, I think the offenders, were those that abused the privilege of seeing the pictures and acting on them professionally.'

The said commentator adds: "The question is: when exactly does nudity become obscene? Here is a poster in a hospital depicting effects of sexually transmitted infections (STI's), and showing the affected genitalia? Or, instruction of usage on a condom wrapper? Or, a teacher delivering a lesson on sexual reproduction? Or, nude studies in most art schools? Then, there are anthropological studies of primitive tribes where nudity is not a taboo. These are filmed and shown on television. Lastly, what's your take on states where pornography is legalized as 'Adult Entertainment'?"

Suffice it to say, section 177(1) of the Penal Code of Zambia makes it a criminal offence to carry on or take part in any business, whether public or private, concerned with pornographic materials, or to deal in any of these materials in any manner whatsoever, or to distribute the materials, or to exhibit any of them publicly, or to make a business of lending any of them. Likewise, it is a criminal offence to advertise or make known by any means whatsoever with a view to assisting the circulation of, or the trafficking in, any of the pornographic material listed above, or to advertise or make known how, or from whom, any such material can be procured either directly or indirectly. And it is an offence to exhibit publicly any indecent show or performance or any show or performance tending to corrupt morals. But wait a minute, what about the famous Rhumba or Zambian music shows where a female musician might be wriggling and gyrating her waist whilst wearing a tight and short suggestive skirt? Would such performance and show be deemed as 'exhibiting publicly an indecent show or performance, or a show or performance tending to corrupt morals'? Let us think again. A Zambian court can, however, order the destruction or confiscation of pornographic material where an accused person is convicted under section 177(1) of the Penal Code.

Section 177A of the same statute makes it a criminal offence for any person to engage a child or other person in a pornographic performance or in the production of a pornographic film or such other material. It is also an offence for any person to engage a child in pornographic activity of any nature. And a person who sells to a child pornographic material, or compels a child to watch a pornographic film or view pornography on the internet or elsewhere or in any form intended to corrupt a child's morals, will be guilty of an offence and liable, upon conviction, to a term of imprisonment. If, however, the law offender is also a child, then the culpable child will be liable to such community service or counseling as the court may determine in the best interests of such child.

Given the fast pace at which technology is developing globally, and with the internet hosting all sorts of interactive web forums where people go to chat, many countries and corporations are now regulating the use of the internet. At some companies, you can get fired for watching pornography during or after work hours on a company computer or premises. An employee can also run into trouble for sending or sharing pornography through office email. But then, how do you prosecute in Zambia someone who is posting, say, pornographic material on a Zambian website from his or her foreign base abroad? Likewise, how do you prosecute in Zambia someone who is emailing pornographic material from his or her foreign base to someone based in Zambia? And what would happen if the act committed by the foreign-based person is not a crime under the laws of the country where he or she is emailing from or posting the porn pictures from? Should we still subject such an individual to the Zambian laws even if the *actus reus* was effected elsewhere although it offended the laws of Zambia? These are critical questions that we ought to be pondering on as we look into the efficacy of the law.

In the Zambian Supreme Court case of *Lipimile and Another v. Mpulungu Harbour Management Ltd* (SCZ/8/270/2005) [2008] ZMSC 15; SCZ. No. 22 of 2008 (23 July 2008), the Supreme Court of Zambia upheld a Zambian High Court ruling, throwing out an appeal against the said High Court ruling that the High Court of Judicature for Zambia enjoys extra-territorial jurisdiction to try a Zambian citizen resident in Zambia for an act of contempt of court allegedly committed in a foreign jurisdiction, namely, France. In that case, the two presiding Zambian Supreme Court justices, Justice L.P.

Chibesakunda and Justice C.S. Mushabati, held that: "...the learned trial judge was on firm ground in finding that his court had extra-territorial jurisdiction over the contemnor. On our part, we cannot agree more by stating that it would be a disaster for the administration of justice in this country if this appeal was allowed...We therefore find that this appeal lacks merit and it is hereby dismissed with costs to the Respondents."

Section 102 of Zambia's Electronic Communications and Transactions Act 2009 makes it a criminal offence for a person to produce pornography for the purpose of distributing such material through a computer system. Then, section 2 of that statute defines a 'computer system' as 'a device or a group of interconnected or related devices, one or more of which, pursuant to a program, performs automatic processing of data'. Closely related to that definition, the same statutory provision defines a 'computer' as 'an electronic, magnetic, optical, electrochemical or other high speed data processing device, performing logical, arithmetic or storage functions, or any data storage facility or communications facility directly related to, or operating in conjunction with, such device.'

But, is a smart-phone a 'computer', or does it form part of a 'computer system'? And can a culpable party get away with watching porn on a smart-phone, arguing that the smart-phone is not a computer and cannot in any way be construed as a 'computer system'? Fortunately, the wording of the definition of 'computer' in section 2 of the Electronic

Communications and Transactions Act 2009 is broad enough to include a smart-phone as well as other web surfing devices.

A related offence under section 102 of the Electronic Communications and Transactions Act 2009 is the offering or making available of pornographic material through a computer system even if such pornographic material was produced outside Zambia, or the accused is not involved in the production of the material. Here, it is an offence to distribute or transmit the pornographic material through a computer system, or to procure any pornographic material through a computer system for oneself or for another person, irrespective of where the said pornographic material was produced. It is also an offence to possess pornographic material in a computer system or on a computer data storage medium. As such, foreigners coming into Zambia with computers that have such information or data on them, whether these foreigners are simply sex tourists or not, as well as all other people visiting or living in Zambia should be mindful of this law. If convicted, the convict would be liable to a fine or to imprisonment, or to both.

CHAPTER

29

IS THE ENGLISH COMMON LAW DOCTRINE OF 'PRESUMPTION OF INNOCENCE' RELEVANT IN THE FIGHT AGAINST CORRUPTION?

As the new Republican Constitution is being worked on, we are presented with an opportunity to revisit some troubling realities of applying some precepts of the English common law, such as 'the presumption of innocence', to some white collar crimes in a developing country such as Zambia. While certain norms of the English common law percolate across much of the common law world, extending to such lands afar as Zambia, as much as certain norms of the French civil law system may be found in much of the civil law world, irrespective of the levels of development of the local or host economies, the adaptation of various laws and regulatory models imported from abroad to the local or host environments cannot be over-emphasised. As one famous English judge, Lord Denning, observed in *Nyali Ltd v. Attorney General* [1956] 1QB 1, at pp. 16-17, regarding the applicability of the English

common law to the African continent, while
sounding a warning that extended to other parts of
the world, "Just as with an English oak, so with the
English common law. You cannot transplant it...and
expect it to retain the tough character which it has
in England. It will flourish indeed, but it needs
careful tending. ...In these far off lands the people
must have a law which they understand and which
they respect."

Care and Haller (see: *Journal of South Pacific Law*,
Vol. 8, No. 2, (2004)) argue that Lord Denning's
dictum in *Nyali Ltd v. Attorney General* highlights
the inherent difficulty in applying the common law,
developed over centuries in England, to foreign
countries where very different circumstances
prevail. According to Care and Haller (see: *Ibid*), the
need to take these circumstances into account was
recognised in the provisions applying the common
law to new settings. Care and Haller (*Ibid*) point out
that 'in many countries it was expressed to apply, *so
far only as the circumstances [of the country] permit.*'

Implicit in Lord Denning's dictum is the notion that
developing countries that import or transplant
model laws from abroad to their own local
environments should consider not only the 'wisdom'
of foreign technical experts from abroad, but also the
local insights and peculiarities articulated by some
local experts. Even more worrying is the calibre and
quality of some of the so-called 'foreign technical
experts' who come to Africa riding on the surfeit of
Western ideological opulence. While it is useful for
law reformers or institutional reformers to be awake

to developments pertaining to parallel legislation in different countries, it is also prudent to avoid falling in the chasm that clouds objectivity with subjectivity by steering clear of blind optimism stupefied in Eurocentric models of development. Law, it must be understood, does not operate or exist in a vacuum. It must be situated in its proper socio-economic and political contexts.

In Zambia, like many other common law jurisdictions, the burden of proof in criminal law cases, generally, including cases of corrupt practices, lies on the prosecution. In other words, if someone accuses you of committing an offence of corrupt practices, the burden of proof requires them (*i.e.* the prosecution team) to prove that you have, indeed, violated the law and committed the offence in question (see: *Woolmington v. DPP* [1935] AC 462, as well as many Zambian criminal law cases). The general rule is that 'he who asserts must prove.' The standard of proof here is such that the prosecution must prove beyond reasonable doubt that you have committed the offence (see: *Miller v. Minister of Pensions* (1947), 2 All E.R. 372). By contract, although the burden of proof in civil law cases, like in criminal law cases, lies on the party bringing an action, the standard of proof in civil law cases is lighter and only requires the plaintiff to prove against the defendant on the balance of probabilities.

Under the Constitution of the Republic of Zambia 1996, Article 18(2)(a) codifies the common law doctrine of 'presumption of innocence' in the following manner: "(2) Every person who is charged with a criminal offence – (a) shall be presumed to be innocent until he is proved or has pleaded guilty;..." This constitutional provision refers solely to criminal offences. Closely related to Article 18(2)(a) of the Zambian Constitution 1996 is Article 11(1) of the United Nations Universal Declaration of Human Rights 1948 which postulates as follows: "(1) Everyone charged with a penal offence has the right to be presumed innocent until proved guilty according to law in a public trial at which he has had all the guarantees necessary for his defence."

Both the Zambian Constitution 1996 and the United Nations Universal Declaration of Human Rights 1948 deal with criminal offences only in as far as the doctrine of presumption of innocence is concerned. However, the Universal Declaration of Human Rights does not constitute binding norms of international human rights law. Neither does the declaration have the force of law as a treaty or as *jus cogens* under customary international law. Against this background, can we argue that a State can derogate from, or introduce exceptions to, the constitutionally enshrined doctrine of presumption of innocence when dealing with certain types of white collar crime where an accused person is failing to account for the source of his or her suspiciously acquired wealth? Indeed, can we shift the burden of proof to the accused? Critics of this view would be quick to argue that pursuing such a line of thought would infringe the rights of the accused. But, then, what about offences covered by strict liability? Does strict liability not shift the burden of proof to the accused somewhat? By parity of reasoning, can we argue that offences of strict liability are unconstitutional since they offend Article 18(2)(a) of the Zambian Constitution 1996?

All in all, the problems associated with a higher standard of proof in criminal law cases and with the requirement that the burden of proof should fall on the prosecution inevitably point to a subtle necessity that the prosecution should comprise a team of highly competent and professional lawyers and investigators if they have to get a good chance at winning the case. Notwithstanding the role played by the Task Force in Zambia, which institution I have, in two out of my many scholarly books (see: *K.K. Mwenda, Legal Aspects of Combating Corruption: the Case of Zambia, (Amherst, NY: Cambria Press, 2007)*; and *K.K. Mwenda, Anti-Money Laundering Law and Practice: Lessons from Zambia, (Lusaka: University of Zambia Press, 2005)*), questioned regarding the legal pedigree upon which it operates, the Director of Public Prosecution (DPP) chambers and the Attorney-General's chambers, although having some well qualified professional lawyers, are understaffed. There is need to attract more lawyers to the public service. Most young lawyers prefer practicing law in some obscure small mushrooming law firms to serving in the DPP's or the Attorney-General's chambers. There are also not enough lawyers on the bench and in such public offices as the Anti-Corruption Commission (ACC). It is issues like these that pose a great challenge to the efficacy of the regulatory and institutional framework for fighting corruption in Zambia.

- Kenneth K. Mwenda

Indeed, law policing and law enforcement arms, together with the judiciary, should be allocated more resources if they are to attract adequate numbers of well qualified people. It is worth noting that even if there are very good laws on the statute books, as long as the implementation of those laws is weak, partly due to weak enforcement and weak investigative measures, the fight against corruption will remain a pipedream. A possible way out of this conundrum, it is proposed, would be to introduce legislative changes that shift the burden of proof from the prosecution to the accused so that the accused should now prove beyond reasonable doubt how, where and when he acquired his seemingly dubious wealth. Indeed, the accused should show that he actually amassed his wealth in a lawful and legal manner. This proposal has in it a deterrent element, and the proposal is a logical extension of section 37 of the Anti-Corruption Commission Act 1996, dealing with the issue of 'possessing unexplained property'.

Unfortunately, the Zambian Government has now repealed section 37 of the Anti-Corruption Commission Act 1996 (see Anti-Corruption Commission (Amendment) Act 2010; Act No. 38 of 2010). The said section 37 read in part, "(1) The Director-General, the Deputy Director-General or any officer of the Commission authorised in writing by the Director-General may investigate any public officer where there are reasonable grounds to believe that such public officer – (a) has abused or misused his office position or authority to obtain property, wealth, advantage or profit directly or indirectly for himself or any other person; (b) maintains a standard of living above that which is commensurate with his present or past official emoluments; (c) is in control or possession of pecuniary resources or property disproportionate to his present or past official emoluments; or (d) is in receipt of the benefit of any services which he may reasonably be suspected of having received corruptly or in circumstances which amount to an offence under this Act. (2) Any public officer who, after due investigation carried out under subsection (1), is found to – (a) have misused or abused his office, position, or authority to obtain advantage, wealth, property or profit directly or indirectly; (b) maintain a standard of living above which is commensurate with his present or past official emoluments; (c) be in control or possession of pecuniary resources or property disproportionate to his present or past official emoluments; or (d) be in receipt of the benefit of any services which he may reasonably be suspected of having received corruptly or in circumstances which amount to an offence under this Act; shall, unless he gives a reasonable explanation, be charged with having, or having had under his control or in his possession of pecuniary resources or property reasonably suspected of having been corruptly acquired, or having misused or abused his office, as the case may be, and shall, unless he gives a satisfactory explanation to the court as to how he was able to maintain such a standard of living or how such pecuniary resources or property came under his control or into his possession or, as the case may be, how he came to enjoy the benefit of such services, be guilty of an offence."

Many critics of the Zambian Government maintain
that the repeal of section 37 of the Anti-Corruption
Commission Act 1996 was designed primarily to
protect a number of thieving politicians from
criminal prosecution after they leave office (but, as
soon as the Patriotic Front Party won the 2011
General and Presidential elections, that statutory
provision was reinstated into law again through the
enactment of the Anti-Corruption Act 2012 (Act No.
3 of 2012)). Legally speaking, there was no
reasonable or logical basis for the previous
Government to repeal section 37 of the Anti-
Corruption Commission Act 1996. Besides, section
37 of the 1996 statute was not in conflict with any
other written law, as others may want to claim. If
anything, section 37 merely complemented and
strengthened the position under the Penal Code of
Zambia. Section 99(1) of the Penal Code stipulates
that: "(1) Any person who, being employed in the
public service, does or directs to be done, in abuse of
the authority of his office, any arbitrary act
prejudicial to the rights or interests of the
Government or any other person, is guilty of a
misdemeanour. If the act is done or directed to be
done for purposes of gain, he is guilty of a felony and
is liable to imprisonment for three years."

The difference between section 37 of the Anti-
Corruption Commission Act 1996 and section 99(1)
of the Penal Code is that the former deals with
situations where an individual is in possession of
property whose source or basis of acquisition the

individual cannot explain whereas the latter deals with a general offence relating to the abuse of one's public office, including situations where such abuse involves financial gain. Under the Penal Code, there is no need to show, for example, that the accused maintained a standard of living above that which is commensurate with his present or past official emoluments, or that he was in control or possession of pecuniary resources or property disproportionate to his present or past official emoluments. The focus there is rather broader, and it covers any situation where an individual abuses authority of his public office in pursuance of an arbitrary act prejudicial to the rights or interests of the Government or any other person.

The idea behind section 37 of the Anti-Corruption Commission Act 1996 was that any law offender and would-be-offenders should be discouraged from ever committing corruption offences. And once the burden of proof had shifted to the defence to show how the accused acquired his seemingly dubious wealth, it would no longer be a question for the prosecution to prove beyond reasonable doubt that the accused committed the offence of corrupt practice. Rather, the accused would have to show, beyond reasonable doubt, that he or she legally and lawfully acquired the wealth and did not engage in any offence relating to corrupt practices. Indeed, what would one fear if he or she has not stolen? All you need to do is demonstrate that you have not stolen. Period! In matters of taxation, it is common practice to find legal obligations akin to the proposal for shifting the burden of proof. The same analogy should be extended to matters of corruption and money laundering. Also, we need to understand the link between corruption and money laundering in order to move away from relying principally on the Penal Code which only points us to simple criminal charges of 'theft'.

Admittedly, if implemented, the proposal to shift the burden of proof from the prosecution to the accused would attract strong criticism. But, we are awake to this fact. A notable criticism here could be that implementing such a proposal would have disastrous effects on the rule of law and the constitutionally guaranteed presumption of innocence. Unfortunately, there is a little water in this argument. In some cases, however, especially where the drafting of legislation is not carried out properly, or where there is no due regard to the full spectrum of provisions of the Republican Constitution, the shifting of the burden of proof from the prosecution to the accused could be struck down by the courts (under judicial review of legislative action) as an unconstitutional measure. But, then, what does Lord Denning tell us about importing precepts of the English common law to foreign lands afar? And is it not a precept of the law that to every general rule there is usually an exception? Indeed, what wrong would there be in enshrining in the Republican Constitution, especially in the Bill of Rights itself, an exception to the general rule, stating therein, unequivocally and explicitly, that notwithstanding whatever is contained in the Bill of Rights, the exception to the presumption of innocence applies only to offences relating to, say, corrupt practices, money laundering and/or drug trafficking? To illustrate, the European Court ruled in a matter involving continued pre-trial detention that such detention can only be justified 'if there are specific indications of a genuine requirement of public interest which, notwithstanding the presumption of innocence, outweighs the rule of respect for individual liberty' (*Van der Tang v. Spain*, (26/1994/473/554), July 13, 1993, para. 55). Why then should we shy away from the proposal highlighted above if we really mean well in the fight against corruption?

A second proposal for law reform would be to lower the standard of proof in criminal law cases of corruption from *beyond reasonable doubt* to the civil law standard of *balance of probabilities*. Such a measure would remove the onerous and strenuous task on the prosecution – especially given that law policing and criminal investigation offices in Zambia are understaffed and have limited resources at their disposal – to prove beyond reasonable doubt that the accused committed an offence relating to corrupt practices. Indeed, there are a number of cases in Zambia where an individual cannot even account for the wealth he or she has amassed over a relatively short period of time. Zambia has seen a number of poverty stricken individuals enter politics and suddenly emerge as some of the wealthiest citizens of that country. Whether we choose to stretch our own imagination of who should be deemed a 'public officer' and who should not be seen as a 'public officer', despite such persons enjoying certain immunities against prosecution while in office, and which immunities can only be enjoyed by someone designated in a certain 'public official' capacity, we have a chance to change the course of the future through some legislative re-engineering. Our aim, thus, should be forward-looking, rather than seeking vendettas or trying to settle scores against those perceived to have committed some irreparable public wrongs as evidenced in their past machinations and mischievousness. When the great Maradona scored through that infamous 'hand of god' against England, many thought that FIFA would reverse the referee's ruling. But it was clear that, whether by design or by default, the referee had already ruled in favour of a goal – the same goes with the courts of law! While court appeals can sometimes work, we are here faced with systemic and endemic corruption in society. Time and again, we have seen one cowboy rise up against a fellow cowboy, despite the fact that they both could have been raiding the cornfields together just the other day. We must understand that cowboys only draw guns at each other when they differ or disagree over matters such as how to share the loot. As one fictitious fable would show: "You promised me the Presidency, and I was loyal to you... But, then, you dribbled me and gave the Presidency to someone else! I will never forgive you for that!" Such politics of personal vendettas, which disenfranchise both the villain and the victim from receiving Holy Communion at Church on Sunday, is what is drawing Africa backwards to the era of primitive politics. This is politics of the stomach! Why do some people feel that they are entitled to public office? Is there no retirement in African politics? But that is not to say those already in power should tell lies and deceive their followers that they will hand them the helm of power. The Machiavellian style of political leadership is not always the best option of maintaining political legitimacy. To that end, even NGOs and some opposition political parties must account to their membership and to other stakeholders on how they have utilized much of the donor funds that they have either received or continue to receive from various sources. Those who live in a glass house should not throw stones otherwise things might boomerang at them. Let us not only focus on the one 'mai-kalange' and his famed mai-kalange fairytale. He will outfox his critics again if they are not careful, and thereafter go on to claim more anointments as long as the critics remain obsessed with trying to bring him down! Looking to the future, as a pro-active measure, it is best instead to develop sound legislative, regulatory and institutional capacities to deal with corruption in the long-term. As such, the past will only be useful in informing the present for a better tomorrow. However, given the rigidity in the law, insisting on the presumption of innocence as an absolute and fundamental right, and requiring that 'he who asserts must prove' beyond reasonable doubt, some ostensibly corrupt individuals have never been charged or prosecuted. And where prosecutions have been instigated, these individuals have often been acquitted. So, then, as one non-native English speaker would put it: "What to do now?"

- Kenneth K. Mwenda

CHAPTER

30

APPRECIATING THE LAW
AGAINST POLITICAL INSULTS

The recent outcry in Zambia against the habitual and pitiful tendency of some politicians to hurl offensive language at each other has attracted much public debate. But, what are 'insults'? The American Heritage dictionary defines the verb 'to insult' as treating someone or something 'with gross insensitivity, insolence, or contemptuous rudeness'. This verb is also described as an affront to, or to demean someone. An insult is an absurd speech that offends or insults the intelligence of someone or the audience. The verb 'to insult' has often been associated with behaving arrogantly towards others. As a noun, the word 'insult' is defined by the American Heritage dictionary as 'an offensive action or remark.' It also entails behaving in an obnoxious and superior manner. And when such unpalatable dispositions are made in the realm of domestic politics, they are known simply as 'political insults'.

Now, some of you may be wondering whether the

word 'insult' should be subjected to the examination of some linguistic or phonological experts. Others may contend that what constitutes an 'insult' varies from culture to culture, and that the word 'insult' has to do with language that makes direct or subtle reference to genitals or sexual conduct, and not otherwise. In essence, this school of thought posits that a factual statement about someone's behaviour or conduct cannot be said to be an insult since it is a fact. The difficulty with this viewpoint is that it confuses the term 'insults' with 'defamation'. The latter is a legal term while the former has a stronger cultural connotation. In our part of the world, even a mere disagreement in a cordial discussion with an elder can be construed as an insult, especially where a young man publicly confronts and proves the elder as a liar.

Indeed, in our part of the world, 'elders are always seen to be right, and that they never tell lies' (smile). In fact, elders are said to have all the wisdom. And the young ones simply have to listen. You don't talk back or ask silly questions when an elder is talking to you because that will be construed most certainly as a sign of insolence and disrespect. But there is also a contrasting view, especially where it is actually an elder who has uttered the offensive words or language. As one anonymous commentator observes, "Frank speech sometimes necessarily involves 'insults' that may upset or demean the other. It quite often involves vulgarity, which...is not only meant to provoke thought, but is also a mnemonic device, given a largely non-literate culture...By that token, what is morally reprehensible in one Zambian culture may not be in another, at least not obviously so. And that has been a prominent feature of frank speech in Zambia, in the form that we find it on the Copperbelt: it has been highly influenced by the cultures of the Chibemba speakers from Luapula and Northern provinces, cultures that do not guard speech as tightly as other Zambians might. For example,...I can scarcely curse in my language (I know scarcely any curse words), but can do so with the rest of them in Chibemba. This is an observation and not necessarily a judgment."

The said commentator goes on to add: "Similarly, an 'insult' in one Zambian culture, morally and even legally punishable, may be seen as *'amalumbo'* (*i.e.* 'praises' to eulogise an individual) in another and only mildly offensive...Frank speech provides a critical path to truth except that some societies provide elaborate controls while others do not. Mind you, 'control' here does not mean a lack of freedom; it just means that you expend more time making sure the ill-effects are minimized... Growing up, I hated witnessing some of the insults flying across the streets and *lunsonga* fences, but by the same token, I do not wish to see people being thrown in jail just for insulting others."

Hitherto, having 'established' that elders generally are believed not to tell lies, would it be an 'insult' if a Head of State were to make a public pronouncement during an election campaign, targeting his political opponents, that: "Ba fya-tile fya bo!!!" (*i.e.* To hell with them and their 'things'!!!), and later denying that those words constitute an insult? Think again. Suffice it to say, we shall proceed in this article with the everyday usage of the word 'insult' in the ordinary parlance and vocabulary of many a reasonable man and woman. And in regard to the phrase, "Ba fya-tile fya bo!!!", I must confess that am not an expert in the Bemba language. And neither have I taken any formal Bemba lessons. In fact, I was born in Livingstone, Zambia, back in the 1960s, and only learned how to speak Bemba when I moved to the Copperbelt. At the time, I would only speak Nyanja, English and a bit of Lozi, although my parents are both Ushi and originally from Mansa, Luapula. When my parents got transferred from Livingstone to Luanshya, I was left with no choice but to adapt rapidly. That is how I learned to speak Bemba within a week. And even though I went to Catholic Convent Schools both in Livingstone and Luanshya, I knew that the two environments were totally different.

On the Copperbelt of those days (here, I am talking about the 1970s and early 1980s), I somehow felt vulnerable and that I was not shielded from some of the rough Bemba-speaking boys; that is, ba mwana shi mine (i.e. some sons of the RCM and NCCM (jointly 'ZCCM') miners, back in the days). Things have changed now. Back in the days, many of us had to pretend to be tough in order to fend off some neighbourhood bullies. And my Bemba suddenly perfected itself. I recall that when I first arrived on the Copperbelt, the young boys in the neighbourhood welcomed me by stealing all my toys. I was shell-shocked. In Livingstone, nobody ever stole my toys. I would leave them outside and find them there the next day. I realised quickly that, unlike my experiences in Livingstone, I was in a new territory – the Copperbelt! Those of us that tried to speak English consistently at school were warned by the big boys that: "Mwaice, uka-ponoka...tuka kumona pa 'closing day'..." (*i.e.* Youngman, don't try to be too smart by speaking English. We'll sort you out at the end of the semester year.). Indeed, the end of the semester was often reserved for bully-fights and the settling of scores; that is, 'Uku-iponona' (*i.e.* this word is deemed to be very offensive in the Bemba language, and one which should never be uttered or repeated). And so, I learned quickly how to insult in Bemba, although I did not insult others.

In Zambia, there is no piece of legislation or case law that defines legally the meaning of the word 'insults'. That said, section 179 of Zambia's Penal Code provides that every person who uses 'insulting' language or otherwise conducts himself in a manner likely to give such provocation to any person as to cause such person to break the public peace or to commit any offence against the person, is liable to imprisonment or to a fine. So, politicians, journalists and others, be warned – the police can arrest you if you cause your political foe or adversary to break public peace as a result of your provocative utterances! And the Penal Code is very clear on the term 'provocation'. It is best for one to take some 'anger-management' training if that person cannot control his or her anger or temper.

Further, section 69 of the Penal Code provides that

any person who, with intent to bring the President of the Republic of Zambia into hatred, ridicule or contempt, publishes any defamatory or insulting matter, whether by writing, print, word of mouth or in any other manner, will be guilty of an offence and is liable on conviction to imprisonment. Again, politicians, journalists and others, be warned – the police can arrest you for defaming the President! Boma ni-boma.

And section 137(3)(b) of the Penal Code provides that any person who is found in a building or dwelling-house or in any verandah or passage attached thereto or in any yard, garden or other land adjacent to or within the curtilage of such building or dwelling-house not being a public place, with intent to annoy or indecently to 'insult any woman or girl' who may be therein, will be guilty of a misdemeanour and is liable to imprisonment. So, folks, be warned! Do not insult women anyhow even if you have your own political or ideological differences. Try to exercise restraint and decorum. Lately, we have seen or heard of complaints by some female politicians regarding some unfortunate utterances by some male politicians which make these ladies feel offended and insulted. Be warned, folks, that the police can arrest you if you insult women unlawfully. The law is there on the books even if it is not frequently implemented.

Now, I know what some of you may be thinking: 'OK, what about freedom of expression in the Constitution for those who want to speak out freely?' Yes, that freedom is there, and it is guaranteed in the Constitution as long as you do not insult others or defame them. And for the comfort of the suspecting reader, let it be known that this author is totally impartial and apolitical. Look, even when the UNIP and MMD governments were in power, respectively, many in the opposition could have been arrested and prosecuted for breaching a number of the laws highlighted above. Usually, political expedience of not wanting to be seen as an undemocratic State or government, especially in the eyes of the donor community, places a restraint on many a sitting government not to initiate such prosecutions. But it does not mean that there is no law to deal with political insults. The law is there on the books and can be invoked anytime. As they say in Bemba, ubushiku usheme ne cimbala ci loca (*i.e.* find out what this means).

CHAPTER

31

UNDERSTANDING THE MINDSET
OF A TRIBALIST

At the outset, I would like to acknowledge that any discussion on the concepts of 'tribe' and 'tribalism', respectively, cannot escape the academic disciplines of anthropology and ethnology. And closely related to that are views from disciplines such as psychology and sociology. Now, it is not the purpose of this article to regurgitate the large volume of literature from these disciplines. Suffice it to say, there are various theories that help to explain the strange phenomena of tribe and tribalism. However, my preferred definition of the term 'tribe' is derived from FreeDictionary.com. The said definition postulates that a tribe is a 'social division of a people, especially of a *preliterate* people, defined in terms of common descent, territory, culture, etc'. Then, the term 'tribalism' is defined by FreeDictionary.com as 'a strong feeling of identity with, and loyalty to, one's tribe or group.' These two definitions are sufficient for the purposes of this essay. But, then, how does the mind of a tribalist really work? I know you are all curious to hear what I am about to say.

For us to know fully well how the mind of a tribalist works, we first have to subject it some serious psychiatric and psychological tests. Now, we are not psychologists or psychiatrists, but we can somehow help the psychologists and psychiatrists by teasing out some common and generic environmental factors that tend to influence the mind of a tribalist. And what we are about to outline below are simply generic factors. We recognise, however, that to every general rule there can be some exception(s). And so, we are mindful that there can be some isolated exceptions to a number of factors outlined below. Further, some arguments may appear like they contradict each other, such as when we talk about poverty having a link to racial and tribal prejudices, on the one hand, and then education and wealth, on the other, failing to change the prejudicial mindsets of some racists and tribalists. Indeed, there will always be some incorrigible and stubbornly myopic folks out there. Although this article is primarily about tribalism, the issue of racism comes in only as a helpful comparative. So, here we go.

(a) Rural upbringing: Akin to a higher likelihood of encountering racist views in places such as the US among some older white folks that grew up in the times of the civil rights movement, there is also a similar likelihood of encountering some tribalism among some older Africans that were raised in the African rural areas and villages. Like racism, tribalism has strong connections with and roots in rural life. In the US, for example, the southern States are rather notorious for such prejudices, in contrast to the more cosmopolitan urban areas. In Africa, the same analogy applies when we are dealing with tribalism. The more rural a fella behaves, the more likely that he or she is going to have some tribal dispositions. But do not get me wrong. Not everything about the rural areas is bad. There are also many good things that emanate from the rural areas.

Further, tribalism and racism can be found in the urban areas as well, although they both tend to be inspired mainly by values of primitive levels of development as opposed to the scientific age of modernity. In general, tribalism and racism are both 'closed-minded' ways of looking at life, and they are both tied closely to superstitious and primitive modes of conceiving knowledge. Hence, it is not surprising that, in some instances, acute forms of tribalism have led to civil wars, secessionist claims, cannibalism, witchcraft, sorcery and so forth. Tribalism is very unscientific and quite primitive.

(b) Even education or church can't change some tribalists: As they say, you can take some African to school but you cannot take the bush out of his or her head. The same analogy here applies to racism. You can take some racist to school, but you can't get the racism out of his or her head. It is not easy for a person with such prejudices to drop them just like that simply because he or she has gone to school. You need more than a strong cleansing detergent to clean those prejudices out of their minds. Thus, you will find many educated people that are still racists and tribalists today. Some even have PhDs, and have done many great and admirable works. Yet, they still struggle with the issue of racism or tribalism. Everything for them revolves around the issue of race or tribe. Even in the church, you will find some pastors who are racists or tribalists.

(c) Distorted family values as part of their socialisation: Closely related to the issue of rural upbringing, some parents indoctrinate, or inculcate tribal values in, their children by constantly conjuring stereotypes against certain tribes. For example, it is not uncommon in Zambia for some parents to object to or discourage their daughter or son from marrying someone from a certain tribe. I will not go into details here because some readers might take it personal. But you all know what I am talking about, don't you? (smile) So, if some elders in the family or community are propagating tribal views, these views are likely to influence the young ones negatively. Remember that some of these elders have the tribal and 'rural-upbringing' baggage even though they may appear to be affluent socialites in the urban areas.

(d) Distorted forms of peer-pressure, role models and other related modes of socialisation: Do you know someone who is so obsessed with or who is constantly talking about or hanging out mainly with folks that he or she went to school with in some remote rural part of Zambia many years ago? Such people find it hard to pick up new friends from other tribes along the way. Even when such people have been to university, they still remain loyally close to their village acquaintances or childhood friends who they went with to high school or primary school in the village. Quite often, much of their communication is conducted in their native language even when others around them cannot understand the language that they are speaking.

At times, you might find that you are in a group of people, and you could all be speaking English, but as soon as one of the culpable chaps notices that someone else has joined the group, and that that newcomer speaks his or her native language, then the two of them will immediately switch to their native language, cutting everyone out of the conversation. Such lack of decency and manners is common with people that are not well-cultivated. And you will that find such behaviours are commonplace in workplaces, schools and many other institutions. For example, as soon as someone notices that your name reads as if you are from his or her tribe, they will be quick to reach out to you until they realise that you are not "one of them"! Yes, my name is "Mwenda". And it is found in almost all the ten (10) provinces of Zambia, as well as in many neighbouring countries, including Congo DRC, Malawi, Angola, Tanzania, Kenya and Uganda. So, you can imagine how many times I have come across such inquisitions and prejudices.

But can tribalists cease to be tribalists when they are placed in a different environment such as when they are living abroad or when they are working in a different province in Zambia from that which they emanate from? A common indication of tribal inclinations is where individuals from a particular country want to identify first people from their tribe before they can warm up to people from other tribes from their country. Such people would rather forge bonds with fellow tribesmates first before they can think of the concept of the 'nation'. For a tribalist, he or she has no sense of nationalism or national patriotism. His or her patriotism is parochial and limited to the tribe. And his or her closest friend or ally is often a fellow tribesmate. Tribalists only reach out to others outside their tribe when they are stranded, but, in turn, are reluctant to help people from other tribes.

And a tribalist is often not ready to learn or speak a different language from his or her own (with the exception of colonial languages like English or French). Look, although I am Ushi, I speak Nyanja and Bemba fluently. And I have no difficulties speaking Nyanja with my Eastern friends. I have told myself that I have to be flexible and adaptable. A tribalist, by contrast, is rigid and not flexible. His or her points of reference often oscillate back to the small shops and the unknown aristocrats in his or her native little hometown or home village. And those are the kind of role models that a tribalist will look up to. It then makes it very hard to strike genuine friendship with such people. What to do now? That is where the psychologists, psychiatrists, anthropologists and ethnologists come in.

A reviewer of an earlier version of this article

observes that: "I read your piece on 'tribalism'. As usual it was insightful. I do believe, however, that the terminology you, and many other writers, use is outdated. Even the kind definition you rely on does not mask the assumption that members of a tribe will be backward compared to members of a nation. While a small number of Zambians may fit this definition, I would argue that the majority of our people do not. There are many Zambians who are (for want of a better term) detribalised. You may be interested in a study done by Brock University in Ontario. The study came out a few months ago. It links racism to low levels of intelligence."

There is no doubt that some social scientists have questioned the validity of the concept of tribe. But, as noted earlier, it is not the purpose of this essay to regurgitate such theory. Suffice it to say, there is no dispute on the correlation between racist behaviours and low levels of intelligence. Indeed, the same can be said of tribalism or Nazism. In many cases, individuals that exhibit attributes of tribalism or Nazism tend to have low levels of intelligence.

Let us now close with the views of an anonymous reader from the African continent. The anonymous reader observes: "As usual I enjoyed reading your article. I think it is well laid out in terms of picking the negative attributes of tribalism. It would have been a better article had it also articulated the positive attributes of tribalism, not in its narrow sense (I am mindful of the definition you adopted for your article) but in the sense of building and sustaining national pride, for example. I am not sure there is anyone who is not 'guilty' of this... Another point I found interesting is the one about people disregarding others, and insisting on speaking their language whether others understand it or not. I also identified with people looking at one's name, and trying to put you in a box. It happens to me all the time. People see my name and already conclude that I am Tonga. What most don't realise is that I don't fit in any particular box really because I was raised speaking different languages at the same time. And I feel lucky that I can speak freely about tribe...without feeling constrained that others will take it personal because my ethnicity is truly 'coloured' (Sotho, Shona, Bemba, Tonga, Lozi Scottish). And depending on who I am with, I am either of these things..."

A concluding remark follows from the anonymous reader from Africa: "But my issue is not whether someone speaks their language or not. In fact, I find it quite cute that people speak their languages. My problem is when people use their language/tribe to exclude others in terms of socio-economic mobility. The bigger challenge, certainly in Zambia, lies with our leaders (both in government and opposition) who, in my view, are obliged to ensure that the wealth of the country is distributed equally among all Zambians. In Zambia today there is a growing and dangerous trend that encourages exclusivity, and our politicians are preying on these 'perceived' differences to divide people on tribal lines. We need to have more internal reflection from our leaders on how their actions affect people's lives at a practical level, to ensure that others do not feel excluded. I am not sure we have such leaders at all. And as long as we continue to project our own prejudices on others, this is going to continue."

CHAPTER

32

CHARACTER AS AN ATTRIBUTE OF LEADERSHIP

An abundance of literature exists in management science on theories such as Trait Theory, Behavioral and Style Theories, Situational and Contingency Theories, Functional Theories, Transactional and Transformational Theories, Environmental Theories, Neo-emergent Theory as well as the Leadership and Emotions Theory. Some commentators argue that we cannot transplant leadership models from the corporate world into the political domain. Others confuse the concept of Executive Leadership with that of Management. But not every manager is a leader. And not every leader is a manager. Underlying the main arguments in this article is the concept of 'transferable skills'. Some life experiences, such as senior leadership in the military, can provide an individual with valuable transferable skills that can be adapted to executive decision-making in the corporate world. Also, following the same example, leadership experience gained in a disciplined environment such as the military can help to build and shape an individual's character. And character, as we argue below, is important in effective leadership. Similarly, many ideas pertaining to effective corporate executive leadership can be transferred and applied successfully to effective political leadership. Indeed, there are many areas of congruence between politics and business as much as there are areas of divergence. After all, we live in an inter-connected and interrelated world. We do not live in separatist and reductionist closed worlds. Our worlds are open systems, interacting continuously with other systems and sub-systems.

That said, while a corporate executive leader often inspires and motivates others through a shared vision as evidenced in the crafting, execution and implementation of effective and sound corporate and business strategies, a manager who lacks leadership skills will often be bogged down with tasks related to the accomplishment of an assignment, without taking into account the bigger picture. But, leadership is not all about accomplishing a task. It involves also navigating with tact in the milieu of people-skills. We sometimes hear of phrases such as Intellectual Leadership. What does this mean? Who is a leader? Boje (2000), in his discussion of Transformational Leadership, citing Burns (1978), observes that: "An intellectual leader is devoted to seeing ideas and values that transcend immediate practical needs and still change and transform their social milieu. 'The concept of intellectual *leadership* brings in the role of *conscious purpose* drawn from values' (Burns, 1978: 142). The intellectual leader is out of step with their own time, in conflict with the status quo. The intellectual leader is a person with a vision that can transform society by raising social consciousness."

In essence, leadership is about character, vision and motivation. And character without consistency and competence can be a recipe for disaster. Generally, there are various types of leaders. Some are charismatic and populist. Others lead on the basis of referent power, expert power, legitimate power or coercive power. But politics should be about character as opposed to opportunity. Imbedded within the concept of character are virtues such as integrity, honesty and fair play. That said, it is not the aim of this article to cause any trouble or problems. We are mindful, however, that institutional economics, a school of economics that gained prominence in the US in the 1920s and 1930s, focuses on the evolution of economic institutions as part of the broader process of cultural development. And institutional economists have long been pre-occupied with understanding the roles that evolutionary process and institutions play in shaping economic behaviour. Invariably, there are different strands of institutional economics, including the 'old' or 'original' institutional economics which is critical of mainstream neoclassical (and Marxian) economics. Another form of institutional economics is the new institutional economics which builds on neoclassical and 'old' institutional economics. And much of the old institutional economics draws inspiration from the works of Thorstein Veblen on the instinct-oriented dichotomy between technology, on the one hand, and the normative spheres of society, on the other hand. But can institutional economics tell us much about the role that institutions might play in shaping political leadership?

Although institutional economics emphasizes a broader study of institutions, viewing markets as the result of the complex interaction of these various institutions, namely, individuals, firms, social norms and States, it is not immediately clear what actually constitutes an 'institution' or how an 'institution' is different from, say, an 'organization'. In the social sciences, the word 'institution' can mean different things. But many scholars pursuing new institutional economics subscribe to Douglass North's distinction of institutions from organizations, contending that institutions are the 'rules of the game' and that institutions consist of both the formal legal rules, such as institutional frameworks, and the informal social norms that govern individual behavior and structure social interactions. By contrast, organizations are said to be groups of people, such as firms, universities and clubs, as well as the governance arrangements that these organizations develop when leveraging their team effort against other organizations.

Some institutional economists argue that Immanuel Kant provided, in phenomenal reality, for a sphere for science that was distinct and separate from anything that would relate to morality or religion. Indeed, Kant endeavoured to resolve the confusion and conflict experienced by some people when they try to figure out whether or how science and religion should fit together. But to what extent can science, especially the social sciences, be said to be free of influence of the normative or value judgements? Plato, in his famous treatise, '*The Republic*', spoke of Philosopher Kings. But was Plato's thesis not a preference towards certain ideals in a political leader? A similar concept to that of Plato is espoused in Mwaipaya's book, '*The importance of quality leadership in national development, with special reference to Africa*'. Although the idea of Philosopher Kings has been criticized by some scholars as being too Utopian, it nevertheless sheds light on the issues of morality-character and leadership that we are discussing here. It is important to understand more objectively the relationship between human thought and the social context within which it arises, as well as the effects that prevailing ideas have on societies. Through an intricate grasp of this sociology of knowledge can we gain insights into the broad fundamental questions about the extent and limits of social influences on individual's lives and the social-cultural basics of our knowledge about the world. To this end, whether as intellectual leaders or as political leaders, our thought-process is fundamentally informed by three inter-related issues: (a) facts; (b) theories; and (c) value judgments. We cannot deny that, nor completely divorce ourselves from value judgments. That said, we can, and should aim to, minimize any value-ladden perspectives. Against this background, I beseech your indulgence to reflect more thoughtfully on the following scenario.

If X was faced with a choice of boarding a modern

luxury coach from City A to Lusaka, and that luxury coach was indeed designed and built on the basis of latest scientific knowledge and institutional designs, and that it would be travelling on an excellent road designed and tarred on the basis of great scientific knowledge and institutional designs, it is conceivable that X, like many other reasonable folks, could be hesitant or unwilling to get on the luxury coach if the driver is drunk. The alternative for X would be to remain behind or to board an old dilapidated bus under the 'leadership' of a sober and focussed driver.

It is a truism that institutions are run and managed by human beings. Institutions do not run and manage themselves. They are run by human beings; managers and leaders. And from a Systems Thinking perspective, if we could borrow from sound Management Theory, every organization or institution is an open system influenced at various recursive levels by different variables. To negate or ignore the influence of good leadership (and character) on the efficacy of any social system would be somewhat disingenuous. Besides, any system has to contend with the external and internal environments. And leaders, as human beings, have their value systems and personal character that can help to shape or drive the culture of an institution. By parity of reasoning, the same logic extends to the political realm. Governments, as systems, are run by people. Governments are not closed systems that cannot be influenced by the external environment. Governments are open systems. There are people outside and inside the government that will have an impact on how the government, as a system, performs. And within the field of institutional economics itself, one need not look far to understanding some of the shortcomings of the traditional approach of simple assumptions of economic behavior. The specialty of behavioral economics uses social, cognitive and emotional factors to understand the economic decisions of individuals and institutions when carrying out economic functions. Many behavioral economists are pre-occupied with understanding the choices made by consumers, borrowers and investors, and the effect that these choices have on market prices, returns and resource allocation.

So, even though X may be cognizant of the fact that the institutional mechanisms of a modern luxury coach or bus, including the good road, may reduce prospects for an accident, it still does not give X some good comfort if the driver is drunk. Cognitive and emotional intelligence on the part of X may inform him to be wary of the drunk driver. Thus, X may not get on the bus or he would rather get on an old bus that he knows full well might breakdown along the way but will eventually get there as long as the driver is not drunk. Indeed, it feels safer to ride with a sober driver than a drunk driver. This metaphor helps to demonstrate the role that character can play in leadership. And many scholars in leadership studies agree on the relevance of character in championing effective leadership.

Even in the fight against corruption, although some pundits opine that if a country can come up with strong and efficient institutions, then the levels of corruption in the country would go down because many strong institutions have checks and balances built within them to prevent the abuse and misuse of power, there are many shortcomings to this institutionalist view. In Zambia, for example, the government built so many seemingly strong and well-funded institutions to fight corruption, including the now disbanded all-powerful Task Force on Corruption, but corruption continued. Even with the vast amount of donor support provided financially, logistically and operationally to the Zambian Task Force, corruption persisted. In the Zambian police force, too, there were reports of corruption.

In many countries worldwide, another example where strong and sound institutional set-ups or frameworks seem to fail to stump out corruption is in regard to the functions of some State security and intelligence agencies. These institutions, although often well-funded, powerful and strong, are circumvented at times to the political whims of certain individuals within the State system, sometimes even abused and misused for corrupt purposes and ends. It must be noted that an institution by itself cannot be said to be corrupt. Rather, it is the conduct of those charged with running the affairs of the institution that will be corrupt. So, will improving institutional procedures and processes alone be sufficient to curb the corrupt behavior of individuals?

The development of strong and efficient institutions

is only a fraction of the entire equation. Institutions on their own may be successful in solving or resolving conflicts arising out of defective institutional processes and procedures or conflicts relating to institutional designs, but they may not resolve or solve some of the conflicts that are deeply rooted in institutional politics and institutional culture. And that is why the setting up of so many institutions to fight corruption may not be an answer. Rather, we should be moving from such obsessions to that of building progressive political cultures that are free of corruption. And such developments require the leadership of leaders who have good character and who are willing and committed to fight corruption, without fear, favour or prejudice. We cannot ignore the role that character plays in leadership today. A leader must not only be a visionary, but must also be of *sound and sober character* if he or she is to move society forward. A notable figure in African-American history, Marcus Garvey, writing on the 'Power of Character', observes that:

"When wealth is lost, nothing is lost. When health is lost, something is lost. When character is lost, all is lost. The man of sterling character is the great builder. He is not only a builder of himself, but according to his opportunities he builds around himself. He builds his environments, he builds his community, he builds his country, and sometimes he helps to build a world." Garvey notes further that, "The greatest possession of man is character. He can well afford to lose his wealth, and even his health, because if he has character he can recover them. So few men pay attention to the most essential natural element in good living. If more people had devoted themselves to the development of good character there would have been less misery and less unhappiness in the world."

Indeed, we concur with Garvey that, "All men who have conquered in every walk and sphere of life were fellows with good character, that is to say, they were men who found the noblest in themselves, who felt that self-development and self-growth were the greatest expression of a normal existence...With sterling character, you can destroy a world and rebuild it, you can go down into the depths and then rise to the heights; you can meet adversity and laugh at it on the way back to prosperity. It is only a characterless coward who goes down permanently. The fellow with the sterling worth, with the urge of honesty, of self-confidence, of nobility, sees no defeat, admits of no handicap, nor barriers, he must climb to the surface... The chance of rising above the level of unfortunate men is for everyone who will ennoble himself by forcing out the good that is in him."

CHAPTER

33

APPLYING STRATEGIC THINKING IN FINDING A SPOUSE AND SECURING MARRIAGE

NOT too long ago, when my article, "Being single not a sin", was published in the ***Zambia Daily Mail*** (Thursday, June 28, 2012), I received some warm email feedback from many a reader. One of the readers implored me to do a follow-up article, focusing this time on how a single person can find someone to marry. She insisted: "Even single people have needs... They also need a companion!" I did not contest that assertion. It was too contentious.That said, I am not an expert in marital affairs. And so, I decided to do some consultation with friends and colleagues who are professional marriage counsellors and those that are psychologists with expertise in social relationships. Indeed, I needed a second pair of eyes to look through my thoughts, albeit the fact that many lawyers have valuable insights into intricate aspects of family law.

PERCEPTION

As a fable would show, Sheila is a very good looking single lady in her early 40's. She is highly educated and has a well-paying professional job, but has no man and no child. She worries a lot about this. In her neighbourhood, a good number of her neighbours are constantly gossiping that 'at least if she had a child, that would have been better and different.' Sheila knows that they are talking, and she also knows what they are talking about. And Sheila has just fired her teenage houseboy. So, her place is very quiet. I asked Sheila on the phone: "Why did you fire your houseboy? I thought he was doing a good job looking after your place."

Sheila laughed, and went on: "Kali tumpa sana (he is very silly). Every morning when he reports for work, he comes straight to my bedroom, and he enters without knocking, claiming that he is looking for laundry to wash. I warned him that he should be knocking on the door before entering, and that he will one day find me dressing up. He looked down shyly, and said: 'No Madame, that can't happen. I always pip through the key-hole before entering your bedroom!' I was so shocked. Just imagine, he thought that that was a smart answer. So, I kicked the fool out! I wish I had a man to beat the crap out of him." And so, our discussion changed to the issue of Sheila finding a man to marry.

I explained to Sheila that people marry for different reasons. Some marry out of loneliness or because the person that they are marrying is the son or daughter to a famous Mr. XYZ. Others marry because the person that they are marrying used to live in England or the USA, and has a UK or American accent. But, of course, you can't eat an accent. And then there are those that marry for such other reasons as: "Oh, he works for such and such a company", or "he drives such and such a car and has a big house", without finding out if it is stolen or borrowed money that is on display.

JUDGEMENTS

In short, we all have value judgements. And we choose our partners based on those value judgements. It is never an objective or scientific exercise. But be warned: you must always endeavour to distinguish wolves from sheep. By that, I mean, you should never marry someone on the basis of fake credentials such as lies, exaggerations or untenable promises!

No doubt, choosing a partner is a subjective thing. And not everyone who is married is happy. Some are sad, yet others are happy. Likewise, not everyone who is single is sad. Others are happy just being single. But Sheila could not take any of that. All she was interested in was finding out how she can get a Mr. Right. So, I went on to explain that although many people do not realise it, those that are in happy marriages not only work at making their marriages successful, but did apply also some kind of strategic thinking in finding the right partner. Sheila listened intently, and asked further: "What do you mean?"

HONESTY

I went on to explain that there is no such thing as 'love is blind'. Love can never be blind. I told her that she needed to be honest with herself first, and then map out her own strengths and weaknesses. With that, she can then look into the market, weighing the opportunities that her strengths could generate when pitted against the weaknesses of her competitors as well as the threats that might confront her because of her weaknesses when pitted against her competitors.

Elucidating on the dynamics of strategic thinking as opposed to strategic planning, I also pointed her to the concept of 'transferable skills' in human resources management (HRM) so as to help her understand that you can simulate or replicate and adapt certain skills from the goods and services industry to the market of love. I implored Sheila to do some scenario planning so as to find out where she saw herself in the next 10 to 15 years, and the type of man she would want to be with.

Sheila counter-argued with some economic arguments of supply and demand in the love market, contending that there just aren't many eligible bachelors out there. I explained to her that, with some strategic thinking, she can try to map her terrain more efficiently and effectively so as to survive the competition. To that, she seemed shocked, and asked: "And how does one do that?"

CULTURE

I continued with my theory. Back in the days, things were somewhat different. Your parents would find you a nice lady or guy to marry in the village or rural areas even though the two of you had never met before. And that other person would faithfully wait for you to go and marry her. But such arranged marriages are rare nowadays, except in places like South Asia. One could argue that culture is dynamic, and that people have moved on. A Zambian correspondent and colleague observes: " That old practice of parents finding partners for their sons and daughters to marry/be married to seems to have worked very well. I have a friend whose parents found him a girl to marry when we were at varsity. They got married twenty years ago, and they are still enjoying their marriage to this day! Sadly, I cannot say the same about some of the marriages whereby the two involved found themselves – some ended in divorce after less than five years. Now, should one conclude that our old folks knew how to pick compatible partners for us?"

The said Zambian correspondent observes further: "True, some people fail to find partners to settle down with in marriage because they aim too high. I feel for career ladies as they often are 'avoided' by eligible bachelors. We men usually go for girls who do not challenge us intellectually! To make matters worse for such ladies, most of them don't score highly in the beauty stakes. They need to do a lot of the strategic thinking that you advocated."

But I contend also that money has entered into our

lives so much, forming a core fabric of many social relations to the extent that many people monetarise love and other social relations. And the issue of monetarised marriages is often the fear of many male skeptics, contending that when a man gets married the following is what can happen (*i.e.* the picture below has been doing rounds via email, although the source of the said picture remains unknown).

In many cases, though not all, there is no love without money. As they say, you can't eat love. And where money runs out, love also usually runs out. But I am not trying to be a prophet of doom. That's really not the point. Rather, what I am saying is that there are very few exceptions to this theory of monetarised social relations. As an old adage postulates: "People were created to be loved. Things were created to be used. The reason why the world is in CHAOS is because things are being loved, and people are being used." Even when it comes to funerals of some so-called rich people, many churches are more than willing to offer them a dignified church service despite the fact that the deceased never used to attend church! Ala bwa fya. Money no longer talks, it actually shouts.

Recently, one young Zambian lady remarked thoughtfully, "Ba Auntie got married to this ugly-looking man! Mwandini, he is so ugly! Kwati ca ku-tinisha ko abaice! But, abene ba Auntie says: 'OK, pa menso pena ni ng'anga ba Uncle bobe. But, cali-kwata impiya ci-mdala, umfwa fye...' (OK, your uncle is damn ugly, but he is also very rich)." This type of thinking is very common in many people today. You will find that even some handsome but economically destitute young guy will pick up some old woman who is almost twice his age as long as the woman can provide for him financially and materially. We are living in strange times.

ATTITUDES
Back to strategic thinking. Since many psychologists tell us that many men are primarily attracted to the good looks of a woman more than anything else, if a sister knows that she ain't that good looking then she must try to find an alternative strength (e.g. a good career, a good education, a good and decent personality, genuine and bona fide Christian values, as well as effective and decent social networks, including reliable introductions, etc) that she can leverage to beat her competitors. And, as some men

would say, she may also want to tone down on 'attitudes' if she wants to get married. The Bible is very clear on this teaching, notwithstanding any spirited feminist arguments grounded in Ephesians 5:21. The said Bible verse postulates that: "**Submit to one another out of reverence for Christ.**" Indeed, there is no contradiction between Ephesians 5:21 and Proverbs 21:9. The latter verse provides that: "Better to live on a corner of the roof than share a house with a quarrelsome wife." In short, Proverbs 21:9 is a clarification of Ephesians 5:21. And just like a good husband should not be seen to be irresponsible, abusive or self-centered, Proverbs 19:13 adds that: "A foolish son is his father's ruin, and a quarrelsome wife is like a constant dripping."

Now, as far as strategic thinking is concerned, if a guy knows that he ain't got that much cash, or does not have a sexually enticing muscular body, he should leverage instead some other strength, targeting those that are interested in that other 'brand' or strength. It would be folly for one to be over-ambitious and try to get someone that you can neither reach nor afford. Indeed, that is the difference between utopia and reality. We have to be awake to the obstacles and challenges out there. Also, there are so many prejudices to deal with in life (e.g. racism, tribalism, self-imagined aristocracies, etc). And you have to factor in all this. For example, in a family of three sisters, it is quite likely that the one with a lighter skin complexion might attract more guys than the darker-skin ones. For some reason, some men attribute beauty to light skin complexion, forcing some darker-skin women to apply 'jaribou' on their faces, ending up with badly bleached faces that are accompanied by dark knuckles and ankles.

The bottom-line is that some people find it hard to get a spouse mainly because they aim too high. But isn't it a truism that, as men, for example, we all can't marry Miss World even if we all wanted her? Tali, ku- ipima festi? (Translated as: "One has to weigh his or her chances before presenting his or her love manifesto").

STRATEGIC
A few years ago, a friend of mine was dating this really cute African chic, but they later broke up. They were both not married, though she was a single mom. According to the guy, they broke up because she was trying to rush him into marriage, and that she was somewhat looking for a father-figure for her child. Had she been more strategic in her approach, she might have known from the outset that he was not looking for marriage but simply a relationship.

Closely related to that, if a woman gets married to a man who already has kids, it would be wise for her to treat those children nicely just like her own, otherwise she will be sowing seeds for a disastrous marriage. The same applies to men who marry women with children. They too must show unconditional love to the entire family, without bias or favour.

CHAPTER

34

BEING SINGLE NOT A SIN

You cannot die from being single. Neither is the state of being single an ailment. Yet, many people go to all sorts of lengths to try and get a spouse, or to get on board what is now considered fashionable amongst some social elites, a partner. The truth of the matter is that being single or being alone cannot lead to death. And whatever cannot kill you can only make you stronger. The Bible is very clear in 1 Corinthians 7:32-35: "I want you to be free from anxieties. The unmarried man is anxious about the things of the Lord, how to please the Lord. But the married man is anxious about worldly things, how to please his wife, and his interests are divided. And the unmarried or betrothed woman is anxious about the things of the Lord, how to be holy in body and spirit. But the married woman is anxious about worldly things, how to please her husband. I say this for your own benefit, not to lay any restraint upon you, but to promote good order and to secure your undivided devotion to the Lord."

- Kenneth K. Mwenda

In order to love and serve the Lord without any worldly distraction, as every good Christian would desire, the state of being single and unmarried can help individuals to attain that goal, although married couples too can uplift their marriage spiritually through a prayerful covenant with God. There is nothing wrong with being single or being married. And it is not a sin to be single. 1 Corinthians 7:8 guides us to the teachings of the Lord Jesus Christ: "To the unmarried and the widows I say that it is good for them to remain single as I am."

And 1 Corinthians 7:1-40 continues: "Now concerning the matters about which you wrote: 'It is good for a man not to have sexual relations with a woman.' But because of the temptation to sexual immorality, each man should have his own wife and each woman her own husband. The husband should give to his wife her conjugal rights, and likewise the wife to her husband. For the wife does not have authority over her own body, but the husband does. Likewise the husband does not have authority over his own body, but the wife does. Do not deprive one another, except perhaps by agreement for a limited time, that you may devote yourselves to prayer; but then come together again, so that Satan may not tempt you because of your lack of self-control.'..."

I sometimes wonder why some people panic so much about their state of being single. Many seem to worry most about how society will view them. Some even join churches to search for a spouse, especially if they feel that time is not on their side, and that they are aging very quickly. Yet, the Bible instructs us in Mark 12:25 that: "For when they rise from the dead, they neither marry nor are given in marriage, but are like angels in heaven." And to that, Matthew 19:12 adds: "For some are eunuchs because they were born that way; others were made that way by men; and others have renounced marriage because of the Kingdom of Heaven. The one who can accept this should accept it."

It appears that in many societies that uphold values of patriarchy the state of bachelorhood for a man is less frowned upon than that of spinsterhood for a lady. Yet, both a bachelor and a spinster are unmarried persons, although they may be dating and both may even have live-in partners. I have heard stories of organisations or companies that are reluctant to hire or recruit senior executives that are single or not married. While many countries have now moved forward to ban the discrimination against hiring or promoting gay or lesbian people in the corporate sector, we have not paid much attention to the discrimination against heterosexual single or unmarried people, especially unmarried women. People remain single or unmarried for various reasons. Suffice it to say, in our part of the world, many women that are widowed are treated less harshly at work than, say, a not-so-attractive single mother who has never been married or one who is divorced. There seems to be a bit of public sympathy and empathy towards single women that are widowed than those that have never been married or those that are divorced. For some reason, society seems to place two different standards here, arguing that a widowed woman has, at least, previously held the title of 'wife' respectfully until she lost her late husband. That said, as one anonymous Zambian female commentator observes: "Even though, Biblically speaking, it is not a sin to be single our society has a way of making single ladies feel as though they are committing an unpardonable sin!"

The Zambian female commentator continues: "As you correctly stated, a widow is given more respect than a single mother. I have noticed that a further distinction is made between a single mother and a single childless woman. Single mothers are given more respect because they at least have a child. I know a lady in my neighbourhood back home who has a top position in a bank but she is single and does not have children. I used to hear people say about her, 'nkasako sembe enzeko chabe na mwana ndaba apasako ulemu'. It is as though single ladies without children are not woman enough especially if they are passed the age of 30! This belief is strongly held in both rural and urban areas. During the times I visited my grandmother in the village..., the girls who are my age or younger looked at me as if there is something very wrong with me, because I wasn't married. A few of my cousins would ask if I, at least, had a child!"

Closely related to the foregoing, the court of public opinion is quite harsh on men and women who have gone through a divorce, constantly conjuring up theories, anecdotes and conjectures on what went wrong or who is to blame. But what about single adult men that have never been married, how does society view them? Let us not go the route of eligible bachelor. We live in largely patriarchical societies that are increasingly being challenged by emerging and assertive feminism. Single adult men, though not always viewed in the same way as unmarried women, have also suffered some form of prejudice and discrimination. There is a tenacious and pervasive view in many parts of our society that if an adult man has never been married and continues to live alone, in spite of having a girlfriend here and there, then something is seriously wrong with him.

Generally, in our part of the world, it is considered culturally disrespectful for anyone younger than or not closely related to a single adult man to ask such a man that: "You, why are you not married at your age?" Rather, people will just be gossiping and spreading rumours and innuendos in the background. As one anonymous Zambian male commentator observes: "...I keep receiving these unnecessary comments, and like you put it rightly, innuendos that the man is impotent hence he's alone. I remember a few years back while living...at some apartments, without realizing, my neighbours who were ladies started a story that I was gay just because they had not seen women frequent my house. I think our culture needs to adjust with the common trends of the world, in the past men could easily go about life by just cultivating and producing food for families. In the present day world, one has to think about the future of the unborn children, educational-wise, and food security and other essentials for their growth...hence even the numbers of nuclear families are reducing in size in comparison to the old days when our parents could produce 12 children etc."

Additional prejudices against single adult men are, as noted above, that some organisations and companies are reluctant to hire or recruit as senior executives single or unmarried adult men. In our part of the world, there is a certain age, for men especially, at which society assumes that someone is or must be married. It is different for women. Society does not make the same assumption because there are not just enough eligible bachelors out there.

I recall a story shared by a young Zambian lady whose auntie kept putting pressure on her to get married. She was young and studying for her law degree at the time. She lamented, "Ba auntie bena, awee shuwa. She is so obsessed with marriage. Bena fyonse ni marriage, marriage! Nga wa landa ko ati first mpwishe isukulu, she will shout back, 'Mulee upwako pakuti mwa cindamika ko ubucende'..." (*i.e.* My auntie is constantly putting pressure on me to get married. Whenever I try to explain to her that I need to complete my studies first before I can think of getting married, she will shout back at me, saying that marriage is important because it not only legitimises people's sexual conduct within the institution of marriage but it also dignifies the same). I felt sorry for the young lady when she gave her testimony, albeit respecting her honesty.

For some people, it is acceptable to contend that

'Mulee upwako pakuti mwa cindamika ko ubucende'. But the institution of marriage was not created for the simple reason of legitimising and dignifying sex. Rather, the institution of marriage, though a social institution and a legal construct, is often steeped in deep religious and traditional values. As an old South African Zulu adage goes, "**Umuntu ngumuntu ngabantu**", expressing a profound truth embedded deep within the core of traditional Afrikan values. The adage translates into English as follows: "a person is a person because of people" or "a person is a person through other persons." Through the institution of marriage, families and extended ties are born. It is indeed **about** 'umuntu ngumuntu ngabantu', and not about legitimising or dignifying sex.

While single parenting can also lead to the establishment of family and extended ties, our societies, partly due to African traditional values and norms of patriarchy, do not often approve of single parenting. It is seen as a Western concept. Closely related to the idea that single parenting is a Western concept is the view that adulterous relationships or extra-marital affairs are less edifying than a marital relationship, no matter how many hours that an adulterous couple may be spending together every day. So, what to do now, as they say would say in Russia?

While some would advocate for the use of love potions to win over a married man or a single guy, or to cement an existing marital relationship, it is a criminal offence under section 10 of the Witchcraft

Act 1914 (as amended through to 1994) to profess to use love potions. The said statutory provision states that: "Every person professing to be able to control by non-natural means the course of nature or using any subtle craft, means or device by means of witchcraft, charms or otherwise to deceive or impose upon any other person shall be liable upon conviction to a fine...or to imprisonment with or without hard labour..., or to both." So, those who brag that "inee abalume bandi nali solva, bekala fye pa ng'anda nomba", implying that they have effectively administered love potions on their man can be arrested and prosecuted for professing to control by non-natural means the course of nature through such charms. It suffices that the accused is professing to be able to control by non-natural means such course of nature as love.

As noted above, you cannot die from being single. Not even lust can kill you. Besides, lust alone cannot be the main issue over which to panic. Whoever died of lust? The Bible, in Job 31:1-40, teaches us about the Holy man, Job: "I have made a covenant with my eyes; how then could I gaze at a virgin? What would be my portion from God above and my heritage from the Almighty on high? Is not calamity for the unrighteous, and disaster for the workers of iniquity? Does not he see my ways and number all my steps? 'If I have walked with falsehood and my foot has hastened to deceit;...'."

CHAPTER

35

EXPLAINING THE FRAGILITY OF ALLIANCES BETWEEN AND AMONG POLITICAL PARTIES

The formulation and successful implementation of a political strategy to win an election is an important tool for any worthwhile political party as a country prepares for its presidential and general elections. In this article, we focuss on the emergence of political alliances in Zambia every time when elections are nearing. Many will remember, for example, the collapse of the political alliance against the then ruling party, the Movement for Multi-party Democracy (MMD), by two of the dominant opposition parties in Zambia, Patriotic Front (PF) and United Party for National Development (UPND). Indeed, there have been many other political alliances in Zambia, and we are yet to see more as the elections draw close.

That said, one success story of an effective political alliance in the recent history of Zambia was the formation of MMD to get United National

Independence Party (UNIP) out of power. Different stakeholders from different walks of life all joined hands to end the One-Party State rule perpetuated by the then ruling party, UNIP. Thereafter, the country has never witnessed any other effective political alliance. The question then is: what is it that really motivates political parties and politicians to form these alliances?

A number of political scientists have examined related issues on similar intellectual discourse. And many leading industrial psychologists and management gurus have churned out literature on teamwork as well as on how effective teams are formed and how they function. The Forming – Storming – Norming – Performing model of group development espoused by Bruce Tuckman in 1965 is a typical example of such management theories. However, it is not the purpose of this article to regurgitate such theory. Suffice it to say, we can draw some insights from these theories.

In Zambia, you do not have to conduct a scientific survey for you to understand why many political alliances emerge, especially when general and presidential elections are drawing closer. You do not even need to formulate scientific research questionnaires or interview questions for this. Indeed, there is an abundance of valuable information out there in the public domain that can help you to understand why some of these political alliances are formed, and what often leads to their fragility. Let us take a more reasoned look.

I have provided below a simple picture that has been doing rounds via email, although the source of the picture in the said emails remains undetermined and unrevealed. To that end, I do not in any way claim to hold or have any copyright ownership over the picture. But, as you can tell from the attached picture, it speaks of real teamwork. As they say, together, we can accomplish so much as long as we do not give a damn about who takes the credit.

- Kenneth K. Mwenda

When I first saw this picture, and after noticing that the squatting guy was crying out to his friend, "Come on hurry it, Jack, I also want to wee wee....", I thought to myself for a minute: what if Jack decided to run away soon after he was done with peeing, leaving his friend stranded? As it were, I was not alone with these thoughts. Many commentators that saw or have seen this picture have reacted in a similar way. They have often said things like: "Aaaah, umwina Zambia kuti a-pashika" (i.e. "You will be lucky if the brother does not bolt after peeing"); or "Iya-yi, ani dyela masuku pa mutu, uyu muntu" (i.e. "There is no way I would allow myself to be stepped on like that. That's exploitation and mistreatment?").

This, ladies and gentlemen, provides some insights into why many political alliances crumble in Zambia. The reasons include: (i) a culture of mistrust, suspicion and superstition; (ii) fragile social cohesion; (iii) each political leader wanting to lead the alliance and to become its presidential candidate; (iv) peddling of rumours and innuendos, including secret brokering of side deals by some interests within the alliance; (v) unresolved leadership squabbles; (vi) a general lack of transparency and accountability; and, (vii) the absence of a post-election strategy. In many developing countries, the opposition parties tend to focuss primarily on winning an election, but not on what will happen should they win the election. It is not surprising that if a political alliance were to win an election, it would either crumble due to internal greed or struggle to settle down.

As a general rule, it is unwise and politically unhealthy to have insatiably greedy and power-hungry political leaders within an alliance. Such leaders may not trust each other, and they will be busy hustling and jostling for presidential power. But, an effective political alliance must be built on trust. Where there is no trust among the stakeholders, it is hard to forge a lasting partnership. In Zambia, this issue has contributed significantly to the collapse of many opportunistic political alliances. Also, an effective political alliance must be built on transparency and honesty. It should not be for selfish or opportunistic reasons. Where values of transparency and honesty are missing, you are simply playing for time before failure ensues. Thirdly, an effective political alliance requires all parties involved to make a compromise and to sacrifice their individual vantage points for the common good of the alliance. And where you have some egoistic leaders within the alliance, each not wanting to back down, that is a recipe for failure. Fourth, you have to weed out or discipline individuals that are working against the common good of the political alliance for the partnership to succeed. In short, an effective alliance works well where there is political commitment of and by all stakeholders as well as where there is mass participation in decision-making processes.

Fifth, an effective political alliance should seek to attain political legitimacy through such strategic means as the use of mass communication technology and the timely transmission of appropriate propaganda. To do so, the alliance must have a common and appealing ideology to sell to its members and the public. Without such an ideological base, the political alliance can sink in quicksand. Sixth, a political alliance might suffer a setback where it has the heavy baggage of a 'tribal' tag among some of its leaders or members. If, say, X political party within the alliance were to be seen as a predominantly Bemba-speaking political party, and the other political party were to be perceived as a predominantly Tonga-speaking political party, that can erode the legitimacy of the alliance. Also, political leaders in an alliance that exhibit or have a soft heart for regional and tribal politics are a major threat to the success of the alliance. An effective political alliance must be all-embracing in order to win votes across the country. It calls for openness and good communication within the alliance as well as respect for other team members.

An additional factor that speaks to the successful performance of a political alliance is the presence of a good and visionary leadership. An effective alliance tends to thrive better under good and visionary leadership which does not discriminate or favour stooges or henchmen, but treats everybody fairly. And in many cultures that easily embrace populism, a good leader must also be charismatic. Further, a good leader must be an effective and creative problem-solver, working closely with his or her people. We must understand that effective leadership can help to motivate those that are in the alliance. So, poor or weak leadership can work against the effectiveness of a political alliance.

Finally, effective political alliances are built on teamwork. Scholars such as Marks, Mathieu and Zaccaro, in an article titled, "A Temporally Based Framework and Taxonomy of Team Processes", published in the *Academy of Management Review,* 26 (3): 356–376 (2001), as well as LePine, Piccolo, Jackson and Mathieu, in an article titled, "A Meta-Analysis of Teamwork Processes: Tests of a Multidimensional Model and Relationships with Team Effectiveness Criteria", published in *Personnel Psychology* 61 (2): 273–307 (2008), highlight the importance of the following teamwork processes, namely: (a) transition processes (between periods of action) that include mission analysis, goal specification, and strategy formulation; (b) action processes (when the team attempts to accomplish its goals and objectives) that include monitoring progress toward goals, systems monitoring, team monitoring and backup behavior, and coordination; and, (c) interpersonal processes (present in both action periods and transition periods) which include conflict management, motivation and confidence building as well as affect management. A good leader needs to understand this in order to provide effective leadership to a political alliance.

322

CHAPTER

36

APPRECIATING THE PRIMACY OF LAW AND ETHICS IN MEDICAL PRACTICE

Why should medical practitioners and members of the public worry about knowing some aspects of the law as well as some aspects of ethics relating to medical practice or, rather, medical malpractice? Before turning to issues of the law, let us first examine issues of medical ethics as espoused by the medical profession through the famous Hippocratic Oath. In an Online article titled, "The Hippocratic Oath Today", dated March 27, 2001, and published by *NOVA Beta*, Peter Tyson observes that: "The Hippocratic Oath is one of the oldest binding documents in history. Written in antiquity, its principles are held sacred by doctors to this day: treat the sick to the best of one's ability, preserve patient privacy, teach the secrets of medicine to the next generation, and so on. 'The Oath of Hippocrates,' holds the American Medical Association's Code of Medical Ethics (1996 edition), 'has remained in Western civilization as an

---

- Kenneth K. Mwenda

expression of ideal conduct for the physician.'..."

Indeed, the ethics of the medical profession are predicated mainly on the Hippocratic Oath taken by many physicians at the time of being admitted to practice medicine. Yet paradoxically, as Peter Tyson observes, "...even as the modern oath's use has burgeoned, its content has tacked away from the classical oath's basic tenets. According to a 1993 survey of 150 U.S. and Canadian medical schools, for example, only 14 percent of modern oaths prohibit euthanasia, 11 percent hold convenant with a deity, 8 percent foreswear abortion, and a mere 3 percent forbid sexual contact with patients—all maxims held sacred in the classical version."

By now, many a reader might be wondering; what then are the actual contents of the Hippocratic Oath? Let us take an example of the Hippocratic Oath promulgated by Cornell University's Weill Cornell Medical College. The Oath spells out the following tenets:

"I do solemnly vow, to that which I value and hold most dear: That I will honor the Profession of Medicine, be just and generous to its members, and help sustain them in their service to humanity; That just as I have learned from those who preceded me, so will I instruct those who follow me in the science and the art of medicine; That I will recognize the limits of my knowledge and pursue lifelong learning to better care for the sick and to prevent illness; That I will seek the counsel of others when they are more expert so as to fulfill my obligation to those who are

entrusted to my care; That I will not withdraw from my patients in their time of need; That I will lead my life and practice my art with integrity and honor, using my power wisely; That whatsoever I shall see or hear of the lives of my patients that is not fitting to be spoken, I will keep in confidence; That into whatever house I shall enter, it shall be for the good of the sick; That I will maintain this sacred trust, holding myself far aloof from wrong, from corrupting, from the tempting of others to vice; That above all else I will serve the highest interests of my patients through the practice of my science and my art; That I will be an advocate for patients in need and strive for justice in the care of the sick. I now turn to my calling, promising to preserve its finest traditions, with the reward of a long experience in the joy of healing. I make this vow freely and upon my honor."

So, what happens to a patient who is in critical condition at the Intensive Care Unit (ICU) of a state-run hospital where medical doctors are on strike, complaining of poor remuneration by their employer? Should the doctors abandon the patient and just watch him or her die while they continue to press for their salary increments? Indeed, if such a case were to occur, would that not be an affront to one of the tenets of the Hippocratic Oath, namely, "That I will not withdraw from my patients in their time of need..."? As one physician observes from Zambia:

"An addition to chew on is the historical withdrawal of labour by Medical Doctors throughout Zambia in

the year 2000. Among the key issues was the refusal
by the Drs to attend to patients in an environment
they adjudged to be unsafe for reasonable medical
care. This scenario was characterized by rampant
shortages of medical and surgical supplies, as well
as with 'improvisations' being the order of the day.
The prevailing conditions, at least in the eyes of the
Drs then, was in direct conflict with the Drs oath to
'...above all, do no harm...'; that is, attending to
patients under such conditions constituted an
assault on the patients because most of these
patients were under the mistaken impression that
the Drs were doing the best they could do and that
the said Drs were carrying out the most reasonable
intervention in accordance with their medical skills.
As they say, the rest is history...FTJ (President
Chiluba) summarily fired the Drs, most of whom
have never shown their faces in Zambia again,
despite the huge deficit faced in the Republic for
skilled manpower." What to do now?

And what about situations where a medical doctor
who operates a private clinic as a general
practitioner (GP) decides on his own to carry out a
medical procedure that should only be carried out by
a physician with established expertise in a complex
and specialised area of medicine such as
neurosurgery? Wouldn't that be an affront to the
Hippocratic Oath, particularly the tenet, "That I will
recognize the limits of my knowledge... seek the
counsel of others when they are more expert so as to
fulfill my obligation to those who are entrusted to
my care..."?

It is against such ethical considerations that the law kicks in. But, not everybody can afford to hire a lawyer. Besides, some legal issues can be resolved out of court through some form of alternative dispute resolution. However, it can also help in reaching an amicable solution if the contesting parties have some idea about the correlative rights and duties attached to their dispute. In short, it is easier to agree outside the court system if both parties agree on who is wrong and who is right, notwithstanding that there may be some outstanding issues on the quantum of compensation. Let us take a more reasoned look.

First, medical doctors need to know the law relating to the confidentiality of a patient's medical records as well as the attendant duty of confidentiality regarding the communication between the doctor and the patient. In Zambia, it also means that medical practitioners should adhere to the policies of non-disclosure and professional conduct promulgated by their employers as well as those set forth by the competent authority for regulating the medical profession. Further, the medical practitioners should be seen to be acting in compliance with the relevant aspects of the common law pertaining to their profession and practice, including legislation such as the Public Health Act, the Termination of Pregnancy Act, the Food and Drugs Act, the Human Tissue Act, the National Health Services Act, the Nurses and Midwives Act, the Therapeutic Substances Act, and the Medical and Allied Professions Act. Like the sacredness with which a priest is expected to hold the confession of a faithful, so it is with a doctor and a patient.

- Kenneth K. Mwenda

Secondly, medical practitioners need to know the circumstances that give rise to fiduciary duties of confidentiality between, say, a doctor and a patient, including any exceptions to these duties. For example, when can a medical doctor disclose or furnish a patient's medical records to lawyers requesting for such information in a court matter? In short, can a patient's medical records be disclosed by the hospital or a medical practitioner to the lawyers during the 'discovery' process leading to a court case? And when does a public duty for a medical doctor to disclose such records arise, and to whom should the disclosure be made?

One might be tempted to ask. Is it always the case that a patient's medical records will only be availed to his wife if the patient himself has consented to such disclosure? Let us assume that the patient is suffering from, say, a sexually transmitted disease (STD) like 'aka-swende' (syphilis). And we assume further that the patient is a married man. Should the hospital treat this patient of aka-swende without informing his wife? What if he insists that his wife 'should not know about this', can the hospital go ahead and treat him quietly without alarming his wife? What about the issue of medical ethics here? Don't ethics have a role to play? And is there any legal obligation for the patient to bring along his wife and any culpable illicit sexual partner so that they are all examined for aka-swende? These are some of the legal issues that confront the medical profession today.

Also, what happens if the nurse at the hospital attending to the aka-swende patient actually knows the man's wife? Can the nurse go around gossiping to a third-party, knowing fully well that that third-party also knows the patient's wife, about the patient's venereal disease? The public humiliation that the patient might suffer here can be very hurtful, especially if the patient is, say, a pastor, church elder or choir master. And can the patient then sue the nurse and/or the hospital if his wife decides to divorce him or walk out on him after learning of the aka-swende ailment via the gossip?

Further, let us assume that a male patient is suffering from some 'socially embarrassing' condition like erectile dysfunction, and that the patient is a community elder or a public figure. Can the medical personnel that have access to the patient's medical records go around gossiping that the said man can hardly sustain an erection, especially if the patient has been having some marital problems with his wife? Does the patient have a right to sue the hospital for breach of confidentiality, negligence and emotional pain resulting from such reckless disclosures?

What about cases where a patient undergoes medical surgery and the operation goes awfully wrong? For example, if a female patient is giving birth through cesarean delivery, but a young inexperienced medical doctor ends up cutting into the patient's bladder as well, can a court action be brought against the medical doctor and the hospital? What happens if the culpable medical doctor rudely counter-argues that, after all, he is protected by the principle of vicarious liability in tort law, and that only the hospital can be sued, but not him? What options does the patient have?

A Nigerian friend of mine in Washington DC almost sued a pharmacist after he'd ordered some over-the-counter medication for treating some light environmental allergies. It was spring time in Washington DC. And when it is spring time in the metropolitan area of Washington DC, Virginia and Maryland, the pollen count is usually high. Thus, many people end up suffering from environmental allergies which manifest themselves through symptoms like itchy eyes and sneezing. Now instead of giving him the Claritin that he'd ordered, the pharmacist handed him Viagra. It could have been my Nigerian friend's strong accent that misled the pharmacist. Anyhow, when at home, just before he took the supposedly Claritin, my Nigerian friend paused for a second, with a glass of water in his hand, to read the instructions. It was then that he realized that he had been handed Viagra. His heart sunk with fear and panic, contemplating what would have happened to him had he taken the Viagra mistakenly. He was on his knees thanking God that he had not taken that medication. Otherwise, he would have ended up in hospital in an embarrassing situation, a thing no decent man wants to find himself in.

The example provided above is no different from situations where a wrong dosage of medicine is given or administered to a patient. Forget the African herbs that have no dosage! In modern scientific medicine, the medical folks can be sued if the patient suffers resulting damage from a breach of duty by the medical doctor that provided the wrong dosage. Yes, the patient has every right to sue the medical doctor and/or hospital for negligence. And if the patient were to die, as was the case with Michael Jackson, criminal charges can be instituted against the medical doctor. The analogy here extends to situations where a wrong prescription is provided to a patient, or where a medical doctor comes up with a wrong diagnosis altogether and then provides unwarranted medical treatment to the patient leading to further medical complications.

A closely related issue here has to do with possible liability of a hospital where a patient who is critically ill, and whose life could have been saved, dies partly because he or she has not been attended to early enough by the medical practitioners. And the medical practitioners are now contending that they were too busy with other patients. Also, it is important to look into the Zambian labour laws, including the contracts of employment, regarding those medical practitioners that hardly spend much time at their place of work in government hospitals, although employed by these hospitals, but prefer to spend working time at some private clinic doing some part-time jobs. Yet these medical practitioners are paid full salaries by the government hospitals. Likewise, can a medical doctor use the institutional facilities at a government hospital where he works to treat his patients from a private clinic? What are the legal consequences of and the ethical considerations for dealing with such behviour? And are medical practitioners under any moral obligation to treat patients with such lethal diseases as AIDS or the Ebola virus?

In cases of, say, abortions, legislation in Zambia is very clear on the circumstances under which abortion is permitted legally. Otherwise, abortion is generally illegal in Zambia as stipulated under sections 151, 152 and 153 of the Penal Code. However, under section 3 of Zambia's Termination of Pregnancy Act 1972 (as amended through to 1994), the law permits the carrying out of a safe abortion in a hospital by authorised medical practitioners where, should the pregnancy continue, there would be: (a) a risk to the life of the pregnant woman; (b) a risk of injury to the physical or mental health of the pregnant woman; or, (c) a risk of injury to the physical or mental health of any existing children of the pregnant woman. A pregnancy can also be terminated lawfully where there is a substantial risk that if the child were born it would suffer from such physical or mental abnormalities as to be seriously handicapped. Other situations under which the law (see: section 152(2) of the Zambia's Penal Code) permits the carrying out of a safe abortion is where a female child is raped or defiled and becomes pregnant.

Otherwise, any abortion carried out by a medical doctor outside the ambit of the law, even if the said medical doctor is qualified to carry out such medical operation, would attract criminal sanctions and penalties. Likewise, a medical doctor is not supposed to touch a patient in a manner that raises legitimate suspicion in the mind of any reasonable person, especially if such touching does not correspond with the ailment complained of by the patient and with standard medical practice. For example, where a young and pretty female patient is complaining of a toothache, it would be ill-advised, as well as an affront to the law, for a lustful medical doctor to insist that the female patient should undress completely so that the doctor can carry out a full medical exam, including an examination of her private parts and breasts. It would make no difference here that a female nurse was present when such unwarranted intrusive examination was conducted.

In the case of medical marijuana, the medical practitioners can only prescribe it for a patient where the law explicitly provides for such. In some countries, the smoking of marijuana or ganja is legally permissible for medicinal purposes as a painkiller for certain ailments as long as the smoker has a legal permit issued by an authorized medical practitioner, and that the patient is not smoking or carrying quantities that are in excess of the prescribed amounts.

Another interesting area of the law that medical practitioners need to familiarize themselves with is 'euthanasia'. Can a medical doctor assist a patient who is terminally ill and in so much pain with a quick passage to death? In short, is the termination of life by a doctor at the request of a patient allowed under Zambian laws? The British House of Lords

Select Committee on Medical Ethics defines euthanasia as 'a deliberate intervention undertaken with the express intention of ending a life, to relieve intractable suffering'.

Under section 8(1) of Zambia's Suicide Act 1967, any person who procures another to kill himself or herself, or any person who counsels another to kill himself or herself, and thereby induces him or her to do so, as well as any person who aids another in killing himself or herself, will be guilty of a felony and be liable to imprisonment for life. Essentially, this statutory provision prohibits the carrying out of euthanasia in Zambia.

And what about patients who show up at the hospital with injuries sustained from, say, a fight, does the law in Zambia allow for such patients to be treated even if they do not have a police report on the cause of the injury? Is it good enough an excuse by the patient that the police officers were not that helpful when he went to collect a police report? A possible reason why a patient could avoid going to the police to get a police report is that the individual could be a suspected criminal who has suffered physical assault from irate and enraged members of the public, and hence the injuries on his body. Often times, such victims of instant mob justice will try to avoid reporting to the police the incidence of physical assault that they have suffered for fear of incriminating themselves. What to do now?

CHAPTER

37

FALLING IN LOVE WITH AFRICA

Africa is my place of birth. Africa gave me my parents as well as my extended family members. Further, Africa has given me a wife and my nuclear family. And Africa has given me many friends and colleagues. Yes, I have this very special connection with Africa. It remains unique to me. Africa is a love supreme. I cannot explain Africa fully to someone who has never experienced it. The love of Africa in me brings me to this article today.

It was a bright Saturday afternoon in Washington DC in the autumn of 2002. The precise date was September 14, 2002, exactly ten years ago now. The limousine for the bride and groom was parked outside the church on Pennsylvania Avenue, NW, in Washington DC, not too far away from the White House, the World Bank, the IMF, Georgetown University, and the Watergate as well as George Washington University and the Monument. Many family members and friends had travelled from places afar and near to attend the wedding and to witness the marriage vows. The eminent and opulent matron of honor had already landed from England, Coventry. The United Nations (UN), too, in New York, had already released for us the distinguished presence of a very able bestman. And our prayerful and most loving sister, the maid of honor, was at hand.

As I stood on the altar of St. Stephen's Catholic Church on Pennsylvania Avenue, NW, ready to take my marriage vows, I could see in my mind's eye that what I was about to commit myself to was very serious... I mean, "very, very serious"! It was no child's play. Indeed, marriage is more than just a simple contract. And so, my wife and I were very excited (and we still are to this day). Prior to the wedding, my wife and I had taken some marriage preparatory classes at an appointed Catholic Church in Takoma Park, Washington DC. So, those classes really helped us to get ready. And we both knew that marriage is not just a simple contract but a Holy Sacrament and Covenant involving a tripartite relationship with God, myself and my wife. Indeed, this is what marriage means. God is, and should always be, at the centre of marriage. Marriage is not something that you just wake up to when you are lonely, lustful or horny. And marriage is not something that you just abrogate as and when you feel like or when you get tired or bored. I have come to learn that even when you are flying on a plane, whether you are in First Class, Business Class or Economy, there is bound to be some turbulence at some point. But you must remain calm and focused. Do not attempt to take off your seat-belt. Stay put in that seat. Likewise, when you are sailing on a boat and suddenly there are some strong winds coming towards the boat, you don't jump off or dive into the water. You have to hang on in there until the winds are gone. Never abandon that boat, unless it is sinking.

My wife and I are today celebrating our ten years in marriage. The Christian marriage vows that I took with my wife, Dr, Judith M. Mvula-Mwenda, on that Saturday afternoon in Washington DC still stand today and ever more. Of course, there are many couples out there that have many more years in marriage than us. But every relationship is different. And that is really my point. It is not only for the love of my wife (and son) that I write this article, but also for the Good Honour and the Glory of God our Father.

A few weeks before the wedding, the celebrant priest for our wedding had made a polite request to both my wife and I that we each obtain parental consent from our respective parents before we could get married, notwithstanding that we were adults. At 33, I was not sure if I really needed to get parental consent in order for me to get married. By then, I was already working at the World Bank and had even completed my PhD and taught at many universities in Europe and elsewhere. But, here I was. I was required to get parental consent. I had to humble myself. And I did not protest. My wife, too, although she had already graduated from seven years of medical school at the University of Zambia's Ridgeway Campus (and later completed an MBA degree at the University of Leicester as well as an MPH degree at the University of Manchester), she had to get parental consent. That, we both did. And our parents gave their respective blessings and full written consents.

My wife and I had planned on having a second 'version' of the wedding in Zambia the following year (2003). At the time of the Washington DC wedding, my Dad had some old-age related health issues and thus he could not travel to Washington DC. Unfortunately, the following year, before my wife and I could travel to Zambia for the African version of the wedding, we lost my Dad. It was a very painful loss, comforted only by knowing and trusting that he is with God our Father in Heaven. A very decent and honourable man, my Dad was my most trusted confidant. He was also my greatest role model. Even when I met my wife, it was to him that I turned for advice on prospects for marriage. My Dad gave me some of the best parental advice that a God-fearing and decent parent can ever give to a son, and he continued to do so until his death in August 2003. When he fell ill this time, I had to make emergency travel plans for both my wife and I, as well as for my immediate young brother, Eugene, who is based in the UK, to fly to Zambia immediately. We lost my Dad just when my wife and I landed in Lusaka, Zambia, via South Africa.

Back to the wedding in Washington DC. After church, the bridal limousine sped off, with champagne popping and flowing inside, for a photo session at a lovely flowery park near the White

House. Thereafter, the limo cruised its way, with the wedding convoy behind, to the marina on the banks of the Potomac River in Washington DC. My wife and I had hired a large enough yacht, the Celebrity, for the wedding. And smooth jazz and other swag musical flavas were flowing in the background. You know how it is...(smile)! With the yacht came full catering service for all of our guests by a professional wedding company. And so, we were all now aboard the "Celebrity" yacht. It was at approximately 4:00pm when we sailed off, and the wedding party was on.

As we sailed on the Potomac River, one of the guests called me to the side and said: "M'dalla, zo-ona aba sungu eba-le twensha mu bwato noku tu serving'a ifya kulya na ma drinks kuno ku America! Md'alla uli mwaume sana! Nsha tala mona po... Uku ci-lisha mu Capital City ya ku America naba sungu ba dabwa!" (i.e. the guy could not believe that an African brother, especially from his native country of

Zambia could hire a whole yacht for a wedding, and have white folks serve the black folks food and drinks). But such is life. For me, personally, such prejudices never cross my mind. I am always at home wherever I am.

Some light rain-showers started pouring as a sign of African blessings, but the upper deck of the yacht was well shielded from the rain. The groove went on as the spacious yacht sailed the Potomac River, with a cool mellow breeze of love ricocheting in the air. Although it is now ten years ago, my love for Africa and all that Africa has presented me with is still fresh and strong, albeit being in the diaspora for twenty years now. Today, my wife and I celebrate our ten years in marriage, as we are joined by our loving son. And for everything, I give my deepest thanks and gratitude to God, our Father, the Almighty.

CHAPTER

38

SMOOTH JAZZ AND MY IPOD

As a jazz enthusiast, I love going to watch live smooth jazz concerts. This passion has taken me to many live concerts in the US and elsewhere, covering such top smooth jazz artists as Gerald Albright, Najee, Paul Taylor, Chuck Loeb, Boney James, Dave Koz, Kim Waters, Brian Culbertson, Richard Elliot, Walter Beasley, Keiko Matsui, Marcus Johnson, Earl Klugh, Bob James, and many more. There is just something unique about smooth jazz. A close analogy here is that of love. And throughout this article, I pursue this analogy. Just like love, you have to experience smooth jazz to know it or feel it. Otherwise, it is hard to explain the concept of smooth jazz to someone who does not pay close attention to the sentiments of such music. As they say, it is hard to explain the concept of love to someone who has never loved, or one who has never been loved.

Lately, I have been reading a bit on the philosophy of jazz, although I do not intend to bore you with an academic treatise on jazz. Many scholars have posited that New Orleans, Louisiana, is arguably the root of modern jazz, emanating from the Afro-blues of the creole sub-culture of the time. It is, however, not the purpose of this article to revisit that jazz scholarship. Suffice it to say, in a dissertation titled, "The Philosophy of Jazz", submitted in 2004 to the Department of Philosophy at Haverford College in the US, Michael Johnson contends that what has been said about jazz in philosophy – and there has been precious little – is largely reactive, which is to say dismissive or polemical.

According to Johnson, given this bias and the dearth of writings in general, it is not surprising that nobody has developed an adequate account of the project of jazz from a philosophical perspective. He argues further that what is surprising, none the less, especially considering the state of jazz in philosophy, is that outside the philosophical world – in literary criticism and musicology, for example – writings about jazz are numerous and oftentimes philosophical. Closely related to Johnson's discourse, the renowned scholar Sigmund Freud argued in 1915 that if you analyse any human emotion, no matter how far it may be removed from the sphere of sex, you are sure to discover somewhere the primal impulse, to which life owes its perpetuation. According to Freud, the primitive stages can always be re-established; the primitive mind is, in the fullest meaning of the word, imperishable. Geoff Haselhurst, an evolutionary philosopher, in an Online article (2012) titled, "Philosophy of love, sex and orgasm", argues that it is strange how little philosophers have written on Love, Sex and Orgasm, as it is clear from Evolution that Sex and Survival are the two most fundamental forces driving our continued existence.

According to Haselhurst, what it does show is how our culture, our religious beliefs, and our emotions have prevented us from writing honestly on this most profound subject. Haselhurst contends further: "I would venture to say that it is almost impossible for a human to be completely happy or healthy if they are devoid of a meaningful sexual relationship. Further, evidence suggests that where sex is actively prohibited, as within certain religions, then the sexual urge, being so strong, tends to manifest in abusive ways that cause great harm to human society. (The sexual abuse of children by priests is an obvious example of this.)."

As a discipline within the broader fields of social philosophy and ethics, the philosophy of love attempts to explain through various theories the nature of love, distinguishing between various kinds of personal love. It also asks questions such as, if and how love is or can be justified, as well as the value of love. The philosophy of love examines what impact love has on the autonomy of both the lover and the beloved. Akin to love, smooth jazz often conveys soulful emotions of love, pain and other closely related sentiments. As they say, there is a thin line between love and hate. Inherently, smooth jazz provides philosophical expositions that are equalled perhaps only by the soulful voice of such great black female vocalists as Anita Baker, Regina Belle, Patti LaBelle, Roberta Flack, Mary J. Blige, Sade, Mahalia Jackson, Lisa Fischer, Keyshia Cole, Gladys Knight, Cece Winans, Yolanda Adams, Mbilia Belle, and our very own Angela Nyirenda.

And not to leave out the male vocalists, of course, the balladeer of all balladeers, the ultimate soulful voice, Luther Vandross, remains one of a kind. Voices like that come once in a generation. There are many imitations, but few come close. In all these artists, you tend to notice a certain sense of quiet and composure as they perform. Their lyrics are never vulgar, delivering, with impeccable decorum, a great emotional and sentimental appeal of acceptable finesse and etiquette. Yet, the message gets through. These artists never panic or jump around anyhow on stage. They are in total control of the stage, and they often regulate the emotions of the audience using such great vocal and musical technique.

Likewise, the voice of the saxophone and the whisper of the jazz guitar can soothe a broken heart or blue night. Jazz creates great moments and great memories. It gives full meaning to a great night of dinner, and is a perfect companion to a fine wine. And a great jazz artist knows just that. Like an acclaimed author, a great jazz artist knows how to pitch the notes and how to improvise with an eclectic taste of rhythm and melody.

As a jazz enthusiast, I have tried to capture on my iPod an eclectic taste of smooth jazz as well as other jazz-inspired music globally. It would be good for many of our Zambian musicians to rely less on computer-generated music, and to enhance instead the role of conventional instruments and African percussion. And here the saxophone is one instrument that is often missing from much of Zambian music. Yet it is such a powerful instrument that can convey deep emotions.

A few years ago, I travelled to Zambia on holiday. As I sat in the hotel lounge listening to music on my iPod while waiting for a friend to pick me up, it was not long before my friend showed up and quickly asked what kind of music I was listening to. I smiled and asked him if he really wanted to know what type of music I was listening to. He insisted, and so I explained to him politely: "If I were to lend you this iPod for one night only, you would sire twins by the next morning!" He burst out laughing. So, I handed him my iPod so that he could sample the music for himself.

There are hundreds of carefully selected classics on my iPod, including golden oldies, smooth jazz, some mellow and fine rhumba as well as contemporary soul and R&B. He quickly picked out on an old classic by Luther Ingram, titled If Loving you is Wrong, I Don't Want to Be Right. That then took him to such other great old classics by the likes of Melba Moore and Freddie Jackson (A little bit more) and Sam Cooke (A Change is Gonna come). But what really knocked off his socks, especially that he was going through a strained relationship with his longtime girlfriend in South Africa, was when he listened closely to the various Luther Vandross assortments before catching the flavour of the lyrics on Musiq Soulchild's Teachme. He played that song over and over, and started fearing that perhaps the song was speaking to him. The lyrics went on:

"I was told the true definition of a man was to never cry... Work till you tired (yeah) got to provide (yeah)... Always be the rock for my fam, protect them by all means (and give you the things that you need, baby)...Our relationship is (suffering) trying to give you (what I never had)... You say I don't know to love you baby...Well I say show me the way... I keep my feelings (deep inside I)...Shadow them (with my pride eye)... I'm trying desperately baby just work with me... Teach me how to love... Show me the way to surrender my heart, girl I'm so lost... Teach me how to love... How I can get my emotions involved... Teach me, show me how to love... Show me the way to surrender my heart, girl I'm lost... I was always taught to be strong, never let them think you care at all... Let know one get close to me...Before (you and me)... I den' shared things wit chu girl about my past... That I'd never tell to anyone else (no)...Just keep it to myself, (yes)...Now I know I lack affection and expressing my feelings... It took me a minute to come and admit this but...See I'm really try'na (change now)... Wanna love you better, (show me how)...I'm tryin desperately baby hey...Ain't nobody ever took the time to try to teach me what (love was but you)...And I ain't never trust anyone enough to let em tell me (what to do)...Teach me how to show it and show me how to love..."

I could see tears start to build up in my friend's eyes. As a man, he tried to hold back the tears. But it was not working. The tears came running down his cheeks. He stopped the car, and began to testify about the heartache caused by the woman he loved so dearly I listened patiently, and then said to him: "Here, take my iPod with you. When you get home, try to sock yourself in the smooth jazz, while you sip some fine wine. You will feel better." Indeed, the smooth jazz was the therapy, as he called his girlfriend in South Africa the very next day. The rest is history. They are now happily married. So, smooth jazz remains a great part of the philosophy of love.

- Kenneth K. Mwenda

CHAPTER

39

DEVELOPING EFFECTIVE TEAMS
IN A WORKPLACE

Many a time, I have come across different types of
management and leadership books on how to build
effective teams in a workplace. And from the time
when I studied management at university, new
management theories have since come up and some
old ones have been revised and updated. Yet, not
many managers are in the habbit of staying on top of
things regarding contemporary updates in
management theory and practice. This article is
pitted against that background. It examines how
best to develop effective teams in a corporate set-up,
cognizant of the fact that certain incentive
structures can also have a bearing on the levels of
motivation of team members.

At the outset, we must understand first the industry
in which these teams operate as well as the nature
of the company's core business. An ideal team would
be one that has, inter alia, a well-articulated mission
and vision, with clear goals. Such characteristics of a

team are important if the team has to overcome a performance gap pertaining to some undefined roles of some team members. Indeed, the team members' roles should be clearly defined and must complement the team's missions and goals.

Many teams tend to develop through successive phases of a three-wave pattern. The initial phase could involve the leader identifying dominant trends in the market or industry, followed by a phase of identifying any counter-trend moves. Thereafter, the third stage could involve determining the maturity of a trend. Now, if, in terms of this three-wave pattern, the team's mission and business goals are at the critical stage where a leader should *take-hold of leading* the team and where he or she should *absorb as much information as possible*, so as to help the team articulate a clear mission and actionable goals, then the team's objectives should also be shared with and by the key stakeholders (*i.e.* the team members, senior management, and internal and external customers that are closely related to the team).

Further, timely, adequate and clear communication of the team's objectives as well as the roles of the team members can help to avoid some performance gaps. With a visionary leadership and a well-motivated and disciplined workforce, the team is likely to succeed. Also, a culture of unity with minimal conflicts or power-politics within the team can enhance the team's performance. However, the success of such a team-building strategy should be measured, in part, on whether or not the team has met its goals or targets. And when it comes to visionary leadership, the leader must immerse himself or herself in strategic issues facing the team in order to understand deeply the challenges and opportunities at hand. Indeed, the leader must be able to identify most of the potential big wins. To do so, the leader must spend time on analysis.

The size of the team would depend, in part, on the level at which a particular assignment is expected to be carried out and on the resources (*e.g.* human capital and financial resources) required. These factors will determine the degree or extent to which a leader can delegate tasks to some team members in order to avoid the common performance gap of non-delegation and micro-managing by a team leader. Some assignments can be carried out more efficiently and effectively through larger teams whereas others require smaller teams.

Notwithstanding arguments against sex role stereotypes, there are certain tasks or assignments that might not be *culturally* 'acceptable' to certain individuals due to the high labor intensity of the work involved. For example, in some countries, women are discouraged from engaging in heavy-duty assignments such as construction of civil works or underground mining. That said, an ideal team should encourage diversity and inclusion across gender and race. Failing to do so could lead to discriminatory practices and 'group-think'. The latter often occurs where team members become so over-protective of their own collective group-ideas such that they cannot think outside the box or accommodate dissenting views. This type of behavior is common in teams whose leader is in the habit of hiring only people of his own race or tribe, or hiring only people from a certain favoured ethnic background or gender persuasion. In many cases, group-think deprives a team of heteregenous and competitive ideas, promoting instead a monolithic culture that prevents competition, creativity and innovation. When group-think appears prevalent, a smart team leader should be able to assess not only how the project is doing, but also how the team is performing. It may well be that promoting diversity and inclusion would open up doors to attract the required skills-mix and skills-set.

For larger teams, the team leader can develop some focal groups to focuss on certain tasks or issues so that when the entire team recovenes at plenary, each focal group is given a chance to present its findings or contributions. What is important here is that the different skills-sets of the various sub-teams complement each other, and that there is trust and a common purpose towards the achievement of common goals. The leader must network across the organization so that he or she can attract to the team valuable organizational resources, including information and financial resources, as well as promote the team's agenda across the organization. Further, in terms of the three-wave pattern noted earlier, the leader should (at this stage) be engaging in *re-shaping* the team's strategy. It is not good for a team to have a leader or manager that favours certain team members over others, or one who is not easily accessible.

In the case of smaller teams, which are usually more efficient and much more effective to manage than larger teams, individual team members are expected to participate at more visible and involving levels than in larger teams. In the case of larger teams, there is some risk of some team members not putting in their best and hiding behind the efforts of other members. This free-rider problem can cause a moral harzard whereby some sections of senior management may be deceived in thinking that all team members are putting in their best when only a few individuals are driving the team's success.

Also, the issue of whether individuals should be selected into a team primarily on the basis of their technical competence or on the basis of their warm interpersonal skills (or 'political connections') often arises when setting up teams. From practical experience, it is best to strike a balance between the two to avoid some performance gaps within the team. Some individuals can be brilliant technocrats but cannot work well with others. Such individuals will sometimes have big egos that can distract team performance and get in the way of the team's mission and business goals. Then, there are also those individuals who can be really warm and nice as team members, but cannot just perform. How do you deal with such discrepancies?

Generally, most tasks in industry, except for some that require certain highly specialised skills (*e.g.* like surgeons), do not require someone to be a genius. An individual with above average competence can actually deliver on most of these corporate tasks. And if such an individual has good team skills, and he or she works well with others, it might be better to have this individual on the team than someone who comes highly recommended as a genius but is not a team-player. The latter individual is best left to work as sole practitioner – that is, if he or she cannot change or adapt.

But then, what does it take to build an ideal team? Building an ideal team will obviously involve the identification of characteristics expected of an ideal team. The team leader should communicate to the team what is expected of its members. Their roles, as noted above, should be defined, stressing also the importance of all team members committing to the organizational values. The team leader should also avoid power-distancing so that team members do not feel intimidated, ignored or alienated. If the team members begin to feel intimidated or ignored, they might start avoiding the team leader. And such reactions could lead to what is known as 'derailment'. To avoid derailment, the leader should promote within the team a culture that fosters trust among team members. And the politics of vying for power among the team members should be handled carefully to avoid watering down the existing synergies of team performance. Furthermore, to enhance the scope for innovative and creative thinking within the team, double-loop learning could be encouraged so that the team members are not confined only to skills that they already know, but can also explore new ideas.

Also, scholars such as Marks, Mathieu and Zaccaro, in an article titled, "A Temporally Based Framework and Taxonomy of Team Processes", published in the *Academy of Management Review,* 26 (3): 356–376 (2001), as well as LePine, Piccolo, Jackson and Mathieu, in an article titled, "A Meta-Analysis of Teamwork Processes: Tests of a Multidimensional Model and Relationships with Team Effectiveness Criteria", published in *Personnel Psychology* 61 (2): 273–307 (2008), highlight the importance of the following teamwork processes, namely: (a) transition processes (between periods of action) that include mission analysis, goal specification, and strategy formulation; (b) action processes (when the team attempts to accomplish its goals and objectives) that include monitoring progress toward goals, systems monitoring, team monitoring and backup behavior, and coordination; and, (c) interpersonal processes (present in both action periods and transition periods) which include conflict management, motivation and confidence building as well as affect management.

Closely related to the foregoing, Tuckman's model posits that many teams go through four main stages of team development, namely, forming, storming, norming and performing. The challenge, however, is that somewhere around the performing stage many teams tend to fall into the trap of 'group-think'. When this happens, most team members are reluctant to challenge the traditional ways of doing business, especially if the status quo reflects the team's dominant value system. But a good leader should endeavour to challenge his or her team members to come up with new and better ways of doing business. He or she should encourage the team members not to sit back and think that everything is alright. There has to be a culture of continuous learning and improvement. Often a time, effective leadership is a stimulant and catalyst to motivating teams. And to perform better, teams must be motivated.

CHAPTER

40

UNDERSTANDING
ORGANISATIONAL POLITICS

In Business School, they do not teach you how to manage or survive organizational politics. The closest they get is teaching you about corporate culture and organizational behaviour. But that is not organisational politics as such, although institutional culture is closely linked to the prevailing politics in an institution. Generally, politics is characterised by 'conflict'. And politics is everywhere around us, including at the dinner table when it comes to who should get the biggest piece of chicken at an overcrowded and competitive dinner of extended family members and dependants. Contrasted with politics, culture tells us that: 'This is the way things are done around here, young man. You can't change this place. You just have to take it or leave!'

An old friend of mine recently called me from Amatole Region in Eastern Cape, South Africa. Yes, in case you are wondering, 'Amatole' is a genuine district that stretches along the coastline of the south-eastern part of the Eastern Cape Province. As we spoke, my friend from Amatole district opened up on how his boss, a white man, has been making his life difficult at work. My friend suspected that his white boss was a racist. My friend alleged further that his boss would only promote fellow whites, while more experienced and better qualified blacks remained marginalised in junior positions. He added that when other managers asked his boss why he hardly ever promoted black people in his department, the man would claim that he could not find well-qualified and experienced black people. To help my friend, I explained to him that aside from the organizational culture prevailing at his workplace, there is also the issue of power-politics. But, how does one survive organisational politics without being bruised? Let us take a more reasoned look.

A recent international media report carried a story of how some young South African students were forced to deal with some life-threatening risks just to get a formal education by swimming across a crocodile-infested river to get to and from school every day. Titled, "Crocodile crossing for SA pupils" (Online: March 27, 2008), the BBC report provides that: "A South African village is demanding that a bridge be built across a crocodile-infested river to stop children swimming it to get to school. Students as young as seven have been making the crossing for two months since the community's boat was stolen."

Indeed, the said South African pupils have to

navigate carefully the political terrain of the crocodile-infested waters. Likewise, I explained to my friend, he too has to deal with some individuals or colleagues at work with crocodile hearts and mindsets. As the BBC observes, "…'There are about 70 households on that side of the river but there are no buses and no-one owns a car,' a Kwazulu-Natal local councillor said. To cross safely would require a 20km (12 miles) detour to get to the school. On school days, 150 children from Sahlumbe village in the heart of rural Zululand swim across the river in their underwear using rubber tyres and buckets to keep afloat and to keep their school uniforms and books dry. The older ones help the small ones who cling to the tyres. 'I worry all the time. There are dangerous animals in there, especially crocodiles,' says Thuthukani Primary School headmistress Hlengiwe Mthembu."

Likewise, there are some dangerous people in the workplace. You have to swim carefully, otherwise they will drown you. For those who have never been exposed to such risk, this is a good starting point. Although the South African kids in the above story appear not to be risk-averse, their bravery could be attributed in part to a lack of alternatives. Indeed, what else can they do? The BBC report adds: "The children, some of whom also attend Mabizela High School, often arrive tired and unable to concentrate… 'They sit in class and shiver because of the cold and they can't study well because they are worrying about how they are going to get home. 'It is very hard for them…'." Does that sound familiar with your situation at your workplace? Do you sometimes go home feeling very tired or exhausted from all the so-called 'nonsense' going on at work? Don't panic. Many others are in similar situations.

The BBC report continues: "...'Not all the children can swim so some ride on the tyres or their parents carry them across. The river is too deep for the adults to walk across and not all of them can swim,' Mr Nbatha says. It is not only children who have to face the fast-flowing Tugela River. The only hospital in the area is also situated on the far bank. In 2003 a pregnant woman battling to reach the opposite bank drowned. In 2005, two children from the same family were also taken by the river and drowned. Mr Nbatha says even the stolen boat was not safe and he wants a bridge built in the area. 'It was old and full of holes...'."

As a metaphor, does the experience of the South African children sound familiar with the situation you are faced with at your workplace? Do you feel surrounded by some crocodile-mentality infested people who are constantly trying to keep you down? As the BBC report concludes, regarding the school children that are forced to cross the crocodile-infested river: "'...It's very frustrating. You can see the school from the opposite bank but you just can't reach it.'" Likewise, my friend from Amatole district could see the various opportunities for promotion at work, but he just could not reach them! Although these lofty jobs were being advertised now and again, he still could not reach them, despite his good education and work experience. It is called organisational politics, and is sometimes fueled by issues such as bigotry, tribalism, institutional racism, gender discrimination, and egotistic and insecure bosses.

Closely related to the foregoing, it would be tempting to ask: how many prayers, tears and fears do the South African kids need to get to school through these crocodile-infested waters? And how fast should they swim in order not to be eaten up by the crocs? Likewise, how far and how long should you stay from your difficult boss or workmate? Can you afford to constantly evade or avoid him? Or should the South African kids, like your good self, just float along silently, not making any noise or sounds that could attract the beasts? In any event, can the tyres protect the kids from the crocodiles, and do the tyres mitigate the risks? Likewise, can your qualifications and work experience alone protect you from the crocodile-minded people at your workplace?

Further still, you may be thinking: just how predictable is the safety of using rubber tyres or our academic qualifications in crossing a crocodile-infested river or organisation? Can you or the kids control the risks associated with crossing such waters or is this beyond your control? Additionally, just how much information do you or the kids have on whether it is safe to swim in these crocodile-infested waters? These are just a few of the type of questions that come to mind when you are dealing with organisational politics, in addition to wanting to find out who has a hold on the power-politics in the institution, and how you can hook yourself up safely. Indeed, the more useful information you can gather about any risky scenario, the greater the probability that you can make a well-informed decision for an optimally efficient outcome. But, then, information comes at a cost. Do we have the necessary resources and tools to gather such information?

So, I explained to my friend that the situation he was faced with was rather complex. None of us could tell best which side of the river (or the company) he should be swimming in because it was hard to tell when and where the vicious crocodiles (*i.e.* his boss) would strike. That said, where someone has a 'grandfather' or 'grandmother' in an institution, that 'grand' person can help to take care of them. But, in the absence of such a father-figure or mother-figure, you are alone as an 'orphan' and are thus vulnerable to attacks by all sorts of crocodile-minded people. And that is what happened to my friend. His refusal to indulge in corporate hustling was giving him away to his crocodile-minded boss. My friend held very strong views that he should not compromise his principles, especially because corporate hustling, cronyism and patronage are all predicated on a culture of mediocrity. To some extent, my friend was right. As Charles Bukowski once said, "The problem with the world is that the intelligent people are full of doubts, while the stupid ones are full of confidence." And my friend's boss was, indeed, full of confidence. So, what to do now?

An anonymous commentator writes: "I totally identify with your friend from the 'said' region. I was brought in at work by a young and promising manager who was cleaning the house and bringing in new high potential blood. And eight (8) months later or so, she was promoted to a different facility and could only take a few closest with her, and the rest of us are now faced with newer management crocodiles fortifying their reign by surrounding themselves with incompetent people. Yep, I happen to not have a sponsor/mentor in the organization and the upward mobility prospects are virtually zero. What does one do? Exercise some patience, pay some political dues, but stay open to outside opportunities. Getting angry at the situation does not help, but taking it as a character-building 'opportunity' is a way of making lemonade from the political lemon. Better days are coming... We ain't getting any younger, though...and the clock keeps ticking...tick...tick...tick..."

Another commentator adds: "Prof, life in a workplace is difficult in most cases. I think the best of all is to be your own boss, though that has its own challenges. Some crocodile-mentality infested bosses are constantly trying to overshadow young intelligent, hardworking, and ambitious employees. I remember in 2003 when I was applying for study leave to go for my Bachelors degree studies at UNZA, the officer responsible for processing my study leave application bluntly told me that, 'You are too young to go to school. You have worked only three years in the Ministry. You young boys want to use the Ministry as a stepping stone to somewhere else. I will not clear you. Will you please leave my office so that I attend to people who have served the Ministry for twenty (20) years and above...who will not leave the Ministry because they have to wait for their pension benefits...!' Anyway, I left for UNZA without being granted study-leave."

So, as I spoke with my friend who was calling in from Amatole Region, I could tell the frustration in his voice. I tried to calm him down, pointing to an old adage: "Being strong doesn't always mean you have to fight the battle. True strength is being adult enough to walk away from the nonsense with your head held high." And therein lay the panacea to his problems. He just needed to summon his inner strength to realise his true worth.

CHAPTER

41

DEVELOPING THE LEGAL PROFESSION THROUGH MANDATORY CONTINUOUS PROFESSIONAL DEVELOPMENT (CPD) OF LAWYERS

The current debate on prospects for institutional reforms in Zambia's judiciary has become ubiquitous enough not to warrant any additional beating of the drum. Indeed, it is not the aim of this paper to add to the said debate in the manner already pontificated upon by various sources. Rather, I would like to shift the debate to focuss instead on the legal profession as a whole, and how that can affect the type of judges or lawyers that we end up with in legal practice or on the bench.

No doubt, to focuss *solely*, and most *spiritedly* so, on what is going on in the judiciary without taking a broader and systemic look at most of the critical issues outside the judiciary but within the legal profession is somewhat a short-sighted approach

- Kenneth K. Mwenda

because judges are, after all, lawyers. They were never born as judges. So, how then do we ensure that our lawyers are on top of issues especially that it is from the domain of legal practitioners that we often get our judges? In essence, the argument that I am advancing is that the problem that we are currently faced with as a nation stems from the development of the legal profession, as opposed to troublesome issues within the judiciary alone.

While the misconduct of an individual judge cannot necessarily or always be attributed to other judges or to the entire legal profession, it is also a truism that some of this misconduct stems from the way that some lawyers are nurtured in the legal profession as well as from their own personal character, including their value systems and the attendant process of socialization. For example, if many young and budding lawyers are made to think that law practice is all about living large, making fast money, driving fancy cars and dressing fashionably, they will grow up subscribing to such values. And what do you expect when they become judges? Do you expect them to transform overnight? That is why the discussion on the appointment of judges should start with the process of the professional development of lawyers in Zambia.

I propose that, to strengthen the technical skills of many lawyers as they progress in their careers, one way would be for the Law Association of Zambia to introduce some stringent guidelines and requirements that all licensed lawyers in Zambia should demonstrate what is known as Continuous

Professional Development (CPD) every three years in order for each one of them to renew or maintain his or her practicing license. The concept of CPD is used by many professions worldwide. And if a licensed professional wants to maintain his practicing license, many professional bodies require that such a person demonstrates that he or she has not just been making quick money while falling asleep on his or her office desk, but that he or she has also been sharpening and honing his or her technical skills. The argument that a lawyer has been going to court daily is not good enough. Isn't that what most lawyers do, anyhows? And aren't they supposed to be doing that, among other things? So, going to court alone is not a good argument. Also, it is not good enough that once a lawyer passes his or her Bar admission exams at ZIALE, and is thereafter admitted to the Bar, then all he or she needs to do is to ensure that he or she has money to renew the law practicing certificate or license. There has to be more than that if we have to nurture our young lawyers into technically sound and robust professionals who can meet the challenges of the twenty-first century. But, then, how does CPD work?

In setting out the regulations on CPD for licensed attorneys or Advocates, the Law Association of Zambia can insist on a mandatory requirement that every three years each licensed lawyer should demonstrate some aptitude for professional growth through, say, different intellectual dispositions. Such dispositions or endeavours could include attending or participating at conferences. And the Law Association of Zambia can assign different or varying points to different types of assignments, depending on the effort expended, the learning outcome or teaching experience involved. For example, the completion of a major degree programme such as an LLM or PhD, or the attendance by a lawyer of a recognized or professionally accredited short course, can count towards CPD. Closely related to that, valuable publications by lawyers that are of significance or relevance to the legal profession can also be given some weighting depending on the type of publication or the journal in which that publication appears. And the Law Association of Zambia can stipulate a minimum threshold of points for a lawyer to accumulate in order to renew or maintain his or her practicing license.

If, for some reason, a previously licensed lawyer is not able to show that over a period of three years from the last date of issuance or renewal of the practicing certificate or license he or she has engaged in CPD up to or above the minimum threshold, then the lawyer should not be allowed by the Law Association of Zambia to renew his or her practicing license. To put matters in context, let us assume that the acceptable CPD minimum score is 250 points. And let us assume that the publication of a scholarly article, say, in the Zambia Law Journal comprises 60 points, and that the attainment of an LLM qualification comprises 120 points while the completion of a PhD ranks at 220 points. That would mean that to recertify or renew his or her practicing license, a lawyer who completes an LLM degree programme will have to get some extra 130 points through, say, attending some workshops (30 points each) or writing some shorter articles in the Law Association of Zambia Journal (45 points each).

I am mindful, however, that some readers might be wondering: "But where has he seen such things before? Where has it ever happened?" On its website (accessed March 2013), the Law Society of South Australia observes that: "*3. The MPCD Scheme:* The Scheme requires all individual legal practitioners to complete 10 CPD units of CPD activity over the course of the CPD year as a condition of every Practising Certificate issued to an individual in South Australia."

The South Australian Law Society continues that the MPCD Scheme is mandatory because the knowledge and skills needed to practise law are dynamic. According to the South Australian Law Society, (a) Legal practitioners need to keep up with developments in the law and in legal practice; and (b) Legal practitioners need to develop and refine their skills continuously.

A further observation is made that: "All other Australian mainland jurisdictions require legal practitioners to undertake mandatory continuing professional development and this Scheme has been developed consistently with the Schemes operating in those jurisdictions. Other professions (including medicine, engineering, architecture and accounting) have recognised the importance of continuing professional development and made it mandatory for their members."

The South Australian Law Society explains its CPD program in greater detail as follows:

"Each individual legal practitioner must complete a minimum of 10 CPD units of CPD activity, including 3 Required Units, during the CPD year, which runs from 1 April to 31 March.

A CPD unit comprises:

A unit of CPD is:

(a) 1 hour of CPD activity (a) seminar, workshop, conference etc

(b) 1 hour of CPD activity (b) viewing, listening, preparing recorded material

(c) 1000 words of CPD activity (c) publishing, editing, refereeing an article

(d) 2 hours CPD activity (d) attendance at meetings etc."

Generally, it is not uncommon to find other mandatory CPD programmes for lawyers in many Commonwealth jurisdictions such as England, Scotland, India and Singapore. Thus, the introduction of CPD for licensed lawyers in Zambia will help to nurture lawyers that are constantly on top of issues.

(i) APPOINTMENT OF STATE COUNSEL: First, let us take the example of the criteria for appointing State Counsel in Zambia, as well as the qualifications of eligible individuals. Section 19 of Zambia's Legal Practitioners' Act 1973 (as amended through to 2006) provides that: *"...a person shall not be appointed as a State Counsel for Zambia unless he is qualified for appointment as a puisne Judge of the High Court"*, and that this statutory provision "...shall not apply to an appointment of the Attorney-General or Solicitor General as a State Counsel." Then, section 2 of said Legal Practitioners' Act defines a State Counsel as: "...a person who attained the rank of Queen's Counsel for the former Protectorate of Northern Rhodesia" and/or "a person admitted to the Inner Bar of Zambia."

Article 97(1) of Zambia's 1991 Constitution, as amended by the 1996 constitutional provisions, provides that a High Court judge in Zambia must hold professional qualifications specified in the Legal Practitioners Act pertaining to Bar admission, and that such individual must have held those qualifications for a total period of not less than ten (10) years. However, the said Article 97(1) does not say that the individual must have been practicing law for a law firm in Zambia for 10 years. It merely refers to the requirement for 10 years of post-Bar admission. And so, the experience gained after Bar admission could vary from one situation to another, and it could have been gained not only in Zambia but elsewhere too. And such experience need not necessarily relate to legal practice. It could be experience from academia, an investigative agency or a policy institution.

Understandably, that is why Article 97(2) of the constitution allows for the President of the Republic of Zambia or the Judicial Service Commission, as the case may be, to consider someone for appointment as High Court judge where the President or the Judicial Service Commission is satisfied that, by reason of special circumstances, the person holds one of the specified qualifications for Bar admission as set forth in the Legal Practitioners Act, and that the said person is worthy, capable and suitable to be appointed as a judge of the High Court. It is on this basis that even academicians of noteworthy can make the cut as State Counsel or as members of the judiciary. Let us take a more a reasoned look at this argument.

Whereas in the UK, a number of leading and notable senior academics have been conferred upon with the honorary title "Queen's Counsel (Hon)", and mindful that the concept of "State Counsel" in Zambia under Zambia's Legal Practitioners' Act is inspired mainly by British traditions, there is, however, no single Zambian legal scholar who has been appointed as State Counsel based primarily on his or her intellectual leadership. Why is that so?

In the UK, as noted above, it is possible for a senior and leading legal luminary to be appointed as "Queen's Counsel (Hon)" even though that individual is an academic and not practicing law. In essence, are we saying none of our Zambian legal academics are worth the honour of "State Counsel (Hon)" for all the outstanding legal scholarship that they continue to produce or have produced wherever they are?

And if our former colonial masters, the British, after whom we have copied some of these laws and practices have evolved into recognizing the merits of intellectual leadership as part of seniority in the legal profession, why are we adamant and not adapting to the changing times? Does one have to be a legal practitioner always in order to be appointed as State Counsel? Certainly not! That is not the meaning of section 19 of Zambia's Legal Practitioners' Act. Under that statutory provision, all that is required is that the individual '...is qualified for appointment as a puisne Judge of the High Court.' In fact, this very statutory provision does not even require a person to be practicing law in Zambia or elsewhere, or that the individual has renewed his membership with a professional body.

As noted above, the sole requirement under section 19 of Zambia's Legal Practitioners' Act is that the individual should be qualified for appointment as a puisne Judge of the High Court. That's all. So, are we prepared to think outside the box and to move developments in the legal profession to internationally acceptable standards?

It is important that the individuals that we confer upon such honour are distinguished and internationally respected professionals. Otherwise, it dilutes the whole meaning of the title of "State Counsel". And this is where evidence of CPD and leading technical competence comes in when the relevant authorities have to make a determination.

(ii) THE APPOINTMENT OF HIGH COURT AND SUPREME COURT JUDGES: Secondly, mindful that there are many attributes that make a good judge, CPD can also give some probable indications on the likely individuals to make the cut as competent judges technically. In Zambia, like elsewhere, the bench should not, and cannot, be an exclusive sanctuary of former legal practitioners only. There has to be a fine blend between top-notch legal practitioners and outstanding legal scholars. Indeed, the latter bring with them intellectual weight and gravitas that some judges with solely a practitioner-background may not necessarily possess.

The USA, for example, has adopted such a blending practice, especially at the Federal Supreme Court level. Kenya (especially recently), Ghana and Nigeria have also traveled that road successfully. In Zambia, there have been some very modest attempts at the High Court level. But I will not mention names here. Suffice it to say, we can learn from the more grounded experiences of the US, UK, Ghana, Kenya (especially recently) and Nigeria, among other countries, in the type of people that are appointed to the bench. For example, President Obama's last pick for the Supreme Court bench came from Harvard Law School. And in jurisdictions such as the US and the UK, some judges even write serious academic articles in prestigious law journals. These are issues that we should be looking at, among many other qualities in a judge, in strengthening the efficiency of the justice system in Zambia. Otherwise we won't be able to steer the ship in the right direction if our people continue to discount the role of intellectual leadership in the development and effectiveness of the legal profession.

CHAPTER

42

TO LEGALISE OR NOT TO
LEGALISE THE PROFESSION OF
PROSTITUTION

It is the oldest profession in the world, and predates even the evolution of the legal, medical and accounting professions. It is commonly known as 'prostitution', though recently it has acquired some gender-advocacy inspired euphemisms through synonyms such as 'sex work'. At the outset, it must be pointed that I will examine in this paper the legal aspects of the profession of prostitution as it relates to adults, and not to children. I received an email not too long ago from one of the readers of the *Zambia Daily Mail*, imploring me to address a topical issue, namely, the legal aspects of the profession of prostitution in Zambia. The reader, who I will call Mr. X so as to protect his identity, wrote: "I find most of your pieces interesting and highly educative. How about writing something about sex workers who are demanding that their activities be legalised? Recently, there has been a silent cry from such people in Zambia saying that their rights should be enshrined in the constitution. As usual, theirs is a silent voice, and the few comments that have come through from some quarters are all negative."

According to Mr. X, "The main argument from these women is that it is unfair for them to be rounded up by the police for 'shishita' because there is rarely evidence of them being in prostitution (ati kawalala ni pa kuboko). It is like the law on prostitution is not clear enough." Mr. X continues, "Most of these girls (women) argue that sex work is their only livelihood, and they will cite vulnerable backgrounds such as being widowed, divorced, or orphaned. Sex work seems to be their only answer."

Mr. X notes further that another viewpoint advanced by those that want to see prostitution legalised is that sex work plays a leading role in the tourism industry, and that it is an earner of foreign exchange. But what is 'sex work' really? In this era of euphemisms, 'sex work' can hardly be distinguished from 'prostitution'. It is like telling someone not to say that a particular Mr. John was in prison or jail, but rather that he was simply incarcerated. The word 'incarcerated', I am told, sounds better and more sophisticated than 'prison'. Likewise, very few Zambian elites would want to admit, when found entangled in a physical fight with an adversary, that they were actually involved in a fight. They would rather call it a simple 'altercation', making it sound more civilised than a brutal fight involving bare knuckles.

Against this background, I will use the term 'prostitution' as a synonym of 'sex work'. The Merriam-Webster Dictionary defines prostitution as 'the act or practice of engaging in promiscuous sexual relations especially for money.' Although the Penal Code of Zambia does not define the term 'prostitution', section 146(1) of that statute, as amended by Act No. 15 of 2005, provides that, "A person who – (a) knowingly lives wholly or in part on the earnings of prostitution; or (b) in any public place, persistently solicits or importunes for immoral purposes; commits a felony and is liable, upon conviction, to imprisonment..." In essence, section 146(1) makes it a criminal offence to carry out the profession of prostitution in Zambia, notwithstanding the semantics that could arise in the legal interpretation of the phrase 'knowingly lives wholly or in part'. Indeed, what is 'knowingly', and how can we prove it? Suffice it to say there is a lot of case law on the criminal law definition of the term 'knowingly'.

Section 146(2) of the Zambian Penal adds that where a person is proved to live with or to be habitually in the company of a prostitute or is proved to have exercised control, direction or influence over the movements of a prostitute in such a manner as to show that the person is aiding, abetting or compelling the prostitution with any other person, or generally, that person will be deemed, unless the person satisfies a court of law to the contrary, to be knowingly living on the earnings of prostitution. In essence, section 146(2) entails that, if, say, a prostitute is keeping up with, or is being looked after by, her elderly parents, then they will be held liable for 'living with' a prostitute even if they are not compelling her to engage in prostitution. It is an offence to keep a prostitute in your home or to be habitually seen in her company, whether or not she is your relative. Here, the law requires you to 'discriminate', sad as it may seem, against any prostitute. What a law!

Further still, section 146(2) of the Zambian Penal Code, when read together with section 147(1), as discussed below, criminalises the pimping of a prostitute. If, say, a police officer or a security guard is seen to be providing security for a prostitute at night while she is busy servicing her male customers, with the hope of getting some sexual 'bonuses' from the prostitute at the end of the day, the culpable police officer or security guard will be deemed to have committed an offence if it is proved that he was aiding, abetting or compelling the prostitute to engage in or to carry on with prostitution.

As noted above, section 147(1) of the Penal Code establishes the offence of a pimp living off proceeds of crime through pimping. An individual who knowingly lives wholly or in part on the earnings of prostitution of another person, or who is proved to have, for the purpose of gain, exercised control, direction or influence over the movements of a prostitute in such a manner as to show that that individual is aiding, abetting or compelling the prostitute to provide services of prostitution to anyone, will be deemed to have committed a felony and will be liable, upon conviction, to imprisonment. This offence can trigger a secondary offence of money laundering under the Prohibition and Prevention of Money Laundering Act 2001. And that brings on board the Forfeiture of Proceeds of Crime Act 2010 to recover moneys earned through pimping. This means that a pimp can actually be arrested and charged for the offence of money laundering if he is seen to be profiting from proceeds of crime through pimping prostitutes.

Closely related to the foregoing, the idea of some guest houses in Zambia serving as brothels of some sort is likely to offend section 149 of the Penal Code. The said statutory provision mandates that any person who keeps a house, room, set of rooms or a place of any kind for purposes of prostitution will be deemed to have committed a felony and is liable, upon conviction, to imprisonment. In essence, section 149 prohibits the operation of brothels in Zambia. And section 148 complements section 149 by providing that if it appears to a magistrate, by information on oath, that there is reason to suspect that a house or any part of it is being used by a woman for purposes of prostitution, and that a person residing in or frequenting the house is knowingly living wholly or in part on the earnings of the prostitute, or is exercising control, direction or influence over the movements of the prostitute, the magistrate can issue a warrant authorising a police officer to enter and search the house as well as to arrest such a person.

Now, given the increasing calls by some quarters in Zambia to legalise prostitution, is it possible to have sex workers' rights enshrined in the Constitution? If so, what are these rights? And should sex workers be required to obtain a practicing license from the State in order for them to operate legally? Also, should they be required to undergo mandatory blood tests?

It could be argued that while the current criminalisation of sex work or prostitution in Zambia is not unconstitutional, as it does not infringe upon the existing constitutional rights enshrined in the Constitution or the rights promulgated through human rights treaties ratified or acceded to by Zambia, the Zambian Parliament is at liberty to debate and determine whether sex work should be legalised and elevated to a constitutional level as a human right.

Be that as it may, with the declaration of Zambia as a Christian nation, as evidenced in the preamble of the 1996 Constitution, it is highly unlikely that the Zambian Parliament would be swayed into elevating sex work or prostitution to a constitutional pedigree of human rights. And if that be the case, then the question of licenses and blood tests also falls away. Indeed, only when sex work has been legalised can we go into secondary issues of whether or not sex workers need to get licensed or to undergo blood tests. But Mr. X insists: "...a number of guesthouses have sprouted around the townships raising suspicions of brothels. This is what's making sex workers to say, 'Look, this is for real. Let's not pretend that these things are not happening. Give us rights that will protect us from police harassment and gender based violence so that we have the freedom to operate freely....'."

Admittedly, in some States, such as the State of Nevada in the US, prostitution is legal, although it is regulated. It has also been reported that elsewhere, in such countries as Argentina, Austria, Belgium, Belize, Benin, Bolivia, Brazil, Burkina Faso, Cape Verde, Central African Republic, Colombia, Costa Rica, Cote d'Ivoire, Cyprus, Czech Republic, Denmark, Dominican Republic, Finland, France, Germany, Italy, Lebanon, Netherlands, Poland, Portugal and Senegal, prostitution is thriving without much legal constraint. But can Zambia do the same? It would require a major paradigm shift, notwithstanding the good argument that: 'Look, this is for real. Let's not pretend that these things are not happening.' Many people in Zambia, especially the outspoken merchants of morals, would rather pretend that nothing of that sort ever happens, notwithstanding that some of them could be regular patrons of guest houses.

CHAPTER

43

DEMYSTIFYING THE DIATRIBE AGAINST FOREIGN AID

Quite often, developing countries are recipients of donor funds from developed nations. Sometimes, donor funds are earmarked for budget support or to strengthen poverty reduction programs that are being supported by some multilateral development bank or international financial institution. Donor funds, therefore, are a constituent element of the broader framework of foreign aid. But, then, there has been so much hullaballoo on the issue of foreign aid to Africa, whereby some skeptics have strongly challenged the relevance and usefulness of foreign aid to African countries. It is, however, not the purpose of this paper to revive such debates or to indulge in the polemics related to the same.

Suffice it to say, Sandra F. Joireman, in an Online article titled, "Still Hungry!", and dated December 29, 2009, puts it succinctly: "Zambian economist Dambisa Moyo has attracted a lot of publicity for her proposal, in *Dead Aid*, that foreign assistance to

Africa should be cut off completely. Instead of taking foreign aid, she says, governments should seek money through the international financial markets, pursue ties with China, press for freer trade in agricultural commodities and develop microfinance institutions. Aid is harmful to Africa, Moyo claims; it not only fails to alleviate poverty, it causes poverty: 'Millions in Africa are poorer today because of aid; misery and poverty have not ended but have increased. Aid has been, and continues to be, an unmitigated political, economic and humanitarian disaster for most parts of the developing world.' Because regular people are not benefiting from aid, she says, they will not suffer from its cessation."

In her rebuttal, Joireman continues: "The contention that foreign aid does not alleviate poverty is not terribly controversial. Scholars and policy makers have been discussing the problem for well over a decade. But Moyo takes the argument a step further by suggesting that aid causes poverty. This assertion sets a high threshold for proof—which this book, targeted at a popular audience, does not provide. Moyo's argument pertains only to what she calls systemic aid: government aid and development banks' direct transfers to governments. This narrowed definition of foreign aid allows her to discount assistance that goes from governments to nongovernmental organizations (NGOs)."

Closely related to Joireman's rebuttal, other voices have added their protest against the notion that foreign aid to Africa should be discontinued. For example, Sachs and McArthur, in an article in the

Huntington Post, titled, "Moyo's confused attack on aid for Africa," published on May 27, 2009, observe that: "Ms. Dambisa Moyo's recent Huffington Post article exposes the confusions that underlie her slashing attacks on aid. Most importantly, she seems to believe that sub-Saharan Africa was economically prosperous and then was pushed into poverty by aid."

According to Sachs and McArthur, "She makes the following statement: 'No surprise, then, that Africa is on the whole worse off today than it was 40 years ago. For example in the 1970's less than 10 percent of Africa's population lived in dire poverty – today over 70 percent of sub-Saharan Africa lives on less than US$2 a day'. Let's parse that statement for a moment. World Bank researchers Shaohua Chen and Martin Ravallion prepare the benchmark under-$2-a-day historical headcount data going back to 1981. According to their figures, headcount poverty under $2 a day was 74 percent of the population in sub-Saharan Africa in 1981 and 73 percent in 2005. Other prominent estimates that go back to 1950 or 1970 also contradict Moyo's statement, by showing high and persistent poverty. All of the macroeconomic time series by Maddison, Summers and Heston, and others tell the same story: the majority of Africa's population started out impoverished at the time of national independence in the 1960s and 1970s, and a majority remains impoverished till today."

Closely related to Sachs' and McArthur's thesis on foreign aid, Barder, in an Online article titled, "Yet another review of 'Dead Aid' by Dambisa Moyo", and dated, March 31, 2009, observes that while Moyo's book, *Dead Aid*, is about some important questions, it makes no useful contribution to the debate. According to Barder, Moyo's arguments and her use of evidence are at best lazy, and at worst mendacious. Even more scathing is the critique from Bunting in an article titled, "The road to ruin", published in the Guardian on February 14, 2009: "The danger is that this book will get more attention than it deserves. It has become fashionable to attack aid to Africa; an overdose of celebrity lobbying and compassion fatigue have prompted harsh critiques of what exactly aid has achieved in the past 50 years. Not all of the criticism has been unjustified – $300bn of aid has gone to Africa since 1970, yet average incomes across much of the continent have stagnated or fallen. *Dead Aid* offers a disastrous history of how aid was used as a tool of the cold war."

Bunting continues, arguing that this kind of analysis (much of which is now only of historical relevance) provides ammunition for those who are skeptical of international responsibilities and always keen to keep charity at home. According to Bunting, Moyo's book is 'an erratic, breathless sweep through aid history and current policy options for Africa, sprinkled with the odd statistic.' Bunting posits that there are so many generalizations in Moyo's book that skid over decades of history, such frequent pre-emptory glib conclusions, that it is likely to leave you dizzy with silent protest. Pitted against these criticisms, the wholesome condemnation of foreign aid to Africa seems to be somewhat misconceived. Taken in its wider context, foreign aid has included programs of capacity-building in Africa, as well as the provision of academic scholarships and fellowships for graduate training abroad, including the provision of funds to support and sustain crippled health sectors in many developing countries.

It is, therefore, our humble contention that a missing link in the development puzzle that confronts Africa today lies not in stopping foreign aid to Africa, but rather in improving the soundness of the governance systems as well as in strengthening the robustness of anti-corruption initiatives. And for such efforts to succeed and bolster, not only should a country's macro-economic conditions be right, but there also has to be the necessary political will from the State as well as the effectiveness of government leadership. If much of Africa can get these institutional and structural fundamentals right, that could help the continent to monitor and supervise effectively the administration of foreign aid, while not abandoning altogether the underlying quest for economic growth and independence. It is, therefore, not entirely correct to assume that foreign aid will necessarily bring about wrong incentives that could wilt the political will of the State to stimulate a country's economic growth. With sound and robust governance systems in place, the reverse is actually possible. Foreign aid, especially where capital markets and financial markets are weak, underdeveloped or almost nonexistent, can provide an alternative stimulus to sustainable economic growth.

CHAPTER
44

DEBUNKING STEREOTYPES IN A QUEST FOR OBJECTIVITY

Whereas the disciplines of psychology and sociology offer some helpful insights into the meaning of the term 'stereotype', the discipline of philosophy underlies the belly of the social sciences in directing our inquiry into the realms of 'objectivity'. The nexus here is not only fascinating, but also an illuminating intellectual discourse among and between the disciplines.

Generally, there are many forms of stereotypes, including sex-role stereotypes and those regarding racial prejudice. Dictionary.com defines the term 'stereotype' as a simplified and standardized conception or image invested with special meaning and held in common by members of a group. The term 'stereotype' is also understood as a conventional, formulaic, and oversimplified conception, opinion, or image of or about someone or a group of people. A stereotype is thus regarded as embodying or conforming to a set image or type. And stereotypes, generally, are an affront to objectivity. They are stupefied in subjectivity as an anti-thesis of objectivity. Sometimes, stereotypes can grow out of rumours, propaganda or lies that are repeated all too often. Legend has it that the great philosopher, Socrates, once confronted the issue of rumours in the following manner.

One day, Socrates met an acquaintance who ran up to him excitedly and said: "Socrates, do you know what I just heard about one of your students...?"

"Wait a moment," Socrates replied. "Before you tell me, I'd like you to pass a little test. It's called the Test of Three."

"Test of Three?" asked Socrates' acquaintance.

"That's correct," Socrates continued. "Before you talk to me about my student let's take a moment to test what you're going to say. The first test is *Truth*. Have you made absolutely sure that what you are about to tell me is true?"

"No," the man replied, "actually I just heard about it."

"All right," said Socrates. "So you don't really know if it's true or not. Now let's try the second test, the test of *Goodness*. Is what you are about to tell me about my student something good?"

"No, on the contrary..."

"So," Socrates continued, "you want to tell me something bad about him even though you're not certain it's true?"

The man shrugged, a little embarrassed.

Socrates continued, "You may still pass though because there is a third test – the filter of *Usefulness*. Is what you want to tell me about my student going to be useful to me?"

"No, not really..."

"Well," concluded Socrates, "if what you want to tell me is neither *True* nor *Good* nor even *Useful*, why tell it to me at all?"

The man was defeated, felt ashamed and said no more. This legend, it has been argued, is one of the reasons why Socrates was considered such a great philosopher. Now, it is not the purpose of this paper to deliver an academic lecture. Rather, the purpose of the paper is to breakdown the relevant concepts by communicating through some erudite but easily discernible practical illustrations.

A Nigerian friend of mind invited me to a cocktail party at his mansion in the affluent neighbourhood of Potomac, Maryland, USA. It was a lavish party, with many elites and wannabes in attendance. The event was punctuated with an abundance of all manner of aristocracy and elitism. Expensive wine and champagne was flowing. And jazz and classical music in the background was setting the stage. One could hear people conversing about different places they've been to and what they own, or where they studied. It was a snobbish environment, quite alright. My friend studied at Harvard. And his Dad went to Oxford. His wife is Princeton and Stanford educated. Well, there I was in the midst of all this splendour and pomp. I sat next to a group of Nigerian, Kenyan, Ugandan and Cameroonian guys.

As the evening drew on, one Nigerian guy in the group, who had driven in from New York, was overheard explaining to the host in an audibly loud and confident voice: "Oh, Oga, I bought the new Lexoz, ooo". As he spoke in his thick native accent, he was at the same time pacing around confidently and swinging the Lexus car-keys in his right hand for all to see. The host smiled, and retorted: "It's not 'LEXOZ'...! It's 'LEXUS'...!" Everyone around burst out laughing, but that did not deter the Nigerian man from New York. He rebutted confidently and spiritedly: "Ahhh, Oga, you have deee (the) pronunciation, but I have deee car!" That left us all in stitches with laughter. What a man! He was back on his feet. He refused to be outdone, notwithstanding his thick accent. When I later asked the host who the guy was, I was told that: "Oh, don't mind him. He talks big all the time. He is an Igbo man. These, our Igbos brothers, they are like that! We are used to them. For us Yorubas, we don't brag that much...even if I have my Harvard degree." And standing right next to me was a Kenyan guy. He quickly chipped in with his Kenyan accent: "Ahhh, this is now a saaacus (circus)! Faaast (first) of all, let me see. You mean that the Igbos are like the Kikuyus in my country?" To which we all turned and asked for an elaboration. Then, the Kenyan guy went on: "You see, the Kikuyus love money too much. But, us, the Luos, we used to be most educated among the Kenyan people." Hearing that, a Cameroonian chipped in: "Just like the Bamileke in my country. They are like the closest cousins of the Igbos in Nigeria. And the two share some common ancestral background especially that their villages are close to one another on the border areas between Nigeria and Cameroon."

The Ugandan guy and I were the only two in the group who did not push any stereotypes about our native country, although I could tell that, like the Kenyan guy, the Ugandan also spoke with the "saaacus" accent from East Africa. Likewise, in South Africa, Botswana, Lesotho and Swaziland, you need not get freightened when you are invited to eat a "snake" because they actually mean a "snack". So, the pronunciation of the word "Lexus" as "Lexoz", or the word "circus" as "saaacus", was not strange to me. After all, even in Zambia, the name "Mwanza" from Zambia's Eastern Province is often mispronounced as "Mwansa" by many natives of Luapula and Northern Provinces. And so it is with the simple English expression of, "And me...", often mispronounced in some parts of Zambia's Southern Province as "Andiii mhhh-eee". But both these linguistic presentations mean the same thing.

Turning back to the issue of stereotypes, I remember as a young adult growing up in Zambia how I would hear about different stereotypes concerning people from this tribe or the other. It was not uncommon to hear things like: "Never marry a woman from that tribe. They are not strong morally, and they usually cheat on their husbands."A friend of mine from Kenya expressed similar views about some women from a particular Kenyan tribe whose name I will not mention. But such stereotypes are merely generalizations predicated mainly on some form of inductive reasoning. In Zambia, it is not uncommon to hear things like: "Men from that tribe like marrying many wives. They are usually polygamists. And men from that other tribe can be alcoholics! They drink a lot." And so, the stereotypes would go on and on. Some would contend fiercely that never marry a woman from that tribe because those people are too tribal in their dealings, and that they only accept people from their traditional cousinship tribe. Others would argue that: "Men from that tribe are like accountants...they are so stingy! They can have several herds of cows, but will not sell any to pay for their children's school fees. They would rather be seated and drinking their local beers while counting the numbers of animals even if it means their children not going to school."

A few years ago, I recall meeting some Zambian colleagues in London. One of them asked me: "This name, 'Mwenda',...which part of Zambia are you from?" I smiled and explained to the elderly man: "That name is perhaps one of the few internationally recognized names from the African continent because you will find it in almost all the ten (10) provinces of Zambia, as well as in almost all the neighbouring countries of Zambia, extending even to places as far as Uganda and Kenya." The man marvelled. And he looked perplexed. I did not want him to associate me with any tribal tag. So, I kept him guessing. The problem is that when you are associated with a tribal tag, stereotypes by some people immediately creep in. So, I am glad that my surname does not give me away easily, not even among some people from the neighbouring countries.

As noted above, stereotypes come in various forms. Sometimes, you meet people who will not support the aspirations of a friend or colleague to ascend to a particular station in life simply because of that aspirant's gender. They will say things like: "Ahhh, voting for a woman? I would rather vote for someone else!" Even some women do advance such sex-role stereotypes against fellow women, making it clear that they would rather vote for a man. But I do not profess to be a psychologist or sociologist to explain why such behaviour occurs. Suffice it to say, the underlying process of socialization and the attendant sociology of knowledge to which such people have been exposed makes them think that a male boss, for example, would do better than a fellow female boss. Sometimes, these cynical people fear that they will not be able to use their power of female attractiveness to get their way around if they are to deal with a fellow female as their boss. They would rather have a male boss who is easily excited with the presence of a beautiful lady at the office, even if there is no intimate relationship involved.

Closely related to the foregoing, in cultures that have a strong affinity towards patriarchical structures, a good number of male chauvinists resent or loathe the idea of reporting to a female boss, especially if that female is younger than them. It's a serious cultural problem whose solution lies partly in marshalling a paradigm shift. Yes, we live in a world of stereotypes. For example, when Zambia won the continental Africa Cup of Nations Soccer tournament this year, a good friend of mine from West Africa put it so nicely: "My brada (brother), deee big boys were not deya (there)! If Nigeria and Cameroon where deya, den (then) Zambia would not win!" But surely, why were Nigeria and Cameroon not deya at the finals? Is it not because they could not make the cut? Such is the problem with stereotypes. And it is not true that Nigeria and Cameroon are the big boys of African soccer. In any event, Zambia is now the biggest boy.

A Zambian PhD student based in California made me laugh the other day. He called me panicking after he had been speaking with a friend of his in Zambia. He told me that his friend in Zambia said that: "Man, mulee chula fye uko ku States! Uka bwele fye, md'ala. Kuno bonse ama guys naba kula ama mansion, mdala" (i.e. You guys are just wasting your time out there in the USA. Just come back to Zambia. We are all doing so well here, and we have even built mansions). The California-based Zambian guy felt like abandoning his PhD studies, especially after his friend told him that, "You cannot eat a PhD! You need to make money!" I had to calm down the California-based guy, advising him that, "Son, be careful. Don't be fooled. There are many people out there who like to talk big. Even if your friend has built the so-called mansions or he is driving a Hummer or Lexus, so what? Is that all there is to life? You need to understand what makes you happy. Do not let someone define your agenda. For example, you will be getting your PhD soon, yet your friend doesn't have one. And he may never ever get one. Do you see my point? What he has, you may not have. But equally, what you have, he may never have. So, don't panic unnecessarily. Besides, it could be mainly inkongole (loans) that your friend is bragging about. So, just relax and take it easy. Don't uku-tina! It is like a dark-skinned Francophone African man who hero-worships being French, and thinks that by speaking French so well or acquiring a French passport then he will have mutated into a white Frenchman, but only to encounter extreme racism on the streets of Paris! Do not be swayed by value-ladden propositions, stereotypes, rumours or cajoleries. Instead, you should seek objectivity!"

CHAPTER

45

FOREIGN CURRENCY PAYMENTS MADE WITHIN ZAMBIA CONSTITUTE ILLEGAL TENDER OF PAYMENT OF MONEY

Some landlords in Zambia are in the habit of demanding that rental payments should be made in US dollars. It is also alleged that some of the chief executive officers in some major parastatal companies and those in certain private sector companies are paid salaries and/or allowances in US dollars. But are such payments permissible under the Zambian law? Closely related to the foregoing, some lawyers in Zambia are reported to be in the habit of charging legal fees in US dollars, especially when they are dealing with a wealthy client such as some local politician who could have amassed wealth dubiously, or when they are dealing with a client who is a foreign investor. But are demands that legal fees be paid in US dollars permissible under the law? Some Zambian hotels too are said to be in the habit of occasionally accepting US dollar payments. But what does the law say in Zambia?

- Kenneth K. Mwenda

At the time of going to the press for the publication of this book, the Zambian monetary currency, the Kwacha, had just been rebased. Also, the country's Minister of Finance had promulgated earlier Statutory Instrument No. 33 of 2012 to ensure that all manner of foreign currency are not used in Zambia as a tender of payment. Later, the Minister backtracked and revoked Statutory Instrument No. 33 of 2012. Today, a debate is looming for the reintroduction of Statutory Instrument No. 33 of 2012 to ensure that the Zambian Kwacha remains the only recognized currency to serve as legal tender of payment in the country. In this chapter, we will proceed as though Statutory Instrument No. 33 of 2012 continues to be in force in order to understand and appreciate the extent of the contentious legal reforms should Statutory Instrument No. 33 of 2012 be reintroduced.

Against this background, unlike some neighboring countries that permit the use of different types of currencies as forms of legal tender of payment of money, section 33(1) of the Bank of Zambia Act 1996 permits only the use of the Zambian Kwacha and Ngwee as the legal tender of payment of money in the country. This is so notwithstanding any spirited economic arguments about the international convertibility of certain currencies such as the US dollar and the British Pound Sterling.

Further, section 33(1) of the Bank of Zambia Act 1996 is now reinforced by section 3 of the Bank of Zambia (Currency) Regulations 2012. The said 2012 regulations were promulgated by the Minister of Finance on May 7, 2012, as Statutory Instrument No. 33 of 2012. The promulgation of these currency regulations followed extensive internal debate within the Bank of Zambia. Prior to that, the Bank of Zambia had engaged many stakeholders to discuss the issue. Although the Bank of Zambia finally recommended to the Minister of Finance that some exceptions should be allowed for tourism institutions to tender or accept the payment of money in foreign currency, the Minister turned down these views. And so, there are no exceptions allowed for under the Bank of Zambia (Currency) Regulations 2012.

Although the US dollar, the British Pound Sterling and the South African Rand are strong currencies, the sole legal tender of payment of money in Zambia is the Zambian Kwacha and Ngwee. This view explains why money-remittance agencies in Zambia should only pay out to a recipient of funds in Zambia the US dollar equivalent in Zambian Kwacha even though the money remitted could have originated in US dollars (see, for example, sections 3, 4 and 6 of the Bank of Zambia (Currency) Regulations 2012; and see also generally, Bank of Zambia (Foreign Currency) Regulations (Statutory Instrument No. 44 of 1994, and Statutory Instrument No. 190 of 1996)).

As the Bank of Zambia observes in a communiqué issued by the Head of its Public Relations Department on June 14, 2012, clarifying the implications of the Bank of Zambia (Currency) Regulations 2012,

---

- Kenneth K. Mwenda

"The Zambian economy experienced distortions from the mid-1990's following the liberalization of the economy in general and the financial sector in particular. One of the distortions was in currency management, where there was excessive demand for foreign currency arising in part from the need to settle purely domestic transactions in foreign currency. A number of entities began to quote and demand to be paid in foreign currency for goods and services produced within Zambia. Payment in foreign currency for domestic transactions poses several challenges for economic management, including the effectiveness of monetary policy implementation."

The Bank of Zambia contends further that the promulgation of the Bank of Zambia (Currency) Regulations 2012 should not be mistaken for or misunderstood as an attempt to reintroduce foreign exchange controls in the country. By contrast, as the Bank of Zambia postulates, the trading of foreign exchange in Zambia will continue to be undertaken through commercial banks and bureaux de change.

But can a commercial bank in Zambia open locally a US dollar bank account for any of its bank clients? As long as such a foreign currency account is not being used to make US dollars payments within Zambia, it would appear that the law will not frown upon such banking practice. However, some critics might be wondering what would happen when it comes to payments in Zambia for intra-regional or cross-border international trade transactions. As long as such foreign-originating payments are being cashed out in Zambia, notwithstanding that the money transfer could have been wired in US dollars and to a US dollar bank account in Zambia, the actual over-the-counter payment should appear in Zambian Kwacha. This argument is in line with section 4(2) of the Bank of Zambia (Currency) Regulations 2012 as well as with the communiqué issued by the Bank of Zambia's Head of Public Relations. That said, the Zambian bank account can remain as a US dollar denominated bank account. Here, we should distinguish transactions such as the one described above from situations were an individual goes specifically to purchase foreign currency at a local commercial bank.

What about customs officers at, say, Chirundu Border post or Kenneth Kaunda International Airport? Should they be allowed to ask travellers to make customs payment in US dollars? Indeed, what is the legal tender of payment of money in Zambia? Here, provision should be made for a nearby bureau de change or bank to make the Zambian Kwacha available for the purposes of customs fees. As a general rule, section 33(1) of the Bank of Zambia Act 1996 and section 3 of the Bank of Zambia (Currency) Regulations 2012 both provide that a tender of payment of money will only be treated as legal tender in Zambia if it is in notes or coins made and issued by the Bank of Zambia. It is important to reiterate that the notes or coins must be made and issued by the Bank of Zambia. In making and issuing these notes or coins, the Bank of Zambia can, if it wishes, sub-contract a company to print on its behalf the said notes or coins. In essence, these notes or coins will still be considered to have been made and issued by the Bank of Zambia since the printing agent was only acting on behalf of the principal, the Bank of Zambia.

Now, what type of notes and coins can the Bank of Zambia make and issue? Section 29(1) and (2) of the Bank of Zambia Act 1996 stipulates that 'The units of currency of the Republic is the Kwacha (abbreviated as K)', and that 'The denominations of money in the currency of the Republic are the Kwacha and the ngwee (abbreviated as N or as n)'. Read together, these two statutory provisions, sections 33 and 29, remain closely aligned to section 3 of the Bank of Zambia (Currency) Regulations 2012, establishing the Bank of Zambia as the sole competent authority in the country to make and issue Zambian legal tender. And, as noted above, the Zambian legal tender of payment of money is the Kwacha and the Ngwee. Indeed, section 30(1) of the Bank of Zambia makes it a criminal offence for any person, other than the Bank of Zambia, to issue in Zambia notes or coins (or other documents or token) which are payable to bearer on demand or purport to be the currency of the Republic of Zambia or the currency of any other country.

Although the latter part of section 33(1) of the Bank of Zambia Act 1996 stipulates that 'Provided that the Minister may by regulation make restrictions as to any particular maximum amount considered as legal tender' (as is now the case under section 3(b) of the Bank of Zambia (Currency) Regulations 2012, regarding the maximum value of coins that can be considered as legal tender), such a proviso does not mean that the landlord or lawyer in Zambia should now start demanding payments in US dollars if the amount to be paid exceeds the statutory mandated maximum for coins. Indeed, such a demand from the landlord would be against the law. The only recognized legal tender of payment of money under the Bank of Zambia Act 1996 and under the Bank of Zambia (Currency) Regulations 2012 is the Zambian Kwacha and Ngwee. So, what happens when a landlord, lawyer or some hotel folks insist that payment should be in US dollars, especially during times when the value of the Zambian Kwacha is fluctuating or depreciating?

Such forms of hedging against exchange rate risks are not allowed under the Zambian law. Even the Zambian Rent Act 1972 (as amended through to 1994) does not provide for rentals to be paid in a foreign currency. So, what to do now since the landlord wants all the rental payments in US dollars? Is it good enough to say, for example, that 'awee, pantu ba lawyer ba-landile ati mufwile fye mwa lipila mu ma dollars'? That someone is a lawyer, and that he or she says you should simply pay in US dollars, does not mean that he or she is right. Likewise, can a private hospital or clinic in Zambia charge patient fees in US dollars?

It could be argued that, both under section 33(1) of the Bank of Zambia Act 1996 and section 3(b) of the Bank of Zambia (Currency) Regulations 2012, a tender of payment of money that is in notes or coins that are not made and issued by the Bank of Zambia will be considered 'illegal' tender. Indeed, the antithesis of legality here is illegality. So, if a payment is demanded in a foreign currency such as US dollars, and the US dollars are paid, it means that the payment is an illegal tender. Further still, can such an illegal tender be construed as an illegal activity for the purpose of the offence of money laundering?

Section 2 of Zambia's Prohibition and Prevention of Money Laundering Act 2001 defines 'money laundering' as: (a) engaging, directly or indirectly, in a business transaction that involves property acquired with proceeds of crime; (b) receiving, possessing, concealing, disguising, disposing of or bringing into Zambia, any property derived or realised directly or indirectly from *illegal activity*; or (c) the retention or acquisition of property knowing that the property is, derived or realised, directly or indirectly, from *illegal activity*. And the term 'illegal activity' is defined in the same statutory provision of the Prohibition and Prevention of Money Laundering Act 2001 as any activity, whenever or wherever carried out which under any written law in the Republic of Zambia amounts to a crime.

Although the Bank of Zambia Act 1996 does not criminalise the illegal tendering, quoting or receiving of a payment of money in foreign currency within Zambia, such a transaction is illegal because section 4 of the recently promulgated Bank of Zambia (Currency) Regulations 2012 prohibits the tendering, quoting, demanding or receiving of a payment of money in Zambia using foreign currency. Under section 4, it is not only the illegal tendering or receiving of a payment of money in foreign currency that is prohibited, but also the quoting or demanding of such a payment. Therefore, where a business entity in Zambia is quoting prices in US Dollars for goods or services that the business entity is offering while indicating to the public that customers can tender payment in the Zambian Kwacha equivalent, the said business entity will be acting in contravention of the law. Indeed, section 4 of the Bank of Zambia (Currency) Regulations 2012 covers also the quoting of prices in foreign currency, notwithstanding that the payment is expected to be made in Zambian Kwacha.

Closely related to this statutory prohibition, section 6 of the Bank of Zambia (Currency) Regulations 2012 provides that it is actually a criminal offence to tender, receive, demand or quote the payment of money in a foreign currency. Viewed from this angle, a client can, and has the right to, refuse to pay in US dollars even after eating a meal at a hotel. Likewise, a tenant can refuse to pay rentals in US dollars. Instead, both the two payees can opt either to report the matter to the police or simply pay the US dollars equivalent in Zambian Kwacha even though the understanding was that the payment would be made in US dollars.

In insisting that the payee should tender the agreed payment of money in foreign currency, those advocating for such foreign currency payments could be labouring under the impression that section 6 of the Bank of Zambia (Currency) Regulations 2012 is invalid because it exceeds the powers provided for in the enabling statute, the Bank of Zambia Act 1996. This school of thought contends that the excess inherent in section 6 of the Bank of Zambia (Currency) Regulations 2012 is that it attempts to make criminal that which is not criminal under the enabling statute. But such arguments constitute a red herring, as section 57(3) of the Bank of Zambia Act 1996 provides the Minister of Finance with explicit powers to promulgate criminal sanctions through a statutory instrument. Section 57 of the Bank of Zambia Act 1996 stipulates as follows: "(1) The Minister may, by statutory instrument, make regulations for the better carrying out of the purposes of this Act. (2) Without prejudice to the generality of subsection (1), the Minister may, on the recommendation of the Bank, make rules or regulations prescribing any matter which the Bank is authorised by this Act to formulate, regulate or determine. (3) Regulations or rules made under this Act may provide in respect of any contravention thereof that the offender shall be liable to a fine not exceeding one hundred thousand fine units or to a term of imprisonment not exceeding ten years, or to both."

Also, an argument can be made that the criminalization of the tendering, quoting, demanding or receiving of a payment of money in Zambia using foreign currency should have been done through an amendment to the Bank of Zambia Act 1996, as opposed to the promulgation of a statutory instrument. The Bank of Zambia (Currency)

Regulations 2012, some critics argue, is not the best set of instrument through which to carry out such legislative goals, and that the statutory instrument should have focussed instead on setting forth intra vires and reasonable elaborations on the Bank of Zambia Act 1996.

Another argument is that the criminalization through a statutory instrument of the tendering, quoting, demanding or receiving of a payment of money in Zambia using foreign currency is meant to criminalise that which is already 'illegal' under the enabling statute. We have already explored above the issue of illegal payments. Here, suffice it to say, a closely related argument is that, first, the tendering, quoting, demanding or receiving of a payment of money using foreign currency is 'illegal' under the Bank of Zambia Act 1996, and that, secondly, given the Minister's powers in paragraph (c) of section 57 of the Bank of Zambia Act 1996, the criminalisation of the illegal tendering, quoting, demanding or receiving of a payment does not take away or exceed the powers provided for in the Bank of Zambia Act 1996.

Notwithstanding that the legislative draftsman of the Bank of Zambia Act 1996 did not give much thoughtful consideration to the need to criminalize the tendering, quoting, demanding or receiving of a payment of money in Zambia using foreign currency, sections 4 and 6 of the Bank of Zambia (Currency) Regulations 2012 do provide for such criminalization. Thus, the tendering, quoting, demanding or receiving of a payment of money in

Zambia using foreign currency is both illegal and criminal. And so, this illegal tendering, quoting, demanding or receiving of a payment can now serve as a predicate offence of money laundering under the Prohibition and Prevention of Money Laundering Act 2001. Indeed, section 6 of the Bank of Zambia (Currency) Regulations 2012 treats the tendering, quoting, demanding or receiving of a payment of money using foreign currency as a criminal offence.

To strengthen the implementation and enforcement of the Bank of Zambia (Currency) Regulations 2012, the Bank of Zambia, we contend, should work closely with the relevant competent authority for combatting and preventing money laundering in Zambia. Currently, the anti-money laundering unit of the Drug Enforcement Commission (DEC) is responsible for the combatting and prevention of money laundering in Zambia. And this unit of DEC has legal authority to investigate and instigate the prosecution of money laundering offenses, whereas the Bank of Zambia lacks such mandate. On its own, the Bank of Zambia may not have the relevant legal authority for the 'effective' implementation and enforcement of the Bank of Zambia (Currency) Regulations 2012, especially where regulatory breaches are committed by institutions or persons that do not fall under the supervisory jurisdiction of the Bank of Zambia.

CHAPTER

46

SHOULD LEGISLATION OR REGULATIONS BE INTRODUCED ON DEPOSIT INSURANCE IN ZAMBIA?

In my book, "K.K. Mwenda, *Legal Aspects of Banking Regulation: Common Law Perspectives from Zambia*, (Pretoria: Pretoria University Law Press, 2010)", whose electronic copy is freely available Online, I posit that there have been efforts in the past to introduce legislation on deposit insurance in Zambia, and that these efforts are still ongoing.

In the said book, I have provided evidence from the Bank of Zambia where it has been acknowledged that it seems evident from past experience, particularly the failure of three banks in 1995, that banking instability can have serious adverse effects on a nation's economy because it can impair a nation's payments mechanism, reduce the nation's savings rate, diminish the financial intermediation process, and inflict serious harm on small savers (see Mwenda, 2010:70).

- Kenneth K. Mwenda

According to observations made by the Bank of Zambia in 2000, to prevent the aforesaid adverse effects, the Zambian Government had by then created a variety of institutional arrangements designed to preserve banking stability (see Mwenda, 2010:70). These arrangements, the Bank of Zambia argued, included banking laws and regulations that set the ground rules for bank operations while attempting to constrain undue bank risk-taking; the laws and regulations were intended to provide a framework for the supervision and examination of banks to ensure compliance with laws and regulations and lender-of-last-resort facilities designed to prevent temporary bank liquidity problems from turning into insolvency.

In addition to these more traditional arrangements, as the Bank of Zambia contended, "the Government is in the process of developing and setting up a deposit insurance scheme. The primary purpose of the scheme is to preserve public confidence in the banking system, provide the Government with a formal mechanism for dealing with failing banks, and ensure that small depositors are protected in the event of bank failures." (Mwenda, 2010:70). Since then, not much has changed in as far as prospects for the introduction of a legal framework for deposit insurance is concerned.

In a 2004 draft of its Financial Sector Development Plan, the Bank of Zambia repeated its sentiments and desire to introduce a deposit insurance scheme. The Bank of Zambia noted that: "*There are no formal*

structures for a financial safety net in Zambia,
therefore leaving the public exposed to suffer losses
every time there is a bank failure, although an
explicit pay out of K500,000 is in place through Act
No. 28 of 1995 and the establishment of a deposit
insurance scheme is under consideration for
implementation." (p.2).

All said and done, an underlying premise for the
design and establishment of a sound deposit
insurance system is that a well-designed system
should advance the vitality and stability of the
banking sector while minimizing the informational
asymmetries that are often associated with
insurance programs: moral hazard, adverse
selection, and agency problems (see Alsalem, in
Mwenda, 2010:71). Researchers have sought to
create models that guide the development of
effective deposit insurance systems by identifying
specific best practices. One such model, proposed by
Gillian Garcia, is said to have been adopted by the
IMF authorities for use by countries that are
considering the establishment of a deposit insurance
system (see Alsalem, in Mwenda, 2010:71).

Alsalem argues that the Garcia-IMF model is flawed
because it is based only on the lessons from the post-
1991 period in the United States and recent
experiences in other countries. According to Alsalem,
the model omits the long and rich pre-1991
experiences of the Federal Deposit Insurance
Corporation (FDIC), the individual US states, the
failed Federal Savings and Loan Insurance
Corporation (FSLIC), and the National Credit Union

Share Insurance Fund (NCUSIF). Alsalem makes use of this richer history to identify and incorporate additional institutional features that have proven successful in the past. He then shows that his modified Garcia-IMF model better addresses the fundamental problems of operating a deposit insurance system.

Closely related to Alsalem's study, Demirgüç-Kunt and Detragiache (see Mwenda, 2010:72) observe evidence in 61 countries between 1980 and 1997. They argue that explicit deposit insurance tends to increase the likelihood of banking crises, the more so where bank interest rates are deregulated and the institutional environment is weak. According to Demirgüç-Kunt and Detragiache, the adverse impact of deposit insurance on bank stability tends to be stronger the more extensive is the coverage offered to depositors, where the scheme is funded, and where it is run by the government rather than the private sector.

In 2001, Demirgüç-Kunt and Kane (see Mwenda, 2010:72) carried out research pertaining, in part, to several financial and banking crises that occurred in the late 1990s around the globe. As a result of these crises, a growing number of developing countries had been seeking advice about designing and adopting an explicit deposit insurance system. According to the authors, previous research delineated not only the well-known trade-off between banking stability and moral hazard but also the interaction between deposit insurance design features and country-specific elements of a country's financial and governmental contracting environment. Demirgüç-Kunt and Kane documented the extent of cross-country differences in deposit insurance design and reviewed also the empirical evidence on how particular design features affected private market discipline, banking stability, financial development, and the effectiveness of crisis resolution. Their findings suggested that countries with institutionally weak informational, legal, and supervisory environments should refrain from adopting an explicit deposit insurance system until they assess and remedy any weaknesses in their environments.

Later, in 2002, Demirgüç-Kunt and Kane (see Mwenda, 2010:73), observed that deposit insurance is not always good or always bad. The authors argued that deposit insurance can be a useful part of a country's financial safety net. However, the authors further postulated that in institutionally weak environments, designing a deposit insurance scheme that will not increase the probability and depth of future banking crises is hard to do. Hartley (see Mwenda, 2010:73), thus, asks the question whether government bank deposit insurance should be scrapped in favour of a system of bank cross-guarantees. In his findings, Hartley argues that some proponents claim to have found successful cross-guarantees among the banks of antebellum Indiana, Ohio, and Iowa, but a closer examination suggests otherwise.

Analysing shortcomings of the International Association of Deposit Insurers (IADI)'s approach,

Kane (see Mwenda, 2010:73) argues that because of cultural differences among regulators, the IADI cannot effectively consolidate deposit insurers. He finds that the IADI could be more successful in its mission of preventing cross-country spillovers of crisis pressure and improving the exchange of regulatory information if it organized a public market in deposit-reinsurance derivatives. Such a market, according to Kane, would ultimately give signals about which insurance structures were optimal. Thus, individual countries would have an incentive to improve their own deposit insurance structure frequently, not only during a financial crisis.

In general, a number of governments do insure liabilities of major banks in a crisis (see Mwenda, 2010:74). Such deposit insurance is important because the closure of these banks or even an interruption in their supply of credit would be too costly to the economy. Put simply, some of these banks are too big to fail. Indeed, as has been argued before, "People know this (that these banks are too big to fail) and believe that the liabilities of these banks are effectively insured. This is *implicit deposit insurance.* Such beliefs may be supported by past actions of the government and are supported by the actions of other countries." (see Mwenda, 2010:74).

Given the views noted above regarding implicit deposit insurance, it might be better to introduce explicit deposit insurance then. Generally, the introduction of insurance of liabilities of TBTF (too-big-to-fail) banks gives them a competitive advantage over small banks, reducing competition in the banking system. Secondly, it is better to collect insurance premiums in stable periods to build up a fiscal reserve to help meet the expense of covering the liabilities of failed banks. Thirdly, incentive problems will be minimised if the system is explicit and unambiguous. More recently, however, conventional wisdom has come to acknowledge that some 'big banks are too big to rescue', especially if a bank rescue would involve costs which could outweigh the benefits. A detailed and methodological risk analysis is helpful here in determining whether the rescue operation should proceed.

In spite of the many arguments that are advanced in favour of deposit insurance, there are also some shortcomings to such insurance systems. And we have highlighted some of these shortcomings above. Here, suffice it to say, deposit insurance can expose a government to significant contingent expenses. The insurance of deposits entails that insured depositors have very little incentive to monitor banks for risks. As a result thereof, banks can, and often do, take on greater risks. This feature is called the 'moral hazard' problem.

However, as Singh argues, sound banking supervision should endeavour to reduce moral hazard that arises from the role of the central bank as the lender-of-last-resort as well as from other safety-net systems, namely deposit insurance (see Mwenda, 2010:75). Also, constructive ambiguity that arises from the absence of statutory provisions on, or in the lack of codification of, the role of the central bank as the lender-of-last-resort helps to reduce moral hazard since creditors are not made explicitly aware that the central bank has such a function.

A further shortcoming of using deposit insurance is that many banking regulators have limited means to supervise risk-taking by banks. In addition, as Singh observes, the issue of moral hazard is exacerbated by the policy of intervening with financial support if the institution is considered 'too-big-to-fail.' (see Mwenda, 2010:75). Singh argues that: "Some banks may indeed be Too-Big-To-Fail. But it is better to leave some ambiguity about whether or not the government will insure the liabilities of these banks for this provides some element of market discipline, reducing the moral hazard problem. Such a policy is referred to as *constructive ambiguity*... countries that do not adequately regulate and supervise banks ought not to offer generous deposit insurance. They might consider much more limited deposit insurance that lowers the risk of a large loss to the government."

Sleet and Smith (see Mwenda, 2010:75-76) consider issues concerning the design of a banking system 'safety net' when both a deposit insurer and a lender-of-last-resort are present. In their model, both entities have a role to play. Moreover, issues related to deposit insurance pricing are considered relatively unimportant in this context, whereas issues related to discount window access and pricing are not. The two authors discuss when and why (or why not) a lender-of-last-resort should lend liberally but charge high rates of interest. And they raise the possibility that discount window policy may enhance or reduce the scope for multiplicity of equilibria.

It is against the backdrop of all this research and empirical evidence that we in Zambia should try to reflect more thoughtfully on how best to handle the issue of whether or not to introduce *explicit* deposit insurance in the country. There is simply no magic silver bullet to these issues. But we cannot, however, discount or exclude the value in according such issues some *critical* and *erudite* examination.

CHAPTER

47

WHY DO WE REGULATE MARKETS?

Before attempting to draft legislation for the regulation of, say, the professional conduct of those engaged in the media industry or the financial sector, we must first understand the policy bases of introducing such legislation as well as the underpinning objectives of the intended regulatory framework. Also, it is important that the legislative drafters understand the size and structure of a particular industry as well as the role of a regulator in that country. In many cases, a service industry will have different peculiarities and regulatory implications from a goods industry.

Generally, economists have been quick to put pen to paper on various theories pertaining to the regulation of different types of markets while other professionals such as lawyers have somewhat lagged behind in such intellectual leadership and inquiry. But then, it is the lawyers who must come up with the relevant laws and regulations to regulate the markets. It begs the question of promoting cross-cultural and interdisciplinary approaches in developing such multi-faceted frameworks.

Our question is: why do we regulate markets? Should the media industry, say, in Zambia, be regulated by a State mandated regulator or should it be left to self-regulation? In one of my books, "K.K. Mwenda, *Legal Aspects of Financial Services Regulation and the Concept of a Unified Regulator*, (Washington DC: The World Bank, 2006)", using the example of the financial services industry, I have argued that a key objective of financial regulation is to redress the information imbalance that sometimes exists between consumers and financial services businesses in favour of consumers. I have posited further that this objective is usually met by imposing upon financial services businesses minimum standards of business conduct. Moreover, the fairness of the financial markets depends in part on the degree of consumer protection.

By parity of reasoning, the unprofessional conduct of some sections of the media (as evidenced through the dissemination of some malicious falsehoods) must be curbed through media regulation so as to protect members of the public from unwarranted and unfair journalistic assaults. And such curbing of unprofessional journalistic conduct need not be mistaken for an affront to the freedom of the press. Indeed, it is not an affront by any means. The pursuance of every liberty and right carries with it an element of social and moral responsibility. So, notwithstanding that the law of torts does provide for various remedies in matters such as defamation (see also the Penal Code on the criminal offence of defaming the President of the Republic of Zambia), the unprofessional conduct of some sections of the media cannot go unchecked. The question here is not about whether to regulate or not to regulate, but rather about the type and mode of regulation required; that is, State regulation or self-regulation, and at what levels of hierarchical controls?

Overall, regulation attempts to strike a balance, protecting the marketplace from itself without stifling legitimate risk-taking. In the financial sector, for example, one method of doing so is by preventing business failures through the imposition of capital and internal control requirements. These requirements ensure that business entities have sufficient liquidity to meet their obligations, making them less vulnerable to hasty withdrawals by depositors and investors and to other market shocks.

In general, the regulatory framework for many markets often comprises a combination of two or more of the following: (a) primary enabling legislation; (b) secondary legislation issued pursuant to the enabling statute; (c) principles, rules, and codes issued by regulators; and (d) guidance or policy directives issued by the regulatory authority. Though there is admittedly no unified theory of financial services regulation, the following comprise some broad objectives for regulation: (i) protecting investors to help build their confidence in the market; (ii) ensuring that the markets are fair, efficient, and transparent; (iii) reducing systemic risk; (iv) protecting financial services businesses from malpractice by some consumers (such as money laundering); and (v) maintaining consumer confidence in the financial system.

Where the regulatory framework effectively controls market abuses, such as unlawful and unauthorized disclosures, insider dealing, and money laundering, prospects for building investor and consumer confidence in the market are high. Investors tend to target markets that protect them against such risks. By contrast, where there is irresponsible or unprofessional journalistic conduct such type of misfeasance can affect the reputational risk of the affected investors or members of the public.

Generally, when financial intermediaries, market players, and institutional investors are well regulated, through means such as effective Chinese walls and clear codes of conduct, financial services businesses are likely to feel protected against fraudulent activity by consumers. Taken together with the efficient regulation of information disclosure, such efforts can lead to a more fair, efficient, and transparent market. It is also important to ensure that legal rules are enforced so as to promote and maintain consumer confidence. Rules without enforcement are like a tiger without teeth.

In some markets, there are fears of 'regulatory capture'. Regulatory capture occurs when a State regulatory agency, set up to act in the public interest, begins to advance commercial or special interests that dominate the industry or sector it is charged with regulating. In essence, regulatory capture is a form of government failure, as it provides incentives for large firms or large media outlets to control the market and thereby produce negative externalities. In the media industry, for example, there is a two-pronged sword, namely: (a) a fear that self-regulation can lead to some strong private-media interests capturing, dominating and controlling the regulatory system, and thus shielding themselves from effective regulation and supervision; and (b) a fear that State regulation would considerably stifle freedom of the press.

In an article titled "Regulatory Capture: What the Experts Have Found" (Online, dated December 19, 2010), Adam Thierer observes that: "Because regulatory capture theory conflicts mightily with romanticized notions of 'independent' regulatory agencies or 'scientific' bureaucracy, it often evokes a visceral reaction and a fair bit of denialism... Yet, countless studies have shown that regulatory capture has been at work in various arenas: transportation and telecommunications; energy and environmental policy; farming and financial services; and many others."

Thomas Frank, in an article titled, "Obama and Regulatory Capture," which was published in *Wall Street Journal* (June 24, 2009), observes that: "There are powerful institutions that don't like being regulated. Regulation sometimes cuts into their profits and interferes with their business. So they have used the political process to sabotage, redirect, defund, undo or hijack the regulatory state since the regulatory state was first invented."

And, Jeffrey M. Berry, in *The Interest Group Society* (1989: p. 151), notes that: "A persistent criticism by political scientists is that agencies that regulate businesses are overly sympathetic to the industries they are responsible for regulating. Critics charge that regulators often come from the businesses they regulate and thus naturally see things from an industry point of view. Even if regulators weren't previously involved in the industry, they have been seen as eager to please powerful clientele groups rather than have them complain to the White House or to the agency's overseeing committees in Congress."

So, what is the way forward in regulating the media industry in Zambia in light of the discussion above? That is a question that I leave for the reader to answer.

CHAPTER

48

THE CONCEPT OF 'TRUE AND FAIR VIEW' IN ACCOUNTING

A quick and expected reaction from some readers would be to ask: what does a lawyer have to do with, or what does he know about, such accounting principles as 'true and fair view'? But, wait a minute, let me push. In a paper titled, "Irreconcilable Legal and Accounting Views of 'A True and Fair View': An Emerging Alternative from Australian Reforms," Ram Karan observes that despite the dispute over the meaning of 'a true and fair view' ever since it was formally introduced by the UK Companies Act 1948, the concept has not only continued to be integral to financial reporting regimes of many countries, but its application has expanded in recent times. In Australia, Karan observes, the status of the concept of 'true and fair view' has been subordinated by accounting standards, and that its replacement paved by Australian reforms brought about an accounting concept of 'not misleading' that may transcend discordant interpretations and national

- Kenneth K. Mwenda

idiosyncrasies of the true and fair view concept.

VentureLine.com provides a definition of 'true and fair view' as follows: "It suggests that an enterprise should provide a true and fair view about its financial conditions and operating results. The concept of true and fair view does not mean absolute truth about enterprises. Financial statements are a product of management's judgments and estimates. The principle of true and fair view requires comparative truth about the enterprise's picture. True and fair view is rather defined operationally; it is thought to be accomplished by complying with all other lower accounting principles."

The Accounting-Dictionary.com postulates that the principle of 'true and fair view' refers to 'a correct statement of a company's financial position as shown in its accounts and confirmed by the auditors.' However, whereas the definition of 'true and fair view' espoused by VentureLine.com emphasizes 'comparative truth' as opposed to 'absolute truth', the definition set forth by Accounting-Dictionary.com places greater emphasis on 'correctness' of the company's financial statements. But, would financial statements that are comparatively true, although not absolutely true, be deemed to be 'correct'?

In the UK, in its policy pronouncement of May 19, 2008, the Financial Reporting Council (FRC: Online, 2012) observes that: "The 'true and fair' concept has been a part of English law and central to accounting and auditing practice in the UK for many decades.

There has been no statutory definition of 'true and fair'. The most authoritative statements as to the meaning of 'true and fair' have been legal opinions written by Lord Hoffmann and Dame Mary Arden in 1983 and 1984 and by Dame Mary Arden in 1993 ('the Opinions'). Since those Opinions were written, there have been some significant changes in accounting standards and company law which have led some to question whether the views expressed in those Opinions remain applicable."

Accordingly, the UK Financial Reporting Council 'concluded that it would be helpful to its preparers, auditors and users of financial statements if it commissioned a further legal opinion to ascertain whether the approach to *true and fair* taken in the Opinions requires to be revised.' In his requested Opinion, as noted by the Financial Reporting Council, Mr Moore endorsed the analysis in the Opinions of Lord Hoffmann and Dame Mary Arden and confirmed the centrality of the true and fair requirement to the preparation of financial statements in the UK, whether they are prepared in accordance with international or UK accounting standards. Accordingly, "Directors must consider whether, taken in the round, the financial statements that they approve are appropriate. Similarly, auditors are required to exercise professional judgment before expressing an audit opinion. As a result, the Opinion confirms that it will not be sufficient for either directors or auditors to reach such conclusions solely because the financial statements were prepared in accordance with applicable accounting standards."

In Zambia, section 164(6) of Zambia's Companies Act 1994 (see also Second Schedule to said section 164) provides that company directors should cause to be attached to the annual accounts, before the auditor reports on the accounts, a statement made in accordance with a resolution of the directors and signed by at least two directors stating whether, in the opinion of the directors – (a) the profit and loss account is drawn up so as to give a 'true and fair view' of the profit or loss of the company for the financial year; (b) the balance sheet is drawn up so as to give a 'true and fair view' of the state of affairs of the company as at the end of the financial year; (c) there are reasonable grounds to believe that the company will be able to pay its debts as and when they fall due; and (d) the group accounts are drawn up so as to give a 'true and fair view' of – (i) the profit or loss of the company and its subsidiaries for their respective last financial years; and (ii) the state of affairs of the company and its subsidiaries as at the end of their respective last financial years, so far as they concern members of the company; if the company has group accounts.

Closely related to the Zambian position, in the UK, section 393 of the UK Companies Act 2006 requires that the directors of a company must not approve accounts unless they are satisfied that the accounts give a 'true and fair view'. As the UK Financial Reporting Council observes, 'the true and fair requirement has been fundamental to accounting in the UK for many years. It is a requirement of both UK and EU law' (*Note: The requirement that company and consolidated accounts give a true and fair view is recognised in Article 2(3) of the 4th Company Law Directive and Article 16(3) of the 7th Company Law Directive issued by the European Commission. Although these two Articles do not apply for accounts required to give a fair presentation in accordance with endorsed International Financial Reporting Standards (IFRS) under the International Accounting Standards (IAS) Regulation, the true and fair principle underlying them is expressly recognised in Article 3(2) of the IAS Regulation – no IFRS standard can be endorsed if it would conflict with the principle set out in those Articles).*

The current UK approach to the 'true and fair view' principle tends to emphasize 'prudence' and a 'reflection of the substance of a transaction as opposed to the legal form of the transaction.' However, whereas the UK Financial Reporting Council posits that for companies reporting under the UK Generally Accepted Accounting Principles (GAAP), both FRS 18 and company law require that directors make prudent judgements in their consideration of accounts, particularly where there is uncertainty, and that UK GAAP contains a separate standard which requires accounts to reflect the substance of a transaction rather than its legal form (i.e. where this is different), some lawyers may argue that since IFRS do not contain a similar standard, and is more rules-based than UK GAAP in some areas, the principle of substance over legal form has no place in IFRS. A rebuttal to this view, however, is that IAS 8 actually provides that, for information to be reliable, it should be reported in accordance with economic substance rather than strictly in adherence to its legal form.

Against this background, to what extent could it be argued that the principle of 'true and fair view' allows for or prevents creative accounting; that is, accounting practices that, although following the letter of the rules of standard accounting practices, somewhat deviate from the spirit of those rules. Creative accounting is often seen through the use of complicated and novel ways to deal with assets or liabilities, including income, with the intent to influence readers towards the interpretations desired by the authors.

Also, how do we treat certain legal obligations created through, say, a guarantee for a loan? Is a guarantee a liability or an asset, or does it only become a liability or asset upon the crystallization of the underlying debt obligation? Where, then, in the balance sheet, should the guarantee appear 'correctly'? Unlike receivables and future book debts, guarantees present a different set of legal issues that are primarily dependent on what happens to the underlying obligations pertaining to the principal debt.

In the UK, a number of court cases have examined the accounting principle of 'true and fair view'. In *Re Kingston Cotton Mills* No. 2, 1896 2 Ch. 279, for example, an auditor was given a broad discretion to rely on information provided by the management, holding that an auditor is a watchdog and not a bloodhound. More recently, it has come to be accepted that an auditor cannot simply rely on information provided by the management when suspicious circumstances arise. As Lord Denning observed in the case of *Formento v. Seldson Fountain Pen Co.*, [1958] 1 WLR 45, an auditor *'must come to (his task) with an inquiring mind – not suspicious of dishonesty, I agree – but suspecting that someone may have made a mistake somewhere and that a check must be made to ensure that there has been none...'. In Re Thomas Gerrard*, 1967 2 All ER 535, it was discovered that certain invoices had been altered, and the court held that the fact of alteration should have caused the auditors to carry out their own check on the stock, without relying merely on the invoices.

It is such interpretations within the context of the common law that bring lawyers back to their feet on the principle of 'true and fair view'. In the Indian case of *ICAI v. P.K. Mukherji, AIR* 1968 SC 1104, the Supreme Court of India held that: "*The auditor must exercise such reasonable care as would satisfy a man that the accounts are genuine, assuming that there is nothing to arouse his suspicion and if he does that he fulfils his duty; if his suspicion is aroused, his duty is to 'probe the thing to the bottom'...*"

It is now broadly accepted that any departure by auditors from accounting standards to probe further must be well justified, otherwise they will be acting in breach of the accounting standards. As noted in the English case of *Lloyd Cheyham v. Littlejohn*, 1987 BCLC 303, "*they are very strong evidence as to what is the proper standard which should be adopted and unless there is some justification, a departure from this will be regarded as constituting a breach of duty..."*

CHAPTER

49

THEOLOGY ON TAP

At the outset, it must be understood that the term 'theology' is a field of study and analysis that examines critically matters of God and of God's attributes and their relation to the universe. The field of theology examines divine things or religious truth, and commits itself to the understanding of divinity. And theologians, it could be argued, often apply various forms of analyses and arguments in their theological discourses. These discourses draw from philosophical, ethnographic, historical and spiritual perspectives to help us all to understand, explain, test, critique, defend or promote a myriad of religious themes. But, I confess here that am not a theologian. Rather, I am a Doctor of Philosophy and a Doctor of Laws. To that end, I will use the Socratic method in legal pedagogy to address some of the critical issues pertaining to competing arguments on Christianity and atheism.

In a broad sense, atheism is a doctrine that argues that there is no God or gods. Atheism is a disbelief in or denial of the existence of God, a deity or gods. To a large extent, atheism is often associated with, for good reasons or bad ones, many intellectuals or intellects. In an article titled, "Intelligent people 'less likely to believe in God'...", dated June 11, 2008 (available Online), the *Telegraph*, a British newspaper, reported that: "Professor Richard Lynn, emeritus professor of psychology at Ulster University, said many more members of the 'intellectual elite' considered themselves atheists than the national average."

Citing Professor Lynn, the *Telegraph* reported: "A decline in religious observance over the last century was directly linked to a rise in average intelligence..." Interestingly, as the Telegraph notes, "But the conclusions – in a paper for the academic journal *Intelligence* – have been branded 'simplistic' by critics. Professor Lynn, who has provoked controversy in the past with research linking intelligence to race and sex, said university academics were less likely to believe in God than almost anyone else. A survey of Royal Society fellows found that only 3.3 per cent believed in God – at a time when 68.5 per cent of the general UK population described themselves as believers."

Does it mean that when one feels or thinks that, for some awkward reason or otherwise, he or she is too educated or too civilized then he or she cannot believe in God? In this essay, I will refrain making 'intimidating' and lengthy citations from the Bible. That approach is less helpful when engaging in secular debate on religious matters, especially if you are engaging the so-called educated atheists. Theirs is driven mainly by scientific empiricism, dismissing many forms of idealism as utopian and unscientific. The typical atheist intellectual is less likely to be convinced that there is God or a deity somewhere out there in the absence of what he would call empirical evidence or data. He or she will be quick to argue: can you prove to me that there is God or a deity out there? What's your evidence? And by evidence, the atheist is asking for material and empirical facts as opposed to self-proclamations by some Christians that they feel that they are experiencing the power of the Holy Spirit. The atheist will simply dismiss such claims as hallucinations or some kind of psychological delusion. It is against this background that an atheist intellectual friend of mine invited me to what I call 'theology on tap'; that is, a discussion of religion over a pint or glass of beer in a pub. And I accepted the invitation.

At the pub, my strategy was to engage my friend thoughtfully. And so, we both filled our glasses. My friend proceeded to light his cigarette and adjust his professorial spectacles. Yes, he is a professor of physics. Here I was, thinking to myself, what does he have up his sleeve this time? Calmly, he broke the ice: "I remember you as a young Catholic altar-boy back in the days. So, you still go to church?" I responded in the affirmative, and added that I have retained my religious beliefs to this day. He then implored further: "Tell me, why do you go to church? Do you still think that there is a god or God somewhere out there who we all cannot see?"

- *Kenneth K. Mwenda*

I gulped half the glass of Heineken that was firmly held in my right hand. And putting down the glass, I asked my friend: "And why do you doubt that there is God?" Of course, this was not going to settle down well with him. But my strategy was to build the discussion around questions rather than on answers. He responded, "Look, I asked you a question, but you come back with a question instead of an answer. I don't have any reason to believe in someone that I can neither see visually nor prove physically that they exist. Besides, if there was God, then why has He allowed Satan to be causing so much havoc in the world today? Why doesn't God stop Satan once and for all, and then we would all live happily thereafter? Also, if God is so powerful as you religious bigots claim, what is He waiting for when there are so many poor and hungry people in the world today?"

I was calm and took no offence at his nomenclature or poor choice of words when he used the word 'bigot'. But, then, there was some silence between us. I gulped my Heineken and adjusted my seat. I decided to be honest with my friend, and said: "Look, there are many things that you and I do not know. The fact that we have read some books here and there does not mean we know everything. We have to be very careful with what we say or do. There is so much out there that even science does not know. We are all learning, including the scientists, and the process of learning never ends."

My friend then smiled, and looked at me: "I knew

you would pull that one. But that is not a good answer. We need to learn now whether or not God exists. It is a very simple and straightforward issue. I don't know why you are trying to beat about the bush. The question is: does God exist or not?"

In my mind, I could hear the lyrics of Erykah Badu's song, "On and On". The words kept coming back, *"Most intellects do not Believe in God, But they fear us just the same."* I must admit that my friend is a highly accomplished physicist who is a professor of physics at an Ivy League university. He, no doubt, has an impressive CV. But that alone was not going to convince me or dissuade me from my religious beliefs. So, I asked him further: "Let us assume, as economists often say, that there was God. What would you do if you discovered on Judgment Day that God does indeed exist, yet you have been denying Him all along?"

My friend broke out in laughter and said: "How can that be? First, God does not physically reveal Himself to me, yet He expects me to believe that He exists? Surely, I would confront Him and blame Him for that." Although tempted to quote the Scriptures now, especially regarding the Biblical incidence when the disciple Thomas doubted that the Lord Jesus Christ had resurrected and that the other disciples had seen Him, I refrained myself. I knew that that was not going to help matters much. So, I asked my friend instead: "Why do people buy car insurance policy when they are not even sure that their cars will ever get involved in an accident? Can they say that they know for a fact that their cars will be involved an accident one day, and that that is why they are insuring against car accidents? Likewise, many people do buy health insurance policy yet they are not even sure whether or not they will get sick to use that health insurance policy."

My friend looked at me intently, and said: "Go on..." And so, I continued: "I would rather be safe than sorry. Even if we were to stretch our imagination to the fullest, it is better to believe that there is God than not to." To this, he quickly plodded: "Why do you say so?" I knew there and then that he was paying attention to what I was saying. So, I calmly lowered the tone of my voice and said to him: "My brother, our life, as humans, is like the life of a student. The student must prepare for his or her exam. And so, we too are called to prepare for Judgment Day. The only difference is that the student knows when the exams will take place. We don't. Further, the student can take a re-sit if he or she fails. With God's exam, there is no re-sit. You either pass or you fail. That is it. You are not allowed to take that life-exam before God more than once. So, think about it. It's only one shot. And that is the first and last chance you have, though you have a lifetime to get ready for the exam. I would rather be safe than sorry, bro."

My friend was quiet now. I began to suspect that perhaps the beer was starting to take its toll on him or he was preparing for a counter-attack. As he was trying to waddle through the maze, I quickly continued in order to strengthen my argument: "OK, even if you feel right now that there is no God, just think of it this way: it is better to believe that there is God now just in case it turns out true that there is indeed God. You won't be losing anything. But if you deny Him today, and then tomorrow it turns out that He actually exists, bro, where you gonna run to? You know that old reggae song by Peter Tosh, 'Downpressor man' right? As Tosh sings: 'You gonna run to the sea, but the sea will be boiling..., You gonna run to the rocks, but the rocks will be melting..., You gonna run to the Lord, begging Him to hide you..., You gonna run to the Lord, begging Him to hide you..., I don't know where you gonna run to, All along that day. You can't run, You can't bribe JAH JAH..., Can't call him in a bar...drink some... Can't bribe him around the corner...can't... You can't bribe no one... Them no want the money.... 'Cause money gets funny!"

My friend smiled and responded: "You should have been a priest, you know! You have very valid points. There is so much we all, including scientists, do not know." As we parted the night to say goodbyes, my friend shook my hand and said: "As always, you held your own very well. I like that insurance policy metaphor. Where did you get it from?" To which I responded: "I learned from the best. The Real Teacher often used parables and metaphors to the Pharisees and the teachers of the law. There can be no better Teacher or Mwalimu to learn from..."

- Kenneth K. Mwenda

CHAPTER

50

LAW AND THE SOCIAL FUNCTIONS OF RELIGION

Among other things, the field of sociology of religion examines the social functions of religion. At the outset, I must state explicitly that I am not a sociologist. Neither do I claim or profess to be one. I only make a modest attempt to stray into some sociological arguments on religion to help inform the debate on how some social functions of religion will correspond to some social functions of law. There are many theories on religion, including the evolutionist and relativist views, but the main theories relate to the following: (a) substantive (or essentialist) theories that focus on the contents of religions and the meaning ascribed to the contents by the believers; and (b) functional (and in a stronger form reductionist) theories that focus on the social or psychological functions that religion has for a group of people or an individual.

Emile Durkheim (see: *Elementary Forms of the Religious Life*, (Free Press: 1995)) spells out a

- Kenneth K. Mwenda

definition of religion, postulating that the term 'religion' hinges on the distinction between things that are sacred (set apart from daily life) and things that are profane (everyday, mundane elements of society). According to Durkheim, the sacred elements of social life are what make up religion. Some scholars argue, however, that religion attempts to answer existential questions while others contend that religion is simply a form of ideology.

Closely related to the foregoing, we must understand that law does not exist in a vacuum. Its usefulness must relate to some cognate discipline such as sociology. In a sense, the discussion here brings on board salient aspects of sociology of law and that of legal theory. No attempt is made, however, to contest the issue of whether or not God exists. Such a discussion falls outside the scope of this paper.

How then do the social functions of religion relate to the social functions of the law? In the midst of the philosophical dialogue on morality, ethics and other normative value-systems, the law seats with its bride, religion, to inspire and regulate the conduct of individuals in society. Notwithstanding the sometimes glaring chasm between religiosity, on the one hand, and secularization, on the other, in situations where the law is absent or where it shows some lacuna or gap, religion (and morality) will often step in to fill the gap by regulating the moral and ethical conduct of individuals in society. In jurisprudence, the debate turns to salient aspects of the natural law school of thought as opposed to strict positivism. For example, while it is not a crime as such to commit adultery, the Ten Commandments in the Bible prohibit the carrying out or the commissioning of adultery or fornication. Now, whether or not people adhere to these dictates of the Bible is a different issue altogether. Suffice it to say, religion, like the law, attempts to regulate the moral and ethical conduct of individuals in society. To that extent, save for the argument of a deity under religion, both the law and religion share common attributes and goals.

We are, however, mindful that whilst religion may not have an immediate secular State authority to enforce or mete out punishment for anyone infringing the Ten Commandments (*cf.* Islamic States that enforce Sharia law, with punishment being meted out to offenders), in contrast to law enforcement and the punishment of law offenders under secular laws, both religion and the law try to regulate human behavior and conduct to acceptable societal norms.

And while religion appeals to the inner self, and fastens on the conscience of an individual, the law appeals to the external side of an individual. It is the external threat of punishment imbedded in secular laws that often presents itself as a deterrent against bad behavior or an incentive for good behavior. It is, however, more effective to write and engrain the letters of religion in a man's heart than it is to write and engrain the letters of the constitution in a man's heart, especially when we are faced with situations of weak constitutional legitimacy. Seen from this angle, religion can at times be more effective in regulating human conduct than the law, especially where law enforcement is weak or lax, but then you have to have strong and committed believers (as opposed to just religious fanatics and fundamentalists).

That said, we concede that religion can at times run parallel or contrary to the law (e.g. where religious fundamentalism instigates civil war or the violation of human rights). Certain religious dictates can, indeed, offend the law or contradict the law. Likewise, certain religious traditions and dogmas can be an affront to the law. But such issues are not the concern of this paper. We are instead focusing on the usefulness or social function of religion in regulating human conduct where the law also prescribes similar or closely related conduct. For example, the Ten Commandments are against homicide (*i.e.* clearly against suicide bombers who claim to rely on religion). And so is the law. And the Ten Commandments are against theft. And so is the law.

Against this background, where law enforcement is weak, some members of the community, especially those whose lives are guided strongly by progressive religious values or some decent secular norms, will be seen to conduct themselves responsibly in society. In a way, religion has a social function akin not only to the law but also to some progressive values espoused through exposure to certain cultural traditions and educational or learning environments. A good family too (and not a dysfunctional one), as a social institution, can help to nurture such progressive values in the same way some churches would. It is this whole process of socialization and the attendant sociology of knowledge that we are concerned with here. Therefore, even the most spiritedly argumentative atheist who does not believe in God can at least give credit to this social function of religion.

Thomas Rees (Online: 2009) argues that one of the leading theories of why religion is so popular goes by the ominous name of 'Terror Management Theory'. Put simply, this is the idea that people turn to religion to ease their fear of death (see Thomas Rees: 2009). As noted by SociologyGuide.com (Online, 2012), social scientists have analyzed religion in terms of what it does for the individual, community or society through its functions and dysfunctions, and that many of these social scientists are known to belong to the tradition of functionalist thought.

According to SociologyGuide.com, a famous social anthropologist of early twentieth century, Malinowski, saw religion and magic as assisting the individual to cope with situations of stress or anxiety. Like good sex, religion was seen as an effective stress-reliever. Malinowski was of the view that religious ritual can enable the bereaved to reassert their collective solidarity as well as to express their common norms and values upon which the proper functioning of the community depends. It is contended that religion can also supplement practical, empirical knowledge, offering some sense of understanding and control in areas to which such knowledge does not extent.

SociologyGuide.com adds that a more influential tradition of functionalist thought on religion derives from Durkheim, whose *Elementary Forms of the Religious Life* presents a theory of religion identifying religion with social cohesion: religious beliefs and rituals are understood in terms of the role they play in promoting and maintaining social solidarity.

On the other hand, Radcliffe-Brown observes that religious ceremonies, for example, in the form of communal dancing, promoted unity and harmony and functioned to enhance social solidarity and the survival of the society. Thus, religious beliefs contained in myths and legends, Radcliffe-Brown observes, express the social values of the different objects which have a major influence on social life such as food, weapons, day and night etc, and that these form the value consensus around which society is integrated (see SociologyGuide.com)

More recently, it has been observed, "recent functionalism while retaining...notion that religion has a central role in maintaining social solidarity has rejected Durkheim's view that religious beliefs are merely symbolic representations of society. Kingsley Davis argues that religious beliefs form the basis for socially valued goals and a justification of them. Religion provides a common focus for identity and an unlimited source of rewards and punishments for behaviour. Functionalist theories of religion face a problem in the apparent decline in religious belief and participation. What is viewed as secularization in other theories is seen as simply religious change in functionalist terms." (*Ibid*)

A further view is that functionalist theorists argue that religion takes different forms in apparently secular societies, and that it is more individualized and less tied to religious institutions (see: *Ibid*). The character of modern industrial capitalist society, it is argued, particularly its rampant individualism, is seen to be expressed in the differentiated character of religion in a society like the USA. Accordingly, although seemingly having little basis for integration, the celebration of individualism is itself an integrating feature of such diverse religious forms, and that new and distinctive forms of religion may perform latent functions for the system by deflecting adherents from critical appraisal of their society and its distribution of rewards.

As noted below, in many anti-religious societies, such as some communist States, the view presented hereinabove cannot hold. It is argued instead that it is the functional alternatives to traditional religion that take precedence. According to SociologyGuide.com, "other systems of belief such as communism itself fulfill the same role as religion elsewhere. National ceremonial, ritual celebration of communist victories, heroes, etc., meets the same need for collective rites, which reaffirm common sentiments and promote enhanced commitment to common goals. Finally, even in highly secularized Western societies civil religion exists. This consists in abstract beliefs and rituals, which relate society to ultimate things and provide a rationale for national history, a transcendental basis for national goals and purposes. Robert King Merton, a twentieth century functionalist, introduced the concept of dysfunction. Talking about religion, for instance, he pointed out the dysfunctional features of religion in a multi-religious society. In such a society religion, instead of bringing about solidarity, could become the cause of disorganization and disunity."

Apart from pundits such as Merton many other leading sociologists have highlighted the dysfunctions of religion. Karl Marx, for example, regarded religion as a source of false consciousness among the proletariat, which prevents the 'class for itself' from developing. It prevents them from developing their real powers and potentialities. Some contend that the main function of religion in society is simply to control weaker social groups by the more powerful, while others argue that religion has a euphoric function in that it serves to counteract feelings of frustration and loss of faith and certitude by reestablishing the believers' sense of well-being, their sense of the essential rightness of the moral world of which they are a part. That said, whichever way one chooses to argue, we maintain that even the most spiritedly argumentative atheist who does not believe in God can at least give credit to the social function of religion discussed earlier in this paper.

CHAPTER

51

UNDERSTANDING SOME ASPECTS OF OUR CHRISTIAN LIFE

In the Holy Scriptures, the Bible explains to us how our Lord Jesus Christ healed a man who was plagued with leprosy. Mark 1:40-45 (see also Matthew 8:1-4) points out that: "A man with leprosy came to him and begged him on his knees, 'If you are willing, you can make me clean.' Jesus was indignant. He reached out his hand and touched the man. 'I am willing,' he said. 'Be clean!' Immediately the leprosy left him and he was cleansed. Jesus sent him away at once with a strong warning: *'See that you don't tell this to anyone.* But go, show yourself to the priest and offer the sacrifices that Moses commanded for your cleansing, as a testimony to them.' Instead he went out and began to talk freely, spreading the news. As a result, Jesus could no longer enter a town openly but stayed outside in lonely places. Yet the people still came to him from everywhere."

The cured man was told explicitly that *'See that you*

- *Kenneth K. Mwenda*

don't tell this to anyone', yet *'he went out and began to talk freely, spreading the news.'* How many of us today would keep quiet over such a miracle? Indeed, how many of us would keep such information to ourselves? Let us be honest. I opine that this man who had just been cured by the Lord Jesus pretended that he would not tell anyone, but no sooner had he turned the corner than he began to pontificate with great exclamations: "Aaa-sovaa, Yesu... Waa chabe! Endesheni ka-biyeni naimwe for miracles...!!!" (*i.e.* The Lord Jesus Christ has taken care of the situation. Hey, go and check him out too if you need a miracle, and better hurry before he leaves...!!!). Such is our nature. We often fail to keep quiet or to keep things to ourselves. And this was not the only time that the Lord Jesus Christ had asked that His works be not told to anyone.

In Mark 9:2-9, the Bible tells us that: "After six days Jesus took Peter, James and John with him and led them up a high mountain, where they were all alone. There he was transfigured before them. His clothes became dazzling white, whiter than anyone in the world could bleach them. And there appeared before them Elijah and Moses, who were talking with Jesus. Peter said to Jesus, 'Rabbi, it is good for us to be here. Let us put up three shelters – one for you, one for Moses and one for Elijah.' (He did not know what to say, they were so frightened). Then a cloud appeared and covered them, and a voice came from the cloud: *'This is my Son, whom I love. Listen to him!'* Suddenly, when they looked around, they no longer saw anyone with them except Jesus. *As they were coming down the mountain, Jesus gave them orders not to tell anyone what they had seen until the Son of Man had risen from the dead.* They kept the matter to themselves, discussing what 'rising from the dead' meant."

Now, if you and I were present at the transfiguration of Jesus, I am not sure either of us would have kept quiet afterwards, as demanded by Jesus. Perhaps, we would have momentarily pretended to keep quiet, but no sooner had we turned the corner would we have started pontificating: "Tata, waaa chabe! I was there... Abena Moses na bena Elijah ukwisa monekela so. Twali fye nabo tule shimika ne lysahi..." (*i.e.* Man, the Lord Jesus is such a great guy. Imagine the Prophets Moses and Elijah pitched up to talk to Him. I was there. I also joined in the discussion! We had a great time together).

Of course, as humans, we love to add spice to a story. But such was not the case for the disciples. By contrast, for you and I, we could have gone on to tell the whole world, including our many friends on Facebook and Twitter, that we were actually chatting with the Prophets Moses and Elijah when, in fact, we were falling all over on our knees from fear and shock. But, at least, the disciples, Peter, James and John, did not tell a soul what they had seen. Neither did they fabricate any exaggerations of how they too got a chance to mix and hang out with the Prophets Moses and Elijah. Now, how many of us would have been that modest as to not gain political mileage out of such a situation? Let us be honest with ourselves.

- Kenneth K. Mwenda

In John 2:1-11, the Lord Jesus Christ's first miracle is recorded. The Holy Scriptures read: "And the third day there was a marriage in Cana of Galilee; and the mother of Jesus was there. And both Jesus was called, and his disciples, to the marriage. And when they wanted wine, the mother of Jesus saith unto him, They have no wine. Jesus saith unto her, 'Woman, what have I to do with thee? Mine hour is not yet come.' His mother saith unto the servants, 'Whatsoever he saith unto you, do it.' And there were set there six waterpots of stone, after the manner of the purifying of the Jews, containing two or three firkins apiece. Jesus saith unto them, 'Fill the waterpots with water.' And they filled them up to the brim. And he saith unto them, 'Draw out now, and bear unto the governor of the feast.' And they bare it. When the ruler of the feast had tasted the water that was made wine, and knew not whence it was: (but the servants which drew the water knew;) the governor of the feast called the bridegroom, And saith unto him, 'Every man at the beginning doth set forth good wine; and when men have well drunk, then that which is worse: but thou hast kept the good wine until now.' This beginning of miracles did Jesus in Cana of Galilee, and manifested forth his glory; and his disciples believed on him."

Now, if you and I were at that wedding in Cana, perhaps clamouring to and hustling for attention among the VIPs, we would have easily formed opinions about the standards of the wedding when the wine ran out. But such was not the case for Jesus. And if you and I were related, even remotely, to any of the disciples of the Lord Jesus, we might have thought that we have finally found a new 'friend' to brew us some free and great wine whenever we needed to get drunk. But, I am not sure we would have afforded the price of such quality fine wine. Yet we would have been quick to extend invitations to other friends, saying "Just come! We have a great friend who turns water into such great wine. And don't worry about the drinks. He will sort it out." And the whole world would be coming to us, and we would even be charging them some money to get the Lord Jesus to make us some good wine. But, alas, I am not sure that the Lord Jesus would have entertained such irresponsible behaviour. Besides, we would be abusing His friendship. Yet, amongst us mortals, there are many of us who live life like that, exploiting friends and relations. The disciples, though, out of respect and honor, did not abuse the Lord Jesus Christ's miraculous powers. They were all above board, and served obediently. Only one Judas messed up in the end because of his love for money. And thus we often see why sometimes those that will betray us are the same people that we are closely related to or that we associate with regularly. The Bembas say: "Ici-kupempula e ci-kulya..." (*i.e.* he or she that visits you often may actually be your worst enemy).

Many a time, when faced with difficulties or hardship, people turn to God. But when their prayers are answered few look back. All they remember is how great they are or how well they managed to solve the problems they were faced with. Closely related to that, some will seek help from others but not want to acknowledge that they have received any help. Others even get upset and angry when they hear that the person that helped them mentioned to someone else that he or she helped them. Yet, the truth remains that when someone helps you, whether or not that person talks about it is irrelevant. Only your own pride will make you feel upset when you hear that the other person has been talking about the assistance rendered.

Admittedly, while Christianity demands that even the giver or helper should not tout his or her horn, in reality very few givers or donors will remain quiet about the assistance rendered. And very few of them, indeed, can go down on that bended knee of humility like the receiver. If anything, the tax laws of many countries require charitable donors to disclose publicly their donations so that they can get some tax incentives. It is this incentive element that often motivates donors to give. Even among Christians, some tithe knowing that the incentive in tithing is that God will look kindly on our sacrifices. That said, we are awake to the fact that Christianity tells us that we should not be like the hypocrites who go out there preaching to everyone how much they have tithed. Rather, we should tithe quietly from the bottom of our hearts. But in doing so, are we not hoping or expecting that the Good Lord will certainly look with favour and kindness on our tithes? If that is the case, then it brings us back to the issue of incentives, and that there must be some incentive in tithing or giving. Rarely is altruism the sole motivation of many givers.

But do not get me wrong here. I am not supporting

or advocating for the arrogance of the giver, or that the giver should publicize his or her generosity. That is beside the point. Rather, the argument is that receiver should be open-minded and not expect that every giver will or should have a Christian heart of humility. If anything, many givers tend to tout their horns. And if you, as the receiver, choose to shower the giver with 'libanga' (*i.e.* some kind of traditional praise song of appreciation), as they call it in the Democratic Republic of the Congo, then the giver may even render to you more assistance. It's that simple. But if you are too proud to acknowledge that help or if you expect that the giver will also show humility when helping you, then you may end up losing out. He may just decide to help someone else instead. Indeed, it is not for you the receiver to say to the person helping you, '*See that you don't tell this to anyone*'. Rather, it is the person helping that has the prerogative to tell you so. As a recipient of aid or help, you cannot be seen to be attaching conditions upon which you should be helped. Otherwise, you might as well not seek any help from people.

By contrast, what is wrong is when a person is exaggerating the help they rendered. I have heard crazy stories of people who, when in desperate need of help, choose not to ask for help from a particular individual, just because they fear that that person will tell the whole world that he helped them. Now, only pride and arrogance will make someone think like that. For me, if I need help, I don't care whether that someone will stand on top of the mountain to preach that he or she helped me. After all, it's the truth. And I will be the first to acknowledge his or her help without any exaggerations, of course. That way, he or she will understand the extent of my appreciation and gratitude, especially if I can throw away my pride and be humble and honest enough about it all.

It must be told that pride is a sin that many Christians struggle with. Someone once said, "Although I have no food in the house, I cannot go to that guy to ask for help. He will tell everybody that I am broke!" But, my humble view has always been that those walking with such heavy hearts often have a problem themselves. And so, my interjection to the complainant was as follows: "The problem is not him but you. Why should you think like that? In any case, aren't you broke, as a matter of fact? You have to be humble in life if you need help. You can't be asking for help with pride and arrogance. A beggar is not a chooser. And learn to say thank you when someone helps you. But if you are too proud, you will want to belittle or downplay even the many things that someone has done for you. No Christian behaves like that, unless you worship a different god."

The issue of pride also manifests itself in relationships and marriages. Some marriages breakdown partly because either party to the marriage or both of them have too much pride to say sorry when in the wrong. But how Christian can we be if we have no sense of remorse and cannot even have the humility and magnanimity to show penance for our wrongs? Christianity calls for a contrite heart. I am not sure a person who never says sorry and one who never admits mistakes belongs to the Christian family. Admittedly, I may not be the best and rightful judge, but the Lord Jesus Christ teaches us penance and remorsefulness through a contrite heart when we sin. So, in our Christian lives, we can be better beings by not only quoting Bible verses dogmatically with a holier than thou attitude, but rather by reflecting more seriously on the interpretation of modern life against the backdrop of parallel teachings in the Holy Scriptures.

- Kenneth K. Mwenda

462

CHAPTER

52

RECONCILING RELIGION WITH THE LAW

Isaiah 55:8 warns us: "…'My thoughts are not your thoughts, and my ways are not your ways,' declares the LORD." Yet, as humans, we are constantly attempting to decree or promulgate ideas of what we perceive to be the Lord's thoughts and ways. Some of these ideas are not even Biblical but are simply man-made church traditions. I am neither a moral theologian, pastor nor a priest. But, I am schooled in legal philosophy and jurisprudence. Against this background, this article is not a discourse in moral theology or Christian doctrine. Rather, the article examines the sustainability of certain religious dictates when pitted against the law.

Humanity has seen so many atrocities committed in the name of religion. For example, the Rwanda genocide had the complicity of some clerics who would abuse their privileged position as church leaders to fuel anarchy. Closely related to that, the current wave of suicide bombers in some parts of the

- Kenneth K. Mwenda

world is orchestrated primarily on religious grounds.
I once heard of how during the Mau-Mau rebellion in
Kenya some Africans that attacked white
colonialists would be arrested shortly after going to
church for confession. Some priests would secretly
whisper to the police about what they had gathered
during these confessions. Indeed, if not properly
handled, religion can be an instrument of oppression
like was the case under the apartheid regime in
South Africa. As Karl Marx noted, religion is the
opium of the people.

Not too long ago, I read a media report where a
Principal Resident Magistrate in Lusaka,
Zambia, granted an order for a team of medical
doctors at the University of Zambia Teaching
Hospital (UTH) to administer blood transfusion to a
sick child that required blood but whose parents
were objecting to the blood transfusion just because
of their religious beliefs. Such issues have often led
to heated religious debates. But, the Magistrate
made a wise decision. Why should someone think
that they can subject another human being's life to
their own religious belief system? That child has a
right to life. The parents cannot project their own
notions of Christianity on an innocent child. Even if
the child is too young to make a choice, we must step
back and take public policy, good conscience and
equity into account. From a moralists' point of view
and under our African philosophy of "Ubuntu", we
should be asking ourselves: (a) is this the right thing
to do? (b) And, are we really sure that we know full
well what the good Lord thinks about our choices?
Every well-meaning religion, Christianity or

otherwise, should make sense. After all, that is why God gave us humans the power to reason.

In some jurisdictions, it may be a criminal offence to: (i) obstruct the work of a medical doctor where the doctor is about to perform a life-saving medical procedure on a patient that is not in a position to communicate his or her own consent; and/or (ii) support or direct a course of action that would deprive another of his or her life, notwithstanding the religious convictions at stake. Here, public policy would favour the saving of a life rather than the termination of the same, just as in the case of inappropriate abortions. A common secular view is that whereas the Bible is well respected, what raises controversy is not the Bible per se, but the interpretation of the Bible (*e.g.* regarding the issue of celibacy of priests as well as that of talking in tongues in some churches). Many religious groups opposed to the transfusion of blood often quote a myriad of Bible verses to buttress their arguments. But we must look beyond just quoting Bible phrases for the sake of wanting to sound prophetic.

Mindful that the Natural Law School of Thought in jurisprudence proceeds primarily on the notion of the supremacy of a deity whose law is above the laws of men and women, and that other Schools of Thought in legal philosophy and jurisprudence are predicated on different notions of the law, including the positivists' view that true law emanates from a determinate sovereign capable of issuing commands and sanctions, it is the Natural Law School of Thought that provides sanctuary to much of religious devotion. And with religious devotion comes the issue of morality. But, morality alone is hard to enforce. It merely appeals to our conscientious to regulate our social conduct. For example, if you break the wind in public, you cannot be arrested or punished under the law, although it is considered not morally polite to do so.

While positivists are pre-occupied with the question, "What is the law?" or "issues of legal realism", the Natural Law School of Thought is pre-occupied with determining "what the law ought to be" or "legal idealism". The latter view, it must emphasized, draws heavily from moral values and ethics. It jettisons the notion of the superiority of religious dictates over secular norms. The writings of St. Thomas Acquinas, St. Augustine and many others with a moralist approach to the law have given much support to this School of Thought. More recently, scholars such as Professor Ronald M. Dworkin have added their intellectual weight, advancing a theory that law should be understood as integrity and that judges interpret the law in terms of consistent and communal moral principles, especially justice and fairness. By contrast, publicists such as John Austin, Jeremy Bentham and Hans Kelsen have given contrasting accounts of what the law is, as opposed to what the law ought to be. To this list of positivists, Professor H.L.A Hart is an additional luminary. In essence, positivism postulates that there is no *inherent* or *necessary* connection between the validity of a law, on the one hand, and ethics or morality, on the other.

Today, we are experiencing a sustained excitement with human rights as if the concept of human rights has just been discovered in Africa. It is quite intriguing. Mindful that there is a renaissance that has been sweeping across the African continent since the collapse of many military dictatorships and One Party States, it is sometimes baffling to see the way we over-emphasize the issue of human rights at the expense of socio-economic development. While some may argue that the promotion of economic rights is part of realizing socio-economic development, it is also arguable whether economic and social rights are even justiciable or enforceable. One view has been to treat them simply as privileges. But one thing remains clear: human rights alone will not bring food to the table. We are not saying human rights are not important. There are certain fundamental rights that are non-negotiable, such as the right to life. And there are many theories on human rights. Others articulate a theory of different generations of human rights, that is, a first generation, a second generation and a third generation, placing varying emphases in a hierarchical order on the different echelons. Others postulate a theory of relativism whilst some promulgate the concept of universality. Akin to these theories, the requirement in some States to domesticate international treaties on human rights before they become opposable contrasts with the practice of other States where mere accession to, or signing and ratifying, of a treaty makes that treaty opposable to the relevant State.

In this article, we argue that our notion of human

- *Kenneth K. Mwenda*

468

rights should not be imbedded in euphoric excitement with self-centred entitlements. We maintain that every individual's human right has a corresponding and correlative duty. With every right comes a corresponding and correlative duty. This view is akin to the idea of Confucianism in many Asian cultures, promoting the cultivation of virtue and the development of moral perfection so that individuals are encouraged to give up their life, if necessary, either passively or actively, for the sake of upholding the cardinal moral values of *ren* and *yi*. In short, our thesis postulates that X's rights end where the rights of others begin. X cannot go out there in the streets in the nude claiming that he or she is exercising his or her freedom of expression that is constitutionally guaranteed. It is evident that, if X were to do so, his or her nudity would offend other people's right to enjoy non-offensive sightings. So, the public good will prevail over X's idiosyncratic and selfish notions of human rights, thereby imposing on X sanctions imbedded in the criminal law on indecent exposure. X cannot rely on arguments of human rights even if the Constitution is the grund norm of the land. Notwithstanding the doctrine of constitutional supremacy and that of inviolability of the Bill of Rights, public policy would not favour such a view. Many a time, 'What the law is' (e.g. the criminal law on indecent exposure) is a codification of some moral values by a determinate sovereign capable of issuing commands and sanctions. But, then, not all laws are a codification of morality, and not all moral or ethical norms are reflected in the law.

469

I have often argued with some of my learned lawyer colleagues that human rights must be viewed in their proper socio-economic and political contexts, while many argue that human right are human rights no matter where we are. As noted above, there are certain fundamental rights (e.g. the right to life) that are so fundamental that no State or institution can derogate from them. And that is why the underlying considerations for death penalty in homicide cases continue to attract debate, notwithstanding some long-standing theories of punishment such as deterrence and retribution.

By parity of reasoning, in the blood transfusion example provided above, the freedom of conscience (i.e. religion) of the parents ended where the child's right to life started. Nobody, morally or ethically speaking, has the right to permit or authorize the taking of another human being's life. If we all agree that the good Lord gives us life and would thus love the best for what He Himself has created, whether or not there are substitute blood supplements, it is not our calling to make judgments on the type of science that the Lord favours between blood supplements and blood transfusion. And what happens where there are no blood supplements or where the Doctors advice is that only real blood transfusion will work? Remember, Isaiah 55:8 warns us: "…'My thoughts are not your thoughts, and my ways are not your ways,' declares the LORD." Likewise, let us assume that someone goes to a church that does not subscribe to singing the Zambia National Anthem or saluting the Zambian Flag. Can the person argue that singing the National Anthem

- Kenneth K. Mwenda

or saluting the Zambian Flag, notwithstanding the dictates of the Flag Act, will infringe his or her constitutionally guaranteed freedom of conscience?

Or, can X, a homosexual and gay rights activist, claim that his homosexual conduct is protected under the Bill of Rights in Zambia's Constitution, pointing to freedom of expression? In short, does homosexual conduct qualify as freedom of expression under the Zambian Constitution, or should society inject morality into the law by summoning the criminal law that punishes those that engage in sex against the order of nature? There is a marked difference between "What the law is" and "What the law ought to be". It is for the reader to discern the difference. A common analogy I would draw here from moral theology is that while 'procreation' should be understood as the cooperation of man and woman with the good Lord in the transmission of new life into this world, 'reproduction' per se does not always involve the direct cooperation of the Lord. Rather, in the case of reproduction involving, say, an immoral sexual act outside marriage, there are two parallel processes taking place. On the one hand, the child being born has been offended by the parents' sin of fornication or adultery, and, on the other hand, the good Lord has blessed the world with the creation of a new life. These two processes are different, though related in a complex way. Likewise, morality and the law sometimes move on two separate but parallel lanes, while at other times the two are in full cooperation.

CHAPTER

53

CRIMINALIZING ADULTERY IN
A CHRISTIAN NATION

The title of this article will obviously catch the interest of many a reader. It is understandable. Many people love juicy topics and juicy gossip. No need to protest. That is what makes us human, after all. But hearken to my humble plea. It is not my intention here to cause any trouble. I was, in fact, reluctantly dragged into the topic by a correspondent from Zambia who implored me to address this topic from a legal point of view. So, I do not profess to be a merchant of morals here. Neither do I profess to stand on a pedestal of the holier than thou. That is not me. I am merely a writer and a scholar, communicating ideas to uplift society.

While the Constitutions of many English common law jurisdictions do not have a Preamble provision that states that a particular country has officially declared itself a Christian nation, the Preamble of Zambia's 1996 Constitution declares Zambia a Christian nation. Also, as *Lusaka Times* reported on

September 25, 2011, in a web article titled, *'President Sata thanks Church for peaceful polls and promises to base his rule on the 10 Commandments'*, the President of the Republic of Zambia, Mr. Michael C. Sata, promulgated a public policy statement to the effect that his Government would be 'governed by biblical teachings based on the Ten Commandments.' And we know full well that one of the Ten Commandments in the Bible holds that, 'Thou shalt not commit adultery'. So, this is where the argument begins.

President Sata's pronouncement elevates the national moral standards by which he expects to run the country. It is no longer a matter of a simple declaration in the Preamble of the Constitution that Zambia has been declared a Christian nation. Rather, the issue has now been given full weight by President Sata's policy statement that the Zambian Government will be administered on the basis of the Ten Commandments. But one wonders: what would happen if any of the Ten Commandments were to be in conflict with any of the rights enshrined in the Bill of Rights?

Indeed, if the Zambian Government will be run on the basis of the Ten Commandments, and given that the Preamble of the Constitution declares Zambia a Christian nation, one would opine reasonably that it may not be too far-fetched to argue that Zambia should legislate against and criminalize adultery. This postulate is not an extremist or religious fundamentalist view. Rather, it is a simple proposal to regulate moral conduct in society. After all,

Christians must not be seen to be condoning adultery even in a democratic society. Arguably, the criminalization of adultery will not take away from or offend any other religions in the country. Ideally, since the proposed criminalization of adultery is expected not to infringe the constitutional right to freedom of expression and conscience in Zambia, there may be no good cause for any religion to worry. I would imagine that there is no decent religion out there that advocates for adultery. If anything, many religions, except for some cults, prohibit adultery.

I have examined elsewhere the constitutionality of declaring Zambia a Christian nation (see: Zambia Daily Mail, August 24, 2011). Here, suffice it to say, the Bible, in John 8:3-11, teaches us the following: "The teachers of the law and the Pharisees brought in a woman caught in adultery. They made her stand before the group {4} and said to Jesus, *'Teacher, this woman was caught in the act of adultery. {5} In the Law, Moses commanded us to stone such women. Now what do you say?'* {6} They were using this question as a trap, in order to have a basis for accusing him. But Jesus bent down and started to write on the ground with his finger. {7} When they kept on questioning him, he straightened up and said to them, *'If any one of you is without sin, let him be the first to throw a stone at her.'* {8} Again he stooped down and wrote on the ground. {9} At this, those who heard began to go away one at a time, the older ones first, until only Jesus was left, with the woman still standing there. {10} Jesus straightened up and asked her, *'Woman, where are they? Has no one condemned you?'* {11} *'No one, sir,'* she said. *'Then neither do I condemn you,'* Jesus declared. *'Go now and leave your life of sin.'...*"

As one can imagine, those elderly men must have left the scene cursing in shame, accusing the young man, Jesus, of lack of respect for the elders. Yet, Jesus only asked a simple question. And they all failed to answer the question. All that was required of them was to respond to his challenge. It had nothing to do with 'umwaice wa mu-salula sana' (*i.e.* the young man is full of insolence) or that 'umwaice ta-kwete mucinshi' (*i.e.* the young man lacks respect for the elders). Truthfully, the young man just asked a simple question which the elders and the teachers of the law could not answer, but rather walked away in guilt and shame. Now, imagine if there were other young people around listening and watching what was happening. How could the elderly men have felt? One could reasonably fear that Jesus was courting trouble. Or, imagine that some of the humble wives of these same elderly men had followed behind to witness the stoning of the prostitute but only to find their husbands retreating in shame. What would have gone through the minds of these noble women? Now, you understand why those guys started plotting against Jesus, right? In their mind's eye, they felt that 'ta-kwete mucinshi nelyo panono' (*i.e.* Jesus was seen as being disrespectful to the elders and the teachers of the law). But who are we to judge?

Whereas certain crimes against morality have been criminalized under the Zambian Penal Code as well as under other Zambian statutes, not all acts of immorality constitute criminal offences. But why is this so? It all depends on who is the passing the law or how the people passing the law feel. If they feel that passing such a law may get them too, they will not pass the law. It is that simple. We can go around in circles arguing on the polemics of morality and the law in legal theory and jurisprudence, but the bottom-line is that if those that are entrusted with powers to pass the law feel that passing such a law will affect them too, then they will not pass that law. Likewise, if a person or individual is entrusted with constitutional powers to assent to a particular draft law, and the individual fears that the law in question will affect him or her if it comes into force, then that individual may opt not to assent to the draft law.

So, the question of whether or not we can criminalize adultery in Zambia depends a lot on the value system of those that make our laws. Otherwise, it is not entirely impossible to criminalize adultery. The criminalization of adultery has been done in some religious jurisdictions before. However, the English common law will obviously frown upon such an approach because those that developed the common law knew full that many wealthy folks of the time tended to have some concubines here and there, and the law had to protect these illicit relationships. And that is why even today, in common law jurisdiction such as Zambia and the United Kingdom, despite there being legislation such as a Wills Act, the common law allows for the admission of a testamentary bequest given secretly outside the will by the testator for the benefit of a secret beneficiary.

An adulterous man can leave some property secretly until he dies for the benefit of his concubine through what is known as a 'secret trust', without specifying anything or any fuller details in his will. And his wife may not know until the man is dead. But is such conduct not unchristian really? Yet, the courts of law, if convinced on the evidence, will uphold such 'secret trusts' as valid. Not many people in Zambia are aware of this. Yes, you can create a half-secret trust or a full secret-trust if you do not want your wife to know who else will benefit from your estate upon your death. Usually, although not always, the beneficiaries of a half-secret trust or a full- secret trust will be concubines of the deceased man or his illegitimate children born out of wedlock. In the olden days, the English even had statutes such as the Special Bastards Act 1235. One would have thought that those that brought Christianity to Africa should have been the first to show that Christianity cannot and will not uphold legal arrangements promoting illicit sexual affairs and for the benefit of concubines in the form of secret trusts. Others use some euphemism here through words such as 'his lady-mistress'. But it all comes back to the same thing – illicit sexual relationships!

In many common law jurisdictions, including the US and the UK, adultery is not a crime. But in Africa, although adultery is not a crime as such, African customary law deals with adultery differently. In many African countries, if an aggrieved spouse sues a concubine or male lover to a female spouse, the accused can be fined by the local court or asked to pay compensation if he or she is found guilty of having committed adultery with the complainant's spouse. The burden of proof in cases of African customary law is usually on the accused to show or prove that he or she did not commit adultery, especially where the complainant begins his or her submission with some evidence against the accused. To illustrate, if a man by the name of Mr. Banda is seen coming from Mr. and Mrs. Mulenga's home after midnight, and it is evidently clear that Mr. Mulenga is out of town, the onus is on Mr. Banda to show to the court what he was doing that late in the night to be coming from Mr and Mrs Mulenga's home when Mr. Mulenga is out of town. The court will not entertain arguments from Mr. Banda that the accuser should instead prove that he committed adultery. It is enough evidence that Mr. Banda was coming from Mrs. Mulenga's home late in the night when Mr. Mulenga was not there.

Likewise, the following fable helps to demonstrate that the burden of proof in African customary law cases often lies on the accused. A man is embroiled in an argument with his wife who accuses him of having an extra-marital affair. His wife points out to him that she has noticed lately that he comes home late in the night and looking very tired. She makes further accusations that even though his pubic hair looks nicely shaven, she is suspicious as to who could have been the barber because she herself did not shave his pubic hair! According to one African legend and custom, it is the wife who should shave her husband's pubic hair. Irritated with the accusations, the man decides to ignore his nagging wife and goes out the next day for a drink again. But, on his way back home from the drink, he notices an unusual sight of several old bicycles and some dilapidated cars parked outside his house. He begins to wonder what is happening. As he approaches his house, he sees his youngest son, Chileshe, playing outside the house on the veranda. He whispers quietly to Chileshe, asking what is going on. Chileshe replies that he just saw grandpa, grandma and many other relatives start arriving. The man queries his son further as to what the heck in the world is going on with all these old-looking bicycles leaning against the walls of his mansion. But the son, being young and naïve, innocently and unsuspectingly replies: "Katwishi, naine nshi-shibe... (I also don't know...) Na chu-mfwa fye ba mbuya bale landa ati, pano pa ng'anda na pa luba aamaso... (I just overheard grandma complaining that, at this house, pubic hair has gone missing)!"

In the fable presented above, the onus is on the accused to tell his wife (and the elders) where he has taken his pubic hair because it is a preserve of his wife to shave those delicate hairs. No girlfriend, workmate, neighbour, maid, classmate or doctor or nurse is allowed to rob a married man of his pubic without his wife's knowledge and consent. Such is the rule under African customary law in many parts of the country. So, it is not for his wife to prove that he has committed adultery. Rather, it is evidence enough that he has committed adultery if he comes home without his pubic hair! The problem, though, is that in many societies that are riddled with pockets of male chauvinism or those under patriarchical cultures, some men will justify their adultery through the imposition of old age adages like: 'Ubu-cende bwa maume tabu toba ng'anda...' (*i.e.* unlike the adulterous act of a married lady, the adultery act of a married man does not wreck a home). In short, it is seen as acceptable for a married man to commit adultery under such customary norms. This view is buttressed by the fact that African customary law generally deems customary marriages as potentially polygamous. But, of course, there is a need to qualify this view.

To say customary marriages are potentially polygamous is not tantamount to encouraging adulterous behavior under African customary law. Indeed, a person need not have sex before marriage. If too horny, the person may consider invoking masturbation instead. But then, masturbation is arguably a sin, although some religious folks dispute the point that masturbation is a sin, arguing instead that masturbation is OK since it is not specifically prohibited in the Bible. But he who sins by thought is as wrong as he who sins in deed. For masturbation to work, it is often accompanied by sinful thoughts.

Granted that in Christianity there is no such thing as a polygamous marriage, and that you only marry one wife and are expected to commit to her only, the secular law governing Christian and statutory marriages is silent on the consequences of committing adultery but only speaks out when a married man tries to go a step further by marrying a second wife. Only then does the criminal offence of bigamy kick in. Before that, the law is strategically mute, as intended by those who drafted it. Yet, we say we are a Christian nation. Why should the law governing statutory marriages under the Marriage Act not speak out against adultery? Even in England and the US such laws are generally silent on adultery. Why? It appears we have something in common with our friends from the UK and the US.

Some commentators against the criminalization of adultery assert that, 'Where have you seen such laws? Ta kwaba!' Others add that we are now operating in a liberalized and free market economy, and that it is all about supply and demand. And if, for example, you ask some sisters in favour of adulterous affairs, they will tell you that: "Ala iweee, naine ba mfwaile fye... Bushe ninee na betile?" (*i.e.* He just came after me by his own volition. I did not force him). But the sad part is that although adulterous relationships tend to benefit the recipients of 'foreign aid' as the adulterous married man often spreads his 'wealth' across many homes, it is his first family that often suffers. The hijackers here often have no mercy.

But in Matthew 5:32, the Lord Jesus Christ tells us that: "But I say to you that everyone who divorces his wife, except on the ground of sexual immorality, makes her commit adultery, and whoever marries a divorced woman commits adultery." In short, marriage is a lifetime commitment to the full exclusion of adultery. Yet others may cry foul, saying: "What about fornication, or even homosexuality? Why not talk about that, too?"

In the Bible, Jude 7 instructs us that: "Just as Sodom and Gomorrah and the cities around them, since they in the same way as these indulged in gross immorality and went after *strange flesh*, are exhibited as an example in undergoing the punishment of eternal fire." In short, as we often say in Bemba to keep a child away from hot things, '*pye-pye*'! The problem really with adultery is that whatever makes you smile today will one day make you cry. Perhaps Christian nations like Zambia should be showing leadership in this area by criminalizing adultery. But I know that this is a lone cry in the desert, especially that no one is perfect and that we have all fallen short of the glory of God.

On Monday, March 26, 2012, the *Zambia Post* newspaper reported in its On-line edition that: "NGOCC (Non-Governmental Organizations Coordinating Council) board chairperson Beatrice Grillo says there is no moral reason for men to abandon their children. Commenting on Mafinga MMD Member of Parliament, Catherine Namugala, who urged the government to enact legislation that should compel men to be penalised for abandoning their own children, Grillo said it was immoral for anyone to abandon their own children. She said she totally supported Namugala's comments, adding that men abandoning their children should be dealt with severely. Grillo said children were a gift from God. She wondered why men went around fathering children whom they could not look after. 'Any action has consequences and men should know that; why should they leave the responsibility to women only?' Grillo asked. 'For these men to be where they are, their parents looked after them and if some of them were abandoned, it should be the more reason why they should look after their own children.' She advised both men and women to be responsible."

Although section 169 of Zambia's Penal Code provides that, "Any person who being the – (a) parent; (b) guardian; or (c) person in charge; of a child that is unable to provide for itself, refuses or willfully neglects to provide, being able to do so, sufficient food, clothes, bedding or other necessities for such child, and thereby injures the health of such child, commits an offence and is liable, on conviction, to a fine...or to imprisonment ...", we need not wait until such parental or guardian refusal or neglect 'injures the health of the child'.

In many cases, children that are born out-of-wedlock or through adulterous relationships or fornication are abandoned by their biological fathers even where their mothers have not re-married or where the custody and support of the child has not been granted to some other man by, say, a court order. The poor woman is often left to fend for the child alone. In a way, this explains the increasing number of street kids in Zambia today. Some of these street kids have relatively wealthy or financially comfortable fathers who, upon impregnating the kid's mother through, say, an adulterous relationship, will dispute paternity so as to avoid parental responsibility. Usually, these men do not want their wives to know about such adulterous affairs or the illegitimate child born out of the illicit sexual relationship. So, what to do now, as a Christian nation? Of course, just talking and talking alone will not solve much. The issue is: how can we strengthen the law to curb such conduct of irresponsible men and women who fail to provide for their children?

484

CHAPTER

54

APPRECIATING THE LAW AGAINST CRUELTY TOWARDS ANIMALS

It is not an uncommon sight in Zambia to see a cow or dog that is thinner than its owner. Some cows actually look like they are just recovering from malaria, with protruding collar bones sticking out in their hide. Yet the cow-owner will be busy over-loading the attendant ox-wagon with all sorts of cargo, expecting the malnourished cow to summon some inexplicable strength to pull the mighty heavy wagon. Closely related to this, many dogs in Zambia have become professional hustlers at garbage bins and other places of refuse disposal. And if the owner of the dog has spent a night out partying, so will the dog. Both could have gone 'hunting' for something similar, but who dares mention what it is! The owner and the dog will end up converging at the gate of the house in the wee hours of the next morning when returning from their social escapades. And they simply look at each other like good old buddies, with no one to blame the other. Sadly, the owner of the dog looks much more well-nourished and well-dressed than his dog.

It would be interesting to find out whether, in many households in Zambia, a dog is considered a pet or it is meant to provide security only. Here, I am trying find out the place or role of a dog in some Zambian homes. In a minute, you will understand why. For now, suffice it to say, in certain parts of the world, many dogs are considered part of the family and some even inherit wealth through testamentary dispositions or wills. Other dogs play the role of a secret-lover to some wealthy but lonely humans. In Zambia, it would be helpful to understand the role or place of a dog in the home if we are to examine objectively the issue of controlling cruelty against such domestic animals as dogs. If, on the one hand, a dog is considered a domestic (home) pet, where and how does it spend most of its nights? And does the dog even get regular and adequate meals or some occasional dog pedicure and dental floss?

One anonymous commentator observes: "Aside from the actual beating of an animal and the overloading of an ox-wagon for a thin and weak cow to pull, everything else becomes relative. Well maybe not so fast because the lines are somewhat blur. First, I wouldn't consider not providing a guard house or a mat for a dog a cruel thing. I think that dogs were designed to live that way. Even where such is provided for, you will see a happy dog digging away in the garden or even sleeping in the muddy hole. I have an issue with the way dogs are sometimes looked after in the West – i.e. as pets. Dogs get castrated or sterilized only for the benefit of the owner, but not for the benefit of the dog itself. Also, those lonely humans that have a tendency of sleeping with dogs, including those that are in the habbit of engaging in bestiality, have escaped the crime of rape because animals do not talk, and that, as a result thereof, it is hard to tell if the animal actually consented. While humans can go to court and win cases of rape or sexual assault, no one is speaking out for poor Spotty, the dog."

Perhaps, the issue of sterilizing dogs to stop their potential to breed is best resolved by the English common law rule in the case of *Rylands v. Fletcher* (1868) L.R. 3 H.L. 330. In that case, the defendants, mill owners in the coal mining area of Lancashire, had constructed a reservoir on their land. The water broke through the filled-in shaft of an abandoned coal mine and flooded connecting passageways into the plaintiff's active mine nearby. In 1865, the trial court found that the defendants were ignorant of the abandoned mine shaft and free of negligence and decided the case in favor of the defendants. In 1866, on appeal by the plaintiffs, the Exchequer Chamber decided to reverse the lower court and imposed strict liability on the defendants, but the case did not readily fit within the existing tort theories. Justice Colin Blackburn, comparing the situation to trespasses involving cattle and dangerous animals, declared: "The true rule of law is that the person who for his own purposes brings on his lands and collects and keeps there anything likely to do mischief if it escapes, must keep it in at his peril, and, if he does not do so, is prima facie answerable for all the damage which is the natural consequence of its escape."

If, on the other hand, a dog is kept only for the purposes of providing security at the home, should the dog be made to sleep outside in the cold at night without any guardhouse or shelter for it, especially when there are heavy thunderstorms and rains? And can we simply take it that, after all, dogs are used to resting their torso on the hard 'concrete-cement' of the veranda, with ceaseless ticks and fleas tormenting them? And what are the nutritional levels like for most dogs in Zambia? Are they provided with decent meals by their owners or do most dogs have to hustle it out and fend for themselves at the garbage bins? Indeed, what does the law say?

The Prevention of Cruelty to Animals Act 1920 (as amended through to 1994) provides for the prevention of cruelty to animals. The statute also criminalizes cruelty towards animals. And the term 'animal' is said to refer to any horse, mare, gelding, bull, cow, ox, heifer, steer, calf, mule, ass, sheep, lamb, hog, pig, sow, goat, fowl, ostrich, dog, cat, or any other domestic animal, fowl or bird, including any wild animal, fowl or bird in a state of captivity. Then, the said Prevention of Cruelty to Animals Act 1920 defines 'owner' of an animal as including any person having the charge, custody or control of the animal.

Under the Prevention of Cruelty to Animals Act 1920, any person who cruelly beats, kicks, ill-treats, over-rides, over-loads or tortures an animal, or causes an animal to be so used, or drives or uses an animal which is so diseased or so injured, or in such a physical condition that it is unfit to do any work, or by wantonly or unreasonably doing or omitting to do any act, or causing or procuring the commission or omission of any act, causes unnecessary suffering, or, being the owner, permits in the manner aforesaid unnecessary suffering to be caused to the animal, will be guilty of the offence of cruelty. Now, let us take a more reasoned look at this statutory provision.

If, say, a dog's owner does not provide it with regular and proper meals, other than, say, nshima left- overs and some salty water, the owner's conduct can be construed as ill-treatment of the dog. It is no good excuse for the owner to claim that many people are facing economic hard times, and that he too cannot afford a decent meal. The owner of the dog ought to know that owning or keeping a dog calls for responsibility under the Prevention of Cruelty to Animals Act 1920, and that ignorance of the law is no defence. In short, do not own a dog if you cannot maintain it financially. Many people like to crave for things that they cannot afford or things that they cannot maintain financially. Yet, the Holy Bible reminds us in Proverbs 12:10 that: "A righteous man cares for the needs of his animal, but the kindest acts of the wicked are cruel."

Indeed, if a dog sleeps on hard ground most of the time and has no proper and decent doghouse, such treatment can be considered as ill-treatment of the animal. But wait a minute. Some critic might be tempted to ask: kanshi, what constitutes 'ill-treatment'? Well, since the Prevention of Cruelty to Animals Act 1920 does not provide a definition of 'ill-treatment' we are left to look to the English common law on the rules of statutory interpretation. In its ordinary meaning, the term 'ill-treatment' can be best understood by referring to the day-to-day Bemba parlance of 'uku-cusha ifi-tekwa.' Does that help?

The Prevention of Cruelty to Animals Act 1920 also prohibits, among other things, causing or promoting dog fights. It is an offence to cause, procure or assist at the fighting of an animal, or keep, use, manage, or act or assist in the management of a premises or place used for the purpose, or partly for the purpose of fighting animals, or permit any premises or place to be so kept, managed or used, or receive or cause or procure a person to receive money for the admission of a person to such premises or place. Let us think through this statutory provision more thoughtfully. Would it be an offence if some mischievous young boys hanging out in the neighbourhood threw some stones at, or caned with a heavy bamboo stick, the intersection of a sexually-locked female dog and male dog involved in passionate copulation?

It would appear that such cruel act by the mischievous young boys would be deemed as 'cruelly beating' the two copulating animals. And the cruel beating of an animal, as noted above, is considered an offence under the Prevention of Cruelty to Animals Act 1920. As shameful or embarrassing as the sexual act of the dogs might seem to the public, people passing-by should just look elsewhere and pretend that they have not seen what is going on.

Further still, it is an offence to cause or procure, without reasonable cause or excuse, or, being the owner, permit such administration of, poisonous or injurious drug or substance to an animal, or without reasonable cause or excuse, cause such substance to be taken by an animal. What does this mean? If, say, a dog is in the habit of stealing from and eating eggs in the poultry house, the law does not allow for or give the dog's owner the right to force a boiling egg in the mouth of the dog as a deterrent measure to stop the dog from stealing and eating the eggs. Such conduct is deemed cruel, and it is a crime under the Prevention of Cruelty to Animals Act 1920. Indeed, there is no reasonable excuse for causing or forcing the dog to eat and swallow the boiling egg. Rather, what might be helpful here is for the dog to undergo some training and to receive regular and adequate meals.

The Prevention of Cruelty to Animals Act 1920 also prohibits the killing of an animal in the sight of other animals waiting to be slaughtered. In essence, what this means is that when a cow is being slaughtered at the abattoir, for example, the people in-charge of this exercise should ensure that other cows waiting to be slaughtered do not see the incident, otherwise the other cows will be too traumatised. But, then, what about some weird incidents of bestiality that have been reported in the Zambian media, involving some arrests of suspects that have been caught having carnal knowledge of, say, a cow, pig or goat? Can such acts be considered as cruelty to animals?

Arguably, unless there is evidence adduced on the cruel nature of the act, such as where a man is forcing himself sexually on a chicken, bestiality may not immediately qualify as a cruel act. And bestiality is usually neither an act of beating, kicking, over-riding or over-loading an animal. However, in some instances, bestiality can be considered as ill-treatment or torture of an animal, depending on the facts of the case. Also, under section 155 of the Penal Code, it is a criminal offence for a person to have carnal knowledge of an animal, whether or not the animal is enjoying the act. To put matters in context, this means that if, say, a lustful man is found in a compromised position in a poultry house, with a fearful hen in his hands, he will not escape the force of the law. Indeed, it is no good excuse for him to argue that he was trying to avoid human sexual partners for fear of contracting sexually-transmitted diseases that can be lethal and fatal.

CHAPTER

55

SLEEPING WITH YOUR BOSS
TO GET AHEAD

That it is not a crime in many countries for two consenting adults, a male and a female, working for the same institution or company, to indulge in a sexual relationship does not mean that such a relationship is morally and/or ethically alright. Akin to situations where a young lady is offered a job after attending 'carpet interviews' (*i.e.* after rendering sexual favours on the carpet to a hiring boss), it is actually wrong and bad to sleep with your boss. You have to consider also the corporate culture and power-politics of the organisation as well as the relevant human resources management (HRM) policies and any applicable sexual harassment laws. Corporate incest, as it is sometimes known, often shows its ugly face when a male supervisor or manager begins to date or to sleep with a female subordinate, or where a professor starts to sleep with one of his or her students. Occasionally, you will find some courageous male subordinate dating or sleeping with a female boss, especially if the latter is desperately looking for a spouse or has difficulties in attracting or finding a suitable male partner. As they say in Bemba, "Iyi-kota, ilya ne cani..." (*i.e.* an old lion or old lioness, with no strength to hunt down a fast sprinting prey, will resort to eating grass).

Generally, many supervisor-subordinate relationships exist in different forms and contexts. For example, you can have a supervisor-subordinate relationship between a supervising male medical doctor and a female medical nurse, or between a church pastor and a female church congregant or a female church-choir member. Such a relationship can also occur between a male guardian and a young female dependant in a home, or between a male senior military officer and a female junior soldier.

Sometimes, the female subordinate, or the male subordinate, as the case may be, will be encouraged by the culpable superior to work in a different unit of the company from that being headed by the said superior, with a view of making the sexual relationship appear somewhat acceptable and normal since the subordinate reports to a different manager or supervisor. But, let us take a more reasoned look.

Is it alright to sleep with your supervisor just to get a promotion or to get ahead of others? Or, is it alright for a female subordinate to flirt with her boss, or to be asking him redundant and simple questions now and again just to get his attention, or to be giggling at him whenever he is asking questions with a view of using one's femininity to get ahead of others? Indeed, what are the moral choices that we ought to be making here, especially if one of the parties or both are married? And does this not tie in with the need for moral decency in the dress-code of some ladies at the workplace so that their clothing is not too suggestive and does not expose much of their upper thighs?

Notably, immoral sexual relationships between a supervisor and a subordinate can occur even in homes, especially where a male boss is sleeping with a female maid or where a female boss is sleeping with the houseboy or garden boy. Now, I am not a psychologist to offer any detailed explanation why such behaviour happens, save to say that it has been reported before that some sexually frustrated but 'self-liberated' married or single women have been known to pounce on their male house servants or garden boys, while some lustful male bosses, whether married or not, have been known to coerce or entice some of their female maids through cajoleries or threats. In a number of these cases, some form of sexual harassment tends to be the starting point, especially where some threats are involved. That said, can we contend that mutual consent between the two parties is all we should be concerned with?

While the laws of many countries, including the HRM policies of many companies, do prohibit sexual harassment in workplaces and elsewhere, these prohibitions tend to focuss more on men as the aggressors and women as the victims. To overcome such gender bias, we have to look beyond the law.

We have to try to figure out additionally what the business ethics say. In an article titled, "Sleeping with your boss can 'boost your career and give you a promotion... especially if you're a woman'," which appeared in a British publication, the *Mail Online*, on August 27, 2010, Daniel Bates reports: "It will threaten to destroy your family life and lose you the respect of others. But having an affair with the boss is seen as likely to boost your career, especially if you are a woman. Some 37 per cent of office workers said that from their experience those who slept with their superiors were rewarded with a career boost. And no wonder – no matter how high achieving, female executives will not reach the very top of their profession unless they find a 'sponsor' who will speak out on their behalf, the study for the U.S. Centre for Work-Life Policy found."

So, after all, sex seems to be a big thing in the corporate world, although it is hardly covered on most MBA degree programmes. However, Bates observes further, "More often than not they are in a position of power and influence, and almost always male and married. Despite all the risks, affairs in the workplace are still a common occurrence." According to Bates, some 34 per cent of women in executive positions said they knew a female colleague who had slept with their boss. Even at director level or above, 15 per cent of women admitted to having had an office fling. And in terms of morale, 61 per cent of men and 70 per cent of women said they would lose respect for a leader involved in an affair. As Bates observes, "Don't expect that your colleagues will have no idea what is happening – 60 per cent of male executives and 65 per cent of female executives suspect that salary hikes and plum assignments are being traded for sexual favours."

Yes, we live in a crazy world! And while much of the corporate world looks quite rosy from outside, things are quite muddy from the inside, with many folks entangled in corporate hustling and jostling so as to position themselves favourably for promotions and all. The evidence presented by the *Mail Online* is quite revealing. Bates continues: "Some 48 per cent of men and 56 per cent of women feel animosity towards the involved couple, and 39 per cent of men and 37 per cent of women see a fall off in productivity as the team splinters."

According to Bates, relationships expert Jean Hannah Edelstein noted that: "Office affairs are a bad idea. Your boss already has a lot of power over you...so once you start sleeping with him, how do you know that he's going to fulfil his end of the bargain? Even if it happens in the short term, everyone will know what's going on and you'll lose their respect. It poisons the atmosphere and in the long run it is not worth it and will follow you around the industry."

Edelstein is quoted as saying further: "In some jobs that are boring you're sitting there all day and you want to fancy someone, or in some high-pressure jobs there is nowhere else to meet people, so these things do happen. If it does, be prepared to leave your job if it goes sour, it can be that serious. You really have to ask yourself: 'Am I that into this person I'd be prepared to lose my job over it?' If the answer is no, then don't do it.'..."

Cherise Fantus makes observations similar to Edelstein's in an article titled, "Why sleeping with your boss will knock you to the bottom," dated February 6, 2011, and published Online in the *Scribe*, "You have a sexy boss. He's tall; he's handsome; he's unattached; and best of all, he's in a position of power. You've no doubt spent a lot of time fantasizing about him in a slightly different position of power. Well, stop it. Sleeping with your boss is almost always guaranteed to end badly."

According to Fantus, "Monica Lewinsky should have taught us that. She slept with the most powerful man in the country. Maybe she simply couldn't resist that kind of power. Maybe she thought it would advance her career." Fantus contends further that most people, like Lewinsky, sleep with their bosses in hopes of advancing their positions or receiving a raise. The reality, though, Fantus argues, is that you will likely lose your job because 'either somebody will find out, there will be a scandal, and your boss' boss will fire you; or, you will develop a relationship'. Also, what if the sex turns out to be terrible? Can you imagine, as Fantus rightly observes, having to look him in the eye the next day? "Uh... sir, can you approve these TRS reports?" Fantus concludes that, by contrast, should the sex turn out to be great, it will eventually end. Although, legally speaking, your boss cannot fire you because you broke up with him, he can always find another reason to fire you. Or he can transfer you "downstairs to Storage Unit B. Either way, you're screwed. Figuratively, not literally, of course." So, what to do now?

It is not always the case that bottom-power will get you to the top. Sometimes it can land you into problems. Some possessive married bosses will not allow their subordinate sexual partner to get herself a spouse to marry. The poor subordinate will remain the boss' concubine, especially if the boss is now fathering children with her or is taking care of most of her financial needs. Likewise, a male subordinate who has been sleeping with his female supervisor will find it hard to break away from that relationship. If he dares try, he might end up being fired or demoted instantly by the upset female boss, or she will deliberately make his life a living hell or a nightmare. So, what to do now? As the Bembas say: "Aka-fupa utemenwe eka kusha umu-cene." And as an old African-American adage goes: "Son, whatever makes you smile gonna make you cry"!

500

CHAPTER

56

POSITIONING ZAMBIA'S HUMAN CAPITAL STRATEGICALLY IN INTERNATIONAL RELATIONS AND DEVELOPMENT

For the 2012 Africa Cup Soccer Finals, many African teams summoned their professional players based in Europe and elsewhere to come and win them the Africa Cup of Nations. Zambia was no exception. We summoned some of our boys from the African soccer giants, TP Mazembe of Democratic Republic of Congo, as well as from China, Russia, Switzerland and South Africa. Otherwise, had we shunned those in the diaspora and just relied solely on input from those in the domestic soccer league, I doubt that we would have brought the Africa Cup of Nations to Zambia.

By parity of reasoning, this year, 2012, Nigeria became the first African nation to attempt to have one of its nationals as President of the World Bank. Yes, the distinguished and highly accomplished lady, Dr. Ngozi Okonjo-Iweala, came from the diaspora. A

Harvard educated economist, with a PhD in Economics from MIT, she has previously worked for the World Bank as a Country Director, a Vice-President and a Managing Director. Dr. Ngozi Okonjo-Iweala joined the World Bank as a Young Professional many years ago. At one time, after serving as a Vice-President at the World Bank, she took time off to serve as Finance Minister of Nigeria (her current position) and then later as Minister of Foreign Affairs. And after her stint in the Nigerian Federal Government, she returned to the World Bank as a World Bank Managing Director before going back to Nigeria again early this year as Minister of Finance and Planning. The story of Dr. Ngozi Okonjo-Iweala is not the only one in terms of how some African countries have utilized the technical expertise of their distinguished nationals from the diaspora.

A few years back, Malawi's now deceased former Head of State, Dr. Bingu wa Mutharika, brought on board his younger brother, Professor Peter Mutharika, from the diaspora to boost his administration. A law graduate of the esteemed Yale Law School, Professor Peter Mutharika is a tenured law professor at Washington University in the US. In Malawi, he has served as Minister of Justice, Minister for Education, Science and Technology, and finally as Minister of Foreign Affairs.

In Ghana, the Supreme Court benefitted from the appointment to the bench, as Supreme Court judges, of Professor A. Kodzo Paaku Kludze of Rutgers University in the USA, who has now retired from the

Supreme Court, and the late Professor Tawia Modibo Ocran, who at the time of his appointment was a senior professor at the University Of Akron School Of Law in Ohio, US. Of Professor Kludze, Kwame Mbroh, writes in the *Modern Ghana* (Online: 2002):

"The University of London has conferred on Dr. A. Kodzo Kludze, a distinguished Ghanaian Professor of Law at Rutgers University in the United States, a Higher Doctorate degree in Law. This highest degree (higher than a PhD) in the books of the University of London..., was conferred...this summer for his exceptional academic contribution to African Law. He is the first Ghanaian to be awarded such a degree based solely on academic excellence. Even Dr. J.B. Danquah, one of our foremost learned academics, did not have the opportunity to be awarded this highest honour in the academia... Dr. Kludze received his BA and LLB degrees from the University of Ghana, where he graduated at the top of his class... According to a former classmate who identified himself as Edusei, 'the top was always reserved for Dr. Kludze, right from his Adisadel days through Legon.' He reccived his PhD from the University of London in 1969."

A while back, when I visited Uganda, I met one of the senior judges of the Ugandan Court of Appeal. He had previously served as a senior lawyer at the IMF. He was now bringing his international experience to bear on the development of the legal system in Uganda. Likewise, the distinguished Professor Benno Ndulu is now the Governor of the

Central Bank of Tanzania. He is not only a distinguished academic but was also at some point with the World Bank in Washington DC before taking up leadership at the Central Bank of Tanzania. You may be wondering by now what exactly I am trying to say. Well, this is not about personal or self-interest, but rather about national interest for those who care for and love their country. It's certainly not about one Professor Mwenda seeking some hidden personal agenda. That is far from it.

And all these examples that I have given above relate to individuals that did not find themselves in the diaspora through political appointments. They earned their ranks abroad on merit. These are individuals that were able to distinguish themselves competitively against other top nationals from other countries. It's a different story to talk about non-competitive political appointments to some institution abroad. I trust you see my point. While many political appointments tend to be nominal, or at times 'executive', they often lack the technical edge of a full-time technocrat and are thus mostly useful for such endeavors as political aspirations or other non-technocrat but affluent stations in life.

The argument I am advancing here is that Zambia has not done well or succeeded at strategically identifying some of its useful and talented professionals in the diaspora for marshaling a competitive edge when it comes to fielding strong candidates in international organizations as well as in strategic positions back home in Zambia. Here, we cannot place the blame entirely on the Zambian Government. A number of our Zambian professionals in the diaspora have also not made much effort to reach out to institutions back home. I mean, how else will the Government or institutions back home know about what you are doing if you do not have a strategy to introduce your works and efforts?

That said, the Zambian Government can, and should, utilize some strategic pockets of the diaspora in order to bring additional technocratic value to our country. Look, I started this essay with the example of how we won the Africa Cup of Nations. We pulled together both our local and foreign talent. We did not shut the door on the foreign-based players. The same analogy and reasoning can be extended to national development, and also on how we can position our people in international organizations like the UN, FAO, WTO and so forth.

Zambia has benefitted from the talent of only a handful of individuals that have held 'political' appointments through the Zambian Government at such international organizations as the UN, IMF, the World Bank, the African Development Bank, WHO, and the Organization for African, Caribbean and Pacific Group of States. But when these individuals' tour of duty ends and they return home, they are usually abandoned whenever there is a change of government, especially if the said individuals are reluctant to become political cadres of the new government. Their international experience just goes to waste. It is like changing players in the national soccer team every time there is a new coach. You can't win like that. Notwithstanding the need for networking and political lobbying, it explains why it has not been easy for Zambia to find and field strong and competitive candidates for positions such as Secretary-General or President of certain international organizations like the African Union. Other countries will come up with candidates that do not only have local experience but that have also worked in internationally competitive portfolios abroad. You can actually see that the CVs of some of these candidates are far ahead of many of our locally-sponsored candidates.

We have to move away from the retrogressive culture of personalizing issues. And we have to be strategic about the way we maneuver in some of these matters, especially as a nation that is trying to influence international public policy through some of these international organizations. I opine that part of the solution lies in those that are allegedly in the diaspora and are in the habbit of 'insulting' some politicians back home to exercise some restraint by criticizing objectively instead as well as in the Zambian Government identifying both local and international talent among its people. Indeed, we cannot ignore the valuable experience of some pockets of the diaspora. That is how national soccer teams are usually organized if they have to win a major international trophy. They never shun or shut the door on the diaspora even if it means inviting foreign-based players who will come and take-up the jobs of the local players. At the end of the day, all you want is to get the best players on the team, not so? If that be the case, then give a chance also to the best foreign-based players to come and help out the country so as to win you the 'economic' trophy, especially if they are good at what they do wherever they are. Thereafter, they can go back, if they so wish. After all, we live in a globalized world. But we do need international and global experience as well as sound insights into international best practice. Local or regional experience alone is not enough. As they say in Bemba: "Umwana ashenda atasha nyina ukunaya".

508

ABOUT THE AUTHOR

Prof. Kenneth K. Mwenda
PhD, LLD, DSc(Econ)

http://www.kennethmwenda.com

A distinguished thought leader and public intellectual, **Prof. Kenneth K. Mwenda** read law at Oxford as a Rhodes Scholar. He has also taught law at top universities in the United States of America (US), the United Kingdom (UK) and South Africa. A Fellow of the British Royal Society of Arts (FRSA), Prof Mwenda is a recipient of several international academic awards, including a competitive fellowship from Yale University Law School in the US. Most recently, he gave the 2015 Distinguished Lecture at the University of Nairobi Law School in Kenya, and was appointed as Extraordinary Professor of Law in the Faculty of Law at the University of Pretoria, South Africa. He has also held previously the position of Extraordinary Professor of Law at the Centre for Human Rights, the University of Pretoria. Based in Washington DC, Prof. Mwenda is the Program Manager and Executive Head of the World Bank's Voice Secondment Program, a major capacity-building initiative of the Board of Executive Directors of the World Bank.

Prof. Mwenda has had a stellar academic career as well as an outstanding professional life as a leading international development practitioner, travelling to more than thirty countries worldwide. His is a fine blend of theory and practice, with many years of international experience in both academia and international development. Prof Mwenda has maintained a parallel academic and professional life, publishing academic books and other scholarly work in top journals and law reviews as well as holding various senior academic appointments at leading universities internationally, while serving with the World Bank. A member of the editorial boards of several scholarly journals, including the *Journal of*

International Banking Regulation and the *Africa Finance Journal*, he is also an occasional editor of the *Journal of African Business*, and was until recently the joint Editor-in-Chief of the World Bank's *Law, Justice and Development Book Series*.

With sustained thought leadership in academia, in addition to valuable experience in international development practice, Prof Mwenda is a widely recognized authority in his field of expertise as well as a highly sought-after speaker that has been interviewed and quoted by numerous print and broadcast media, including the *New York Times* (US), the *Voice of America* (VOA, US), *CCTV* (US), the *Times* (UK), the *British Broadcasting Corporation* (BBC, UK), and *Sky TV* (UK). In 2008, after a rigorous and thorough examination of Prof Mwenda's selected scholarly books and peer-refereed journal articles by a distinguished panel of top international legal scholars, Prof Mwenda was admitted by Rhodes University, a leading university in South Africa, to the rarely awarded Higher Doctorate degree of Doctor of Laws (LLD). It was the first time ever in the rich academic history of that university that such an award was being conferred in the Faculty of Law! Six years later, in 2014, after another rigorous and thorough examination of Prof Mwenda's other substantial portfolio of scholarly books and peer-refereed journal articles by a distinguished panel of eminent international scholars, Prof Mwenda was admitted by the University of Hull, a leading British university, to the rarely awarded Higher Doctorate degree of Doctor of Science in Economics (DSc(Econ)). It is important to stress that in the entire English speaking world, Prof. Mwenda is arguably the only senior legal scholar to have earned two Higher Doctorate degrees in two different disciplines! Higher Doctorates, it should be emphasized, are never the immediate step after a PhD. Rather, they are reserved for those internationally recognized senior scholars that have made exceedingly significant contributions to a science or body of knowledge through exceptionally insightful and distinctive scholarly publications, earning them recognition as international authorities in the field of research that forms the basis of the degree.

Further, Prof. Mwenda holds a PhD in Law from a leading British university, the University of Warwick. At the World Bank, he has served additionally as Senior Legal Counsel in the Legal Vice-Presidency as well as Senior Legal Counsel in the World Bank's Integrity Vice-Presidency. All in all, Prof. Mwenda has written more than twenty-five (25) scholarly books and over ninety (90) articles in leading law reviews and academic journals. Prior to joining the World Bank, he served as an Assistant Professor of Law at the Faculty of Law, the University of Warwick, in the UK. Prof Mwenda has also taught as Adjunct Professor of Law at American University Washington College of Law (WCL) in Washington DC. His scholarly work is cited frequently as authority not only in academia, but also by the courts of law, most recently by the Supreme Court for the Republic of Zambia in the case of *Ventriglia and Ventriglia v. Eastern and Southern Africa Trade and Development Bank and*

Robert Simeza SCZ NO. 13 OF 2010 (Appeal No. 11/ 2009). His other scholarly work has been seminal in some of the research work and country assessments carried out by the International Monetary Fund (IMF), the World Bank, the Asian Development Bank (ADB) and the Inter-American Development Bank (IADB).

In addition, Prof. Mwenda holds, *inter alia*, the prestigious BCL degree from the University of Oxford (UK) and an MBA degree from the University of Hull (UK), with subsequent executive leadership training from Cornell and Georgetown Universities, respectively. His first professional law degree, a Bachelor of Laws (LLB), is from the University of Zambia where he graduated in 1990 in the top one percent (1%) of his class. He was admitted to the Bar in Zambia in 1991, as the best Bar admission student. Prof. Mwenda is a US Certified Anti-Money Laundering Specialist (CAMS) as well as a Fellow of the British International Compliance Association (FICA). He has served as Visiting Full Professor of Law at a number of leading universities in Europe and South Africa, including the University of Miskolc in Hungary, the University of Cape Town (UCT), the University of Western Cape (UWC) and the University of Zambia. He has also given many lead lectures and presentations at major US universities, including George Washington University, the University of Maryland, Duke University, Temple University, and the University of South Florida.

- Kenneth K. Mwenda

OTHER BOOKS BY THIS AUTHOR

2016

Kenneth K. Mwenda, **Public Intellectualism and Socio-Political Inquiry through Metaphor and Musing**, Vol. 4, (Toronto, Canada: Africa in Canada Press, 2016).

2016

Kenneth K. Mwenda, **Public Intellectualism and Socio-Political Inquiry through Metaphor and Musing**, Vol. 3, (Toronto, Canada: Africa in Canada Press, 2016).

2016

Kenneth K. Mwenda, **Public Intellectualism and Socio-Political Inquiry through Metaphor and Musing**, Vol. 2, (Toronto, Canada: Africa in Canada Press, 2016).

2015

Kenneth K. Mwenda, **Understanding Securities Law and Regulation in Zambia**, (Cape Town, South Africa: Juta Academic Publishers, 2015).

2015

Kenneth K. Mwenda, **Public Intellectualism and Socio-Political Inquiry through Metaphor and Musing**, Vol. 1, (Toronto, Canada: Africa in Canada Press, 2015).

2011

Kenneth K. Mwenda, **Public International Law and the Regulation of Diplomatic Immunity in the Fight against Corruption**, (Pretoria, South Africa: Pretoria University Law Press (PULP), 2011).

2011

Kenneth K. Mwenda, **Contemporary Issues in Zambian and English Company Law: A Comparative Study**, (Amherst, NY: Teneo Press, 2011).

2010

Kenneth K. Mwenda, **Legal Aspects of Banking Regulation: Common Law Perspectives from Zambia**, (Pretoria, South Africa: Pretoria University Law Press (PULP), 2010).

2010

Kenneth K. Mwenda, W. Fischer, H. A. Amankwah and D. Goulding, **German Hyperinflation 1922/1923 – A Law and Economics Approach**, (Cologne, Germany: Josef Eul Verlag, 2010).

2009

Kenneth K. Mwenda and G.N. Muuka (eds), **The Challenge of Change in Africa's Higher Education in the 21st Century**, (Amherst, NY: Cambria Press, 2009).

2007

Kenneth K. Mwenda, **Comparing American and British Legal Education Systems: Lessons for Commonwealth African Law Schools**, (Amherst, NY: Cambria Press, 2007).

2007

Kenneth K. Mwenda and W. Fischer (eds), **Country of Origin – A Law and Economics Approach to the Concept of 'Made in Australia'**, (Cologne, Germany: Josef Eul Verlag, 2007).

2007

Kenneth K. Mwenda, **Legal Aspects of Combating Corruption: the Case of Zambia**, (Amherst, NY: Cambria Press, 2007).

2006

Kenneth K. Mwenda, **Legal Aspects of Financial Services Regulation and the Concept of a Unified Regulator**, (Washington DC: The World Bank, 2006).

2006

Kenneth K. Mwenda**, Combating Financial Crime: Legal, Regulatory and Institutional Frameworks**, (Lewiston, NY: The Edwin Mellen Press, 2006).

2006

Kenneth K. Mwenda, **The Legal Administration of Financial Services in Common Law Jurisdictions: with special attention to the dual regulation system in Zambia**, (Lewiston, NY: The Edwin Mellen Press, 2006).

2006

Kenneth K. Mwenda and V. Mosoti (eds), **Contemporary Issues in International Economic Law**, (Cologne, Germany: Josef Eul Verlag, 2006).

2006

H. Kyambalesa and M.C. Houngnikpo; with contributions from Kenneth K. Mwenda and G.N. Muuka, **Economic Integration and Development in Africa**, (Aldershot, UK: Ashgate Publishing Co., 2006).

2005

Kenneth K. Mwenda, **Anti-Money Laundering Law and Practice: Lessons from Zambia**, (Lusaka, Zambia: University of Zambia (UNZA) Press, 2005).

2003

Kenneth K. Mwenda, and D.A. Ailola, (eds), **Frontiers of Legal Knowledge: Business and Economic Law in Context**, (Durham, NC: Carolina Academic Press, 2003).

2003

Kenneth K. Mwenda, **Principles of Arbitration Law**, (Parkland, FL: Brown Walker Press, 2003).

2002

Kenneth K. Mwenda (ed), **Banking and Micro-finance Regulation and Supervision: Lessons from Zambia**, (Parkland, FL: Brown Walker Press, 2002).

2001

Kenneth K. Mwenda, **Zambia's Stock Exchange and Privatisation Programme: Corporate Finance Law in Emerging Markets**, (Lewiston, NY: The Edwin Mellen Press, 2001).

2000

Kenneth K. Mwenda, **Banking Supervision and Systemic Bank Restructuring: An International and Comparative Legal Perspective**, (London, UK: Routledge-Cavendish Publishing, 2000).

2000

Kenneth K. Mwenda, **The Dynamics of Market Integration: African Stock Exchanges in the New Millennium**, (Parkland, FL: Brown Walker Press, 2000).

2000

    Kenneth K. Mwenda, **Contemporary Issues in Corporate Finance and Investment Law**, (Washington DC: Penn Press, 2000).

1999

    Kenneth K. Mwenda, **Legal Aspects of Corporate Capital and Finance**, (Washington DC: Penn Press, 1999).

FEEDBACK

Now that you have read the book ...

Was it interesting?

Did you enjoy what you wanted to read?
Was there any room for improvement?

Let us know at:
http://www.kennethmwenda.com/feedback

Your feedback is highly appreciated.
Thank you!

- Kenneth K. Mwenda

Would you like to buy a copy of

ANTHOLOGY IN LAW AND THE SOCIAL SCIENCES
by Kenneth Mwenda?

Order Online!

Please visit:
http://www. kennethmwenda.com/books